The Body in Flannery O'Connor's Fiction

The Body in Flannery O'Connor's Fiction

Computational Technique and Linguistic Voice

DONALD E. HARDY

The University of South Carolina Press

Published by the University of South Carolina Press
Columbia, South Carolina 29208

www.sc.edu/uscpress

Manufactured in the United States of America

16 15 14 13 12 11 10 09 08 07 10 9 8 7 6 5 4 3 2 1

Library of Congress Cataloging-in-Publication Data

Hardy, Donald E., 1955–
The body in Flannery O'connor's fiction : computational technique and linguistic voice / Donald E. Hardy.
p. cm.
Includes bibliographical references and index.
ISBN-13: 978-1-57003-698-9 (cloth : alk. paper)
ISBN-10: 1-57003-698-5 (cloth : alk. paper)
1. O'Connor, Flannery—Criticism and interpretation. 2. O'Connor, Flannery—Technique. 3. Narration (Rhetoric)—History—20th century. 4. Women and literature—Southern States—History—20th century. I. Title.
PS3565.C57Z864 2007
813'.54—c22

2007022661

This book was printed on Glatfelter Natures, a recycled paper with 50 percent postconsumer waste content.

For Heather

Contents

Illustrations

Figures

Tables

Acknowledgments

The Body in Flannery O'Connor's Fiction: Computational Technique and Linguistic Voice includes parts of three essays that I have published elsewhere, distributed over various chapters. In all cases the essays have been rewritten. My understanding of the sacramental, the incarnational, and the grotesque has been improved by two books that have been published in the time since I wrote those three essays: Susan Srigley's 2004 *Flannery O'Connor's Sacramental Art* and Christina Bieber Lake's 2005 *The Incarnational Art of Flannery O'Connor.* In all cases of the rewriting and distribution of parts of those essays over various chapters, the statistical arguments are different because of a shift from chi-square and probability testing to log-likelihood rankings and dispersion tests, the latter of which rankings and tests are argued for in chapter 3. The three essays are the following: "*Face* and the Middle Voice in Flannery O'Connor's Fiction," *Journal of Literary Semantics* 32 (2003): 133–50; "The Role of Linguistics in Interpretation: The Case of Grammatical Voice," *Belgian Journal of English Language and Literatures. Thematic Issue: The Linguistics/Literature Interface* 2 (2004): 31–48; "Collocational Analysis as a Stylistic Discovery Procedure: The Case of Flannery O'Connor's *Eyes*," *Style* 38, no. 4 (2004): 410–27. I thank these journals for permission to reprint portions of these essays. I also thank Meredith Larson, who first encouraged and helped me to think through some of the restrictions and methodologies a study such as this would require. And I thank my colleague Doug Flahive at Colorado State University for questions and discussion that motivated my initial research into the statistical literature on randomness and probability that formed the bases of my decision to use many of the statistical methods that I argue for in chapter 3. My deep appreciation goes to the anonymous referees for this book at University of South Carolina Press. Their suggestions have provided me the opportunity to improve the book in several respects. All errors remain my own.

Abbreviations

O'Connor's Works

CS	*The Complete Stories*
CW	*Collected Works*
CWFO	*Conversations with Flannery O'Connor*, ed. Rosemary M. Magee
ERMC	*Everything That Rises Must Converge*
GM	*A Good Man Is Hard to Find and Other Stories*
HB	*The Habit of Being*, ed. Sally Fitzgerald
MM	*Mystery and Manners: Occasional Prose*
VBA	*The Violent Bear It Away*
WB	*Wise Blood*

Grammatical and Statistical Terms

ABS	Absolutive
c	Cell
D	Juilland's *D*
DEC	Declarative
DIM	Diminutive
Diff. Co.	Difference Coefficient
E	Expected Frequency
ERG	Ergative
Freq	Frequency
G^2	Log-Likelihood
ln	Natural Log
MID	Middle
O	Observed Frequency
s	Standard Deviation
ST	Stative
V	Variation Coefficient
χ^2	Chi-Square
x	Frequency
~	Not
*	Ungrammatical
?	Questionable grammaticality

CHAPTER 1

The Body in Flannery O'Connor's Fiction

Symbols are big things that knock you in the face.
Flannery O'Connor (*CWFO,* 59)

An insight of considerable importance and complexity in the critical literature on Flannery O'Connor's fiction is that O'Connor's characters struggle with the divisions of spirit and matter.[1] It is as if O'Connor's characters could take Tom T. Shiftlet of "The Life You Save May Be Your Own" as their confused spokesperson for their common body-spirit problem. In his negotiation with Lucynell Crater the senior for her car in exchange for his marriage to Lucynell Crater the junior, he announces his understanding of the body and spirit: "'Lady, a man is divided into two parts, body and spirit.' The old woman clamped her gums together. 'A body and a spirit,' he repeated. 'The body, lady, is like a house: it don't go anywhere; but the spirit, lady, is like a automobile: always on the move, always'" (*GM,* 62–63). Not only is there an implicit dualism in his philosophy, but also, as Gilbert H. Muller explains, Shiftlet has it a bit mixed up. He has literalized the spirit as a material object, thus "paying homage to Henry Ford" rather than to Christ. Shiftlet's words certainly do not represent O'Connor's beliefs on the body and the spirit. Muller suggests that O'Connor's sympathies more likely align with those of the hermaphrodite in "A Temple of the Holy Ghost": "God made me thisaway and if you laugh He may strike you the same way. This is the way He wanted me to be and I ain't disputing His way. I'm showing you because I got to make the best of it. I expect you to act like ladies and gentlemen. I never done it to myself nor had a thing to do with it but I'm making the best of it. I don't dispute hit" (*GM,* 97). As Muller argues, the hermaphrodite "connects his grotesque agonies with a deeper spiritual order." James W. Horton points out that O'Connor does not use the hermaphrodite as an "ephemeralized metaphor for spirit." Instead, the hermaphrodite quite literally "redeems the bodily state."[2]

As both Susan Srigley and Christina Bieber Lake demonstrate in their respective detailed theological and literary arguments, O'Connor had a sacramental aesthetics and an incarnational art. Lake points out that the terms *sacramental* and *incarnational* as applied to fiction are not synonymous: "Though [fiction] follows the definition of sacrament as an outward manifestation of God's grace, it is not in and of itself sacred." O'Connor's fiction is incarnational, as Lake argues, because O'Connor "shows the God of creation through the beauty of the made." To say that *sacramental* and *incarnational* are not synonymous is not to say that the concepts are unrelated. As Srigley argues, "The sacramental character of O'Connor's Christian aesthetics means that, for her, spiritual reality is present and experienced in the material world; her fiction as an incarnational art is the embodiment of this understanding." Thus, Srigley contends, "Since [O'Connor] believed fiction to be an incarnational art, her stories are the most appropriate means of discovering her sacramental view."[3] I will use both terms throughout *The Body in Flannery O'Connor's Fiction, sacramental* to represent O'Connor's literary thematics of the manifestation of God in matter and *incarnational* to represent the method of signaling the incarnation of spirit in matter. Because this book concerns method more frequently than thematics, I will use the term *incarnational* more often than the term *sacramental.*

The innovative central thesis of *The Body in Flannery O'Connor's Fiction* is that it is possible to illuminate the struggle with the divisions of spirit and matter by a close examination of the interactions of grammatical voice and the body at both the macrolevel and the microlevel of the narrative. As we shall see, O'Connor reminds us of the ineluctable body not only when the body is a macronarrational theme, as many others including Srigley and Lake have noticed, but also when parts of the body act on their own and when characters act on parts of their own bodies as described in very particular sentences. That is, the body parts occur as semantic actors or goals, respectively, normally grammatical subjects or objects. In "Revelation" it is Mary Grace's face, not Mary Grace herself, that as actor launches the physical and spiritual attack on Ruby Turpin's self-righteousness: "Before [Ruby] could utter a sound, the raw face came crashing across the table toward her, howling" (*ERMC,* 206). In "The Train" Mrs. Hosen's actor face seems an alien and unsympathetic witness to Hazel's social awkwardness. The following example includes that witness as well as Hazel's irrelevant and incoherent response to Mrs. Hosen's question of just where he does live if he doesn't live in Taulkinham, where she has assumed that he lives: "He wanted to get away from her. 'It was there,' he mumbled, squirming in the seat. Then he said, 'I don't rightly know, I was there but . . . this is just the third time I been at Taulkinham,' he said quickly—**her face had crawled out and was staring at him**—'I ain't been since I went when I was six. I don't know nothin' about it'" (*CS,* 56; emphasis mine throughout book unless noted otherwise, ellipses in original here). Although the question may be asked of almost all of O'Connor's fiction, Patricia Yaeger asks of *Wise Blood,* "Why this extraordinary focus on wounds, on protuberances, on body parts which seem to have a life of their own?"[4] Yaeger's question gets at one of the very curious patterns of O'Connor's body images: that body parts do sometimes seem to have a will of their own. Both Mary Grace's and Mrs. Hosen's faces in these passages occur as animate and actor subjects of their verbs, reflecting the will of which Yaeger writes. More subtle indications that the faces in O'Connor have a life of their own are cases in which the subject of the verb acts on the face as its own goal body, thus calling attention to the existence of body parts separate from their normally actor human subjects. In "A Good Man Is Hard to Find" the grandmother attempts to entertain her infant grandson during her family's long car trip: "She rolled her eyes and screwed up her mouth and stuck her leathery thin face into his smooth bland one" (*GM,* 12). In "The Displaced Person" the priest has to force his attention away from the revelation he sees in the peacock's "tail full of suns" in order to attend to the displaced family that he has brought to the McIntyre farm: "The peacock stepped off toward the mulberry tree . . . and the priest turned his absorbed face away and got in the car and drove the displaced people down to the shack they were to occupy" (*GM,* 202–3).

It can be shown that many of the constructions in which the body parts of O'Connor's characters seem particularly to have an existence of their own, either as actors or as goals, are grammatical manipulations of semantic variations on the middle voice, a grammatical category of considerable interest in linguistics and recent and intense interest in literary theory and the interpretive humanities in general. *The Body in Flannery O'Connor's Fiction* makes explicit and thoroughgoing connections between the two very well recognized O'Connor concerns of the sacramental and the grotesque on the one hand and the grammar of voice and the body on the other, largely through the techniques of computational stylistics. It might seem not quite believable that such important themes in O'Connor's fiction as the sacramental and the grotesque play out in part at one of the most detailed levels of grammar: that of grammatical relations (for example, subjects, objects) within the clause and the lexical class of body parts. Yet the subtlety of the English voice system in conjunction with the lexicon of the body is an ideal ground for O'Connor's incarnational explorations of body and spirit and the sacramental and grotesque connections between them. Computational stylistics, the use of concordancing programs and basic statistics to explore the construction of literary meaning, is a central focus of the present study as well. *The Body in Flannery O'Connor's Fiction* is, thus, both an examination of the manifestation of the themes of the sacramental and the grotesque in the incarnational bodies of O'Connor's characters as well as an exposition of a method of stylistic investigation. The book should serve to advance not only O'Connor studies themselves but also the field of computational stylistics.

The Body

The body has wide theoretical and critical recognition in both American and British literature, especially in the sense of the problem of the unity of the body and the spirit. Sharon Cameron argues that "American works seem preoccupied with questions of identity conceived in corporeal terms." Among the authors who are most concerned with body and identity, according to Cameron, are Poe, Whitman, Melville, Hawthorne, Faulkner, and Lawrence. Cameron's particular subjects are Hawthorne and Melville. What she says about their fiction might just as well be said about O'Connor's: "They are . . . in a particularly strong position to illustrate the fissures and dualism that are the inevitable consequences of imagining that one could pry the allegorical from the literal, the body from the soul." Among the many other American writers whose focus on individual body parts is striking are Steinbeck, Sherwood Anderson, Hemingway, Nathanael West, and the Southwestern Humorists. Among the critics who have written on body aesthetics in Shakespeare are Jonathan Hall and Sean Benson, the latter of whom writes, for example, of the distorted politics of the rhetorical figure of "Roman authority" as "the grotesque image of a belly" in *Coriolanus.* Malcolm Andrews's analysis of the grotesque body in Dickens's fiction takes both Mikhail Bakhtin and Jacques Lacan as theoretical bases. B. M. Sagar's brief programmatic call for the study of "physical appearance of characters in novels" mentions the foregrounding of body parts such as the face, hand, eyes, and head in Dickens, William Golding, and Emily Brontë.[5]

Critics have commented frequently on the importance of the body and identity in O'Connor's fiction, especially the importance of the maimed body. There is no doubt that a good number of O'Connor's characters, either in part or wholly, are maimed in some way. The infirmities are various: Hulga Hopewell's missing leg, Claud Turpin's ulcerous leg, Rayber's deafness, Tom T. Shiftlet's missing arm, General Sash's infirmity, Mrs. McIntyre's general declining health, including failing vision and voice, Julian's mother's high blood pressure and weight problem, Asbury Fox's undulant fever. And of course there are the even more numerous spiritual and emotional problems that accompany these bodily ills: Hulga's intellectual pride and spiritual emptiness, Rayber's Christ complex, Julian's mother's racism, Asbury's self-centeredness, Shiftlet's moral vacuity. Henry Taylor comments that in O'Connor's fiction "there are a number of characters who are partly distinguishable from their fellows by some obvious physical defect." Most widely known among these characters is perhaps Hulga Hopewell, the one-legged Ph.D. nihilist/romantic of "Good Country People." Another of many who have been examined is Asbury Fox, the failed artist with an incurable case of Bang's disease, itself a consequence of his foolish self-centeredness.[6] Although other body parts are considered in the critical literature, perhaps the most important body part for the unity of the material and the spiritual (that is, incarnational unity) is the eye, whose stylistic significance and patterns will be explored in detail in chapters 4 and 5. The eyes and blindness figure both as symbols and as important plot elements in O'Connor's fiction, most obviously in *Wise Blood.* Mary Glenn Freeman, Miles Orvell, Marshall Bruce Gentry, James Mellard, and Larue Love Sloan all consider the eye the most important body part in O'Connor's fiction.[7] One of the more biographical of bodily details is the fact of O'Connor's long suffering and eventual death from systematic lupus erythematosus, the same autoimmune disease that killed her father. Among the many critics that analyze O'Connor's work with a focus on lupus, most indicate that the body (especially the ill body) functions sacramentally, or at least metaphorically, in her fiction. As Jeffrey J. Folks argues more generally, "the disabilities of her characters replicate the action of Redemption through Crucifixion."[8]

Most studies that explore the body in O'Connor's fiction do so at a relatively abstract level, not treating specific body parts but instead concentrating on O'Connor's supposed disgust, on the one hand, or reverence, on the other, for the body. Josephine Hendin, in particular, sees O'Connor as a sort of malcontent, comfortable neither in the social world nor in the physical world. In an intensely biographical reading, in which Hendin sees O'Connor dramatizing her own frustration with her body, Hendin argues that O'Connor "regards the body itself as repulsive." She specifically contends, "O'Connor consistently opposes the spiritual and physical, keeping them so separate and dual that no one seems to have both a mind and body at the same time." Laurence Enjolras, in a chapter of his 1998 book entitled "Physical Portrait: The Ugly Human Body," points to a permanent "gap between body and mind" in O'Connor's fiction. Martha Stephens is unusual among these critics in commenting on a specific body part in O'Connor's treatment of the "ugly" human body. Stephens argues generally that O'Connor exhibits a "stubborn refusal to see any good, any beauty or dignity or meaning, in ordinary human life on earth." She then comments on the "loathing with which she apparently contemplated the human body," specifically human faces, which we will discuss in detail in chapters 4 and 5. Lake's important and innovative book on the incarnational in O'Connor's fiction is the most extended analysis of the literary and theological importance of the body to O'Connor's fiction. However, aside from a few mentions of the literary significance of body parts such as the eye and the face, most of Lake's attention is on the aesthetic and theological significance of the body in general: "Bodies in O'Connor's stories serve always to remind character and readers of what the Incarnation validates—the inescapable reality of human embodiment." So, for example, it is certainly true, as Lake argues, that Asbury Fox in "The Enduring Chill" "needs to be brought down to earth, brought back to his body." Lake is also interested in a sense of embodiment as a metaphor for place, an interest that is beyond the scope of this study.[9]

Much more rarely noticed than O'Connor's use of individual body parts such as the eyes or the face and the grotesque body in general are her characters' body actions and in particular O'Connor's grammatical patterns in the use of body parts. However, there are isolated studies that explore these issues. Barbara Korte indicates that Manley Pointer uses "intentional" (that is, conscious) body language as opposed to "spontaneous" (that is, unconscious) body language to hide his intentions. Also, for example, she says, Mrs. Freeman in "Good Country People" intentionally uses her facial expressions (neutral, forward, and reverse), the first for "when she was alone" the second "for all her human dealings," such as taking advantage of Hulga's mother and Hulga herself. Korte makes further distinctions between "comitative" body language (that which goes with speech) and "independent" body language (that which is not attached to speech). Consider, then, this passage from "Good Country People," when Manley first appears at Mrs. Hopewell's door to sell her a Bible: "'Oh!' he said, **pretending to looked puzzled** but with his eyes sparkling, 'I saw it said "The Cedars," on the mailbox so I thought you was Mrs. Cedars!' and he burst out in a pleasant laugh . . . 'Mrs. Hopewell!' he said and **grabbed her hand.** 'I hope you are well!' and he **laughed again and then all at once his face sobered completely.** He paused and **gave her a straight earnest look** and said 'Lady, I've come to speak of serious things'" (emphasis in Korte; *GM,* 177–78). Korte says that all of the phrases she has singled out indicate comitative body language, since they "emphasize [Manley's] verbal utterance" while "eyes sparkling" indicates independent body language because the sparkle reveals his real intentions, which he attempts to conceal.[10] The presence of the verb *pretending* can be understood to frame the entire passage with Manley's intentional deception. Further supporting that intentionality is the use of the phrase "**gave** her a straight earnest look" instead of "**looked** at her straightly and earnestly." Korte's nonproblematic major thesis is that body language has a communicative function in literature. A good bit of *The Body in Flannery O'Connor's Fiction* is concerned with the same thesis; however the difference is that my book concentrates not on the intentional communication of the character but on that of the author and does so by exploring the use of particular body parts and grammatical voice to illustrate concerns with the sacramental, the incarnational, and the grotesque. Thus, for example, I will have nothing to say about constructions such as "pretending to look puzzled" because a body part is not mentioned in the construction nor is a *pretending* a verb of interest in the voice system that we will investigate.

In this book I am interested particularly in constructions such as "his face sobered completely" in the passage quoted above from "Good Country People." Korte references Stephen R. Portch's study of body language in literature, which takes a much longer look at the manipulation of body language in Manley Pointer's behavior. Portch in 1985 laments the "vacuum" in the stylistics criticism on O'Connor, indicating rightly that most O'Connor criticism is nonstylistic.[11] There is a great deal of scattered stylistic comment in O'Connor criticism, but very little of it gets to the rock-bottom level of sentence and lexical patterns. Joanne Halleran McMullen notes one of the general patterns that I will explore in great detail in this book: the use of body parts in the subject position in a clause, as in "his face sobered completely." She analyzes examples from three short stories and *Wise Blood.* For example McMullen notes from "The Lame Shall Enter First," "Sheppard's mouth stretched in disgust" and from "Good Country People," "The boy's mouth was set angrily." She uses these examples and others to support her general thesis that O'Connor has a distinctly un-Christian viewpoint, in particular that the significance of this pattern is that it increases "character anonymity," that it is a "distancing technique," and that it prevents the reader from seeing her characters "as whole people who actively take part in the completion of God's scheme." McMullen refers to Geoffrey N. Leech and Michael H. Short's discussion of the same phenomenon in Christopher Isherwood's and John Steinbeck's fiction in which the authors argue that the pattern "is a fairly common device for suggesting that the part of the body involved acts of its own accord" (quoted in McMullen) and that in some circumstances the pattern "can be used to play down the blame attributed to a character for his actions." McMullen also refers to Chris Kennedy's argument that body parts as subject have a "distancing" effect in Conrad's *The Secret Agent.* Similarly, Walter Nash argues that in Lawrence's "Odour of Chrysanthemums" the effect of the body part as subject indicates internal division in a character.[12] There have been other similar stylistic explorations of body parts in fiction. Both M. A. K. Halliday and David Hoover have examined in detail the use of body parts in William Golding's *The Inheritors.* Halliday concentrates on the use of body parts as subjects of intransitive verbs and how those constructions syntactically signal an absence of agency and realization of the entire human, the latter absence being representative of the Neanderthal world of part of the novel. Hoover, on the other hand, sees the use of body part subjects as representative of an "animistic, alien, and primitive fictional world."[13] I will return to McMullen's methodology in chapter 6 as well as to the problem of determining whether there is one literary effect of the body part as subject. In my reading it is too simplistic and reductive to say that O'Connor's isolated body parts reveal an anti-Christian viewpoint. Rather, the grotesque use of body parts manifests mystery just as does the incarnational. In his book on the aesthetics of the medieval grotesque in O'Connor's fiction, Di Renzo creatively paraphrases Bakhtin on the essential agentivity of some (grotesque) body parts—their tendency to make their own connections to the world: "the human body, vulgarly trumpeting its own materiality," becomes "a dynamic part of the body of the world."[14] Grammatical voice provides an arena—although an arena on a comparatively microscopic level—for the dependent interaction of the grotesque and the sacramental. The body (including individual body parts) celebrates its own agentivity and thus demonstrates the spirit in the flesh, or the flesh as spirit.

The Sacramental, the Incarnational, and the Grotesque

Before returning to a discussion of the body, this time as literary symbol, it will be useful to set the particular interpretive stage for *The Body in Flannery O'Connor's Fiction.* Rather than place grammatical voice and its many interpretations at the center of that stage, I will place three of O'Connor's well-recognized spiritual and literary concerns there: the sacramental, the incarnational, and the grotesque. Chapter 6 of this book will demonstrate the critical and theoretical effects of placing grammatical voice at the center of one's interpretive actions.

The particular significance of the incarnational in O'Connor's fiction is highlighted by the contrasting it with Manichaeism, the heresy that spirit and matter are separate and that matter is inherently evil. The dangers of Manichaeism were very much on O'Connor's mind, as is clear throughout her fiction and as is clear from the following comments in her essay "The Nature and Aim of Fiction": "The Manicheans separated spirit and matter. To them all material things were evil. They sought pure spirit and tried to approach the infinite directly without any mediation of matter. This is also pretty much the modern spirit" (*MM,* 68). O'Connor repeatedly claimed for herself directly and indirectly the contrary belief and practice of sacramentalism and the incarnation, which see matter as the manifestation of God's grace, primarily in the figure of Christ (*MM,* 163; *HB,* 341; *CW,* 816, 1099, 1107) and also in the physical world, both human and nonhuman. There has been a fair amount of debate, direct and indirect, on whether O'Connor's fiction is truly incarnational or Manichean.[15] The evidence for O'Connor's Manichaeism is normally taken to be what appears sometimes to be her aesthetic enjoyment of the hideous and the evil. As John Hawkes writes, arguing that O'Connor's narrator has "the devil's view": "Within her almost luridly bright pastoral world—usually created as meaningless or indifferent or corrupted—the characters of Flannery O'Connor are *judged,* victimized, made to appear only as absurd entities of the flesh."[16] There is no question that O'Connor's physical world, especially that touched by fallible human hands, can be hideous. In "The River" "the city [rises] like a cluster of warts on the side of the mountain" (*GM,* 41). However, even the city is a place for miracles. At the end of *The Violent Bear It Away,* Tarwater turns his attention back to it: "His singed eyes, black in their deep sockets, seemed already to envision the fate that awaited him but he moved steadily on, his face set toward the dark city, where the children of God lay sleeping" (*VBA,* 243). The inanimate as grotesque cognizant is also a common trope in O'Connor's fiction. In the first paragraph of "The Artificial

Nigger" O'Connor writes: "The straight chair against the wall looked stiff and attentive as if it were awaiting an order and Mr. Head's trousers, hanging to the back of it, had an almost noble air" (*GM,* 102). The tractor that runs over Mr. Guizac in "The Displaced Person" has its own murderous will. Mrs. McIntyre "saw it move forward, calculating it own path" (*GM,* 249). Throughout O'Connor's fiction, the inanimate invades the human space and the human invades the inanimate space. In O'Connor's world grace permeates both nature and the all-too-human world. The dynamics of O'Connor's Catholic incarnational vision in the Protestant South are illustrated in a letter to John Hawkes in which she discusses the significance of The Misfit's response to the grandmother before he murders her in "A Good Man Is Hard to Find": "Grace, to the Catholic way of thinking, can and does use as its medium the imperfect, purely human, and even hypocritical. . . . In the Protestant view, I think Grace and nature don't have much to do with each other. The old lady, because of her hypocrisy and humanness and banality couldn't be a medium for Grace. In the sense that I see things the other way, I'm a Catholic writer" (*HB,* 389–90). There is, then, in O'Connor's fiction minimally the struggle between her vision and the anti-incarnational view of some of her Protestant readers.

As Edward Kessler suggests, part of the evidence for an incarnational viewpoint in O'Connor's fiction is that O'Connor condemned those characters, such as Sarah Ruth, in "Parker's Back," who rejected the physical world. It is difficult to imagine sympathy for Sarah Ruth: "The skin on her face was thin and drawn as tight as the skin on an onion and her eyes were grey and sharp like the points of two icepicks" (*ERMC,* 219). Monroe points out that O'Connor had an ambiguous relationship to asceticism in early fiction, such as *Wise Blood.* However, he contends that "Parker's Back"—the last story she worked on before she died in 1964—certainly shows "a motif of embodiment, a celebration of healthiness and physical vitality." He notes "the hunger for the physical" even in Sarah Ruth as she delights in the taste of the apple that Parker gives her and as she perhaps unconsciously delights in the imagination of the tattoos that Parker says she can't see. As Monroe points out, "Two circles of red appeared like apples on the girl's cheeks and softened her appearance" (*ERMC,* 222).[17] O'Connor approached the incarnational from many perspectives, including the comic and the tragic. In *The Violent Bear It Away* the characters of both Francis Tarwater and his uncle, Rayber, are defined in part by their hatred of the mundane, in Francis's case manifested in his expectation of great things for his spiritual self, much greater than the mission of baptizing his mentally retarded cousin, and in Rayber's case manifested in his fear of the physicality of the material world. Early in the novel as Francis is procrastinating the burial of his uncle, he feels a sign from God coming on, something that will tell him what his great mission is: "There was a complete stillness over everything and the boy felt his heart begin to swell. He held his breath as if he were about to hear a voice from on high. After a few moments he heard a hen scratching beneath him under the porch" (*VBA*, 12–13). Although Francis hopes for the gloriously nonmundane, he is aware of the power of the ordinary. He refuses to "let his eye rest for an instant longer than was needed to place something—a spade, a hoe, the mule's hind quarters before his plow, the red furrow under him." He wanted "to avoid this threatened intimacy of creation" and expected the voice of God, when it came to him, to be "untouched by any fleshly hand or breath" (*VBA*, 22). Francis's uncle Rayber demonstrates by the desiccated quality of his life the consequences of running from the incarnational world. He is terrified of the "horrifying love" that he in "moments" feels for his son, Bishop: "Anything he looked at too long could bring it on. Bishop did not have to be around. It could be a stick or a stone, the line of a shadow, the absurd old man's walk of a starling crossing the sidewalk" (*VBA*, 113).

While the sacramental and the incarnational are essentially unified and well understood themes in O'Connor scholarship, the grotesque is a bit more problematic. The grotesque is in most discussions considered to be a horrifying mixture of the mundane and the unusual, an invasion of the understood by the impossible to understand. Paula M. Uruburu notes that it is "a genre which derives its effectiveness from paradox, from the fusion of numerous and seemingly incompatible elements—the horrible with the laughable, the sinister with the ludicrous, the mundane with the bizarre."[18] An early story of the grotesque, odd for many reasons, not least of which is O'Connor's note on the typescript that it was "unpublishable," is the 1947 thesis story "The Crop."[19] In it, an amateur writer, Miss Willerton, has a great deal of difficulty writing past the first sentences of her stories, largely because she is constantly on the lookout for the picturesque or the social problem rather than for the gloriously mundane and grotesque. Two of her imagined characters, purely imagined because she never actually writes the story, are the sharecropper Lot and his wife. Whether or not Miss Willerton has ever actually finished a story, it is certainly the case that she has a theory, or even theories, of writing; for example, she has talked to "a group at the United Daughters of the Colonies" about the importance of such things as "phonetic art" and "tonal quality" in the "literary venture" (*CS*, 35). However frustrated or just simply bad Miss Willerton is as a writer, she certainly sees no opportunity for art in her surroundings. In an early instance of O'Connor's celebrated doubling of characters, Miss Willerton encounters the real-life doubles of both Lot and his wife. While earlier, in Willerton's imagination, Lot's wife is described simply as "more or less pretty—yellow hair, fat ankles, muddy-colored eyes," the double is "plump with yellow hair and fat ankles and muddy-colored eyes" (*CS*, 37, 41). More important, the double evinces further details, grotesque details that bring the character aesthetic significance: "She had on high-heel pumps and blue anklets, a too-short cotton dress, and a plaid jacket. Her skin was mottled and her neck thrust forward as if she were sticking it out to smell something that was always being drawn away. Her face was set in an inane grin" (*CS*, 41). In Willerton's imagination Lot himself "would be tall, stooped, and shaggy" (*CS*, 37). The double "was long and wasted and shaggy" (*CS*, 41). Lot would have "sad eyes that made him look like a gentleman in spite of his red neck and big fumbling hands." The double's "shoulders were stooped and there were yellow knots along the side of his large, red neck" (*CS*, 37, 40). Lot would "have straight teeth and, to indicate that he had some spirit, red hair" (*CS*, 37). His double's "hands fumbled stupidly with the girl's as they slumped along" and "he had straight teeth and sad eyes and a rash over his forehead." After the description of the doubles the narrator records Miss Willerton's reaction to them: "'Ugh,' she shuddered" (*CS*, 41). In town, just before she encounters the doubles, Miss Willerton asks herself of the drudgery that she sees around her, "Where was there any chance for self-expression, for creation, for art?" (*CS*, 40). The obvious implication here is that it is at least in part in the more detailed grotesqueness of the body and its parts (for example, "neck thrust forward," "rash over his forehead," "knots along the side of his large, red neck") where art and the possibility for self-expression lie for Flannery O'Connor. The body is also where the incarnational lies, as is clear in the last chapter of *Wise Blood,* in which Mrs. Flood—Hazel's landlady—contemplates the mystery of Hazel's self-blinding: "She could not make up her mind what would be inside his head and what out. She thought of her own head as a switchbox where she controlled from; but with him, she could only imagine the outside in, the whole black world in his head and his head bigger than the world, his head big enough to include the sky and planets and whatever was or had been or would be. How would he know if time was going backwards or forwards or if he was going with it? . . . She saw him going backwards to Bethlehem and she had to laugh" (*WB*, 218–19). In this passage Hazel's head contains the whole world, even after his blinding, and that bodily involvement in the world also makes possible his intense spirituality as he goes "backwards to Bethlehem."

One difficult issue for critics has been the reconciliation of O'Connor's sacramentalism with her intense interest in the grotesque. Among the faults that critics have found in O'Connor, the grotesque, variously called by other names, stands prominent. Ben Satterfield, who includes O'Connor among "provincial dogmatists without charity or compassion," argues against a sacramental effect in her fiction: "The conflict in Haze, as in so many O'Connor characters, is between what is perceived of the natural world and what is taught of the spiritual. There is more than a suggestion in O'Connor that the two cannot be reconciled." Among the many other faults that Satterfield finds with *Wise Blood* is "the lack of meaning in Haze's self-inflicted suffering and his guilt-provoked attempt at atonement." Irving Malin thinks that O'Connor's grotesque might be "pre-Christian" and sees one piece of evidence in support of this split between her grotesque vision and her Christian vision in the narrative failure of Hazel's conversion, a conversion for which Malin feels that the reader is not prepared. Hendin believes that O'Connor allows her "real portraits to overpower her allegorical ones." Thus she argues that Shiftlet in "The Life You Save May Be Your Own" is clearly intended to have symbolic significance since he "forms a crooked cross against the sky" and since he is a carpenter, for example. However, she argues, the grotesque literal world, with a run-down farm in a "dwarfed universe," defeats the "symbolic" world. McMullen argues that the "peculiar imagery" of O'Connor's fiction contradicts the frequent sacramental pronouncements in her letters and essays. McMullen cites Francis Tarwater's "own stricken image of himself, trudging into the distance in the bleeding stinking mad shadow of Jesus, until at last he received his reward, a broken fish, a multiplied loaf" (*VBA*, 91) and argues that this image is "repulsive" and "mocks the reader."[20] O'Connor herself argued that the "Catholic novel" is "one that represents reality adequately as we see it manifested in this world of things and human relationships. Only in and by these sense experiences does the fiction writer approach a contemplative knowledge of the mystery they embody" (*MM*, 172). Both Wilson Yates and Roger Hazelton would agree with O'Connor in their arguments that the grotesque is a manifestation of mystery.[21]

If the grotesque is, as William Van O'Connor argues, a particularly American style, well suited to the disjunction between our dreams and pretension on the one hand and our realities on the other, then the grotesque is equally well suited in O'Connor's world to show the disjunction between a prettified, cleaned-up version of the incarnation and the brutal reality of the bleeding Jesus. Brinkmeyer summarizes many of the critical arguments and argues himself that O'Connor's *Wise Blood* demonstrates the essential tension in O'Connor between the sacramental and the Manichean. He concludes that "the dynamics of *Wise Blood* can be seen to be less Manichean than sacramental, though the novel's sacramentalism is one that cancels the world to celebrate the body." Thus, he argues, it is the incarnational body itself that is O'Connor's site of the celebration of sacramentalism. Hazel blinds himself to the external world to bind his spirit more closely to his own body. As for an explanation of Hazel's self-mortification, Ralph C. Wood probably says it best when he argues that the self-mortification is penance —exactly what Hazel says it is when he says he is "paying"—and that Hazel is "what, borrowing from Augustine, one might call 'a naturally Catholic soul.'"[22] Thus many O'Connor critics see a close connection between recognition of the grotesque and the recognition and acceptance of the sacramental.

The grotesque in itself is not the incarnational solution to the Manichean split between body and spirit; it is the call to the solution, which is at least in part acceptance of both the beautiful and the flawed in the body. Portch contends that "O'Connor uses the body primarily to show its limitations and to reveal how all too often it shapes personality and limits the spirit" as in the case of Hulga and her wooden leg. Specifically addressing the frequent argument that O'Connor was too fond of the grotesque, seeming to revel in it and its negativity, Folks argues that "though she wrote *about* the grotesque, her beliefs were the *opposite* of grotesque." The grotesque is the exaggeration that O'Connor so frequently said was necessary for her readers to see what she intended. Gary M. Ciuba argues that the failure of characters in *Wise Blood* to "see" and appreciate both literal and figurative faces is illustrative of their spiritual failure. Ciuba points out that O'Connor's characters are sometimes reduced to "a set of yellow teeth, a pair of icy eyes, a patch of blotchy skin." That is, O'Connor's incarnational method is not easy on the reader. Among the most challenging grotesque descriptions in O'Connor is the one of Mrs. Watts, the prostitute in *Wise Blood:* "Mrs. Watts . . . was a big woman with very yellow hair and white skin that glistened with a greasy preparation. . . . The pink tip of Mrs. Watts's tongue appeared and moistened her lower lip. . . . Mrs. Watts's mouth split in a wide full grin that showed her teeth. They were small and pointed and speckled with green and there was a wide space between each one" (*WB,* 33–34). Di Renzo's is perhaps the strongest made and supported argument that the grotesque is central to O'Connor's sacramentalism. He writes, "Hers is an aggressively sacramental vision." He sees O'Connor's grotesque to be essentially that of the medieval grotesque, a celebration of the beautiful and the ugly in both human corporeality and spirituality.

Stephens argues that O'Connor's thought is closer to that of medieval Christianity than any. Di Renzo finds that similarity not in what Stephens refers to as the "constant injunction to renunciation of the world" but instead in medieval folk art and the fabliau. Di Renzo argues that, just as in the fabliau, O'Connor's "emphasis on the body—on its needs and vulnerabilities, its sheer fleshiness—undermines all forms of pride and abstraction in her characters." It is important to see the grotesque in O'Connor's fiction and accept it because that acceptance is a sacramental view and an incarnational artistic strategy. Ciuba justifies the connection between the exaggerated grotesque body and incarnation in part by arguing that "if O'Connor's gaze obliterates much, it leaves the essentials of the soul to be seen in the distorted outlines of the body." Near the end of "A Temple of the Holy Ghost" one of the signs that the girl has received some sort of grace is that during the mass she makes the connection between the hermaphrodite and the sacramental. She leaves her intellectual pride and meanness behind: "Her mind began to get quiet and then empty but when the priest raised the monstrance with the Host shining ivory-colored in the center of it, she was thinking of the tent at the fair that had the freak in it" (*GM,* 100). Di Renzo argues effectively that the connection the girl makes here changes her. As he points out, the girl "does not ignore Alonso's ugliness but neither is she repelled by it. It simply is what it is." O'Connor believed that it was important to accept the human body and its limitations, which was especially evident in her comments in "Introduction to *A Memoir of Mary Ann*," the memoir of a small child who was born with a facial tumor and who died young. O'Connor professes irritation with those who want only the beautiful and the easy to look at: "If other ages felt less, they saw more, even though they saw with the blind, prophetical, unsentimental eye of acceptance, which is to say, of faith" (*MM*, 227). In a detailed discussion of "Introduction to *A Memoir of Mary Ann*," Lake makes the incarnational connection between the good and the body: "O'Connor insists that when we truly look into the face of good we are not going to see the purified intellect and a refined abstraction, but a *face*."[23]

The Body as Symbol and the Body as Detail

In some literary discussions the word *symbol* does most of the work, body parts are themselves idiomatic symbols if mentioned at all, as "knock you in the face" is in the epigraph to this chapter for "force recognition," and the grammar of body parts is, whatever that is, not worth commenting on. If the symbols are the big things that knock the reader in the face, the prevalent sentence patterns like those investigated in this book are the small things that brush against the reader like a consistent but barely perceptible breeze. Because they are barely perceptible, the patterns are subtle, but because they are consistent they have great power to support thematic development. In O'Connor's fiction there are many rather obvious, one might say, symbolic, uses of the body, that knock one in the face, so to speak, as does Hulga Hopewell's wooden leg, which "she was as sensitive about . . . as a peacock about his tail" and which she "took care of . . . as someone else would his soul, in private and almost with her own eyes turned away" (*GM*, 192). In one of her occasional essays O'Connor herself commented on the symbolic significance of the leg and Manley Pointer's theft of it: "by the time the Bible salesman comes along, the leg has accumulated so much meaning that it is, as the saying goes, loaded. And when the Bible salesman steals it, the reader realizes that he has taken away part of the girl's personality and has revealed her deeper affliction to her for the first time" (*MM*, 99; quoted in Carol Shloss). The many critical exegeses of the significance of Hulga's leg are all variations on O'Connor's, although they take particular turns in the context of individual arguments. Carol Shloss, for example, nicely points out that the theft of the leg provides the central moment of the grotesque in the story. The theft is grotesque because "the rape plays against expectations." As Shloss points out, Manley doesn't take Hulga's virginity. He takes her "wooden soul."[24] In "The Lame Shall Enter First" Johnson's club foot and the "heavy black battered shoe" that he wears on it are quite symbolically similar to Hulga's missing leg and prosthesis: "The leather parted from [the shoe] in one place and the end of an empty sock protruded like a grey tongue from a severed head" (*ERMC*, 149). Johnson is as dependent on his foot and shoe as Hulga is on her wooden soul. When Sheppard, the self-satisfied and self-righteous do-gooder, takes Johnson to pick up his new orthopedic shoe, Johnson refuses the new shoe with "a glint of triumph in his eyes" (*ERMC*, 176). As Uruburu argues, Johnson sees the club foot as "a sign from God that he is 'special.'"[25] It is also more obviously symbolic of the reality of human existence that Sheppard cannot face. Just as Mrs. Hopewell has difficulty realizing her daughter's condition, Sheppard cannot face the reality of Johnson's spiritual and physical disabilities until it is too late. When the old shoe is going to be taken off, the narrator hits us in the face with the significance of the symbolic club foot and Sheppard's inability to face reality: "The unsheathed mass of foot in the dirty sock made Sheppard feel queasy. He turned his eyes away until the new shoe was on" (*ERMC*, 175–76).

The Christian symbolism of the body can be heavy-handed at times in O'Connor's fiction. Obadiah Elihue Parker's back and the tattoo of the Byzantine Christ on it team up for a powerful symbol of the crucified Christ at the end of "Parker's Back" after Sarah Ruth beats Parker with a broom: "He sat there and let her beat him until she had nearly knocked him senseless and large welts had formed on the face of the tattooed Christ" (*ERMC*, 244). In "The Life You Save May Be Your Own," Lucynell Crater the senior's and Tom T. Shiftlet's bodies both figure their maimed souls: "She was about the size of a cedar fence post and she had a man's gray hat pulled down low over her head. . . . He turned his back and faced the sunset. He swung both his whole and his short arm up slowly so that they indicated an expanse of sky and his figure formed a crooked cross" (*GM*, 54). And Tilman in "A View of the Woods" functions as a rather comic Satan: "Tilman was a man of quick action and few words. He sat habitually with his arms folded on the counter and his insignificant head weaving snake-fashion above them. He had a triangular-shaped face with the point at the bottom and the top of his skull was covered with a cap of freckles. His eyes were green and very narrow and his tongue was always exposed in his partly opened mouth" (*ERMC*, 76).

In the same essay in which O'Connor explains the significance of Hulga's wooden leg, "Writing Short Stories," she bewails the tendency of inexperienced writers to attempt to write with pure unembodied compassion, emotion, or thought. O'Connor argues that the successful writer "has to provide all these things with a body; he has to create a world with weight and extension." That weight and extension are created not only with in-your-face symbols like Hulga's leg or Parker's back or Shiftlet's crooked crosslike body or Tilman's serpentine head, but also with any number of tiny details that one might not think worth commenting on. For O'Connor good fiction is "in the details" and "how [the writer] sees them." She reminds us, "Ford Madox Ford taught that you couldn't have a man appear long enough to sell a newspaper in a story unless you put him there with enough detail to make the reader see him" (*MM*, 92). It is not very difficult to "see" a Hulga Hopewell with a wooden leg, especially given all the other necessary detail that O'Connor provides her.

The Body in Flannery O'Connor's Fiction will be ultimately less concerned with wooden legs, club feet, and snakelike heads and more with the kinds of detail that make real the "colored boy" from the drug store in "Revelation," a character who is there for reasons that are far more complicated than selling a newspaper or delivering drugs or even standing as a symbol; however, that complexity is possible only first because of the details. One of the common patterns in O'Connor's fiction is directed attention of the narrator to the physicality of characters who frighten, or even sometimes, attract other characters. This pattern is especially common in directing the attention of white characters toward black characters. In "Revelation," which has one of the most concentrated collection of racist characters in O'Connor's fiction, the white characters spend a good bit of time in the first part of the story talking about how they are "tired of buttering up niggers" and swearing that they "ain't" going to "love no niggers." Then a "colored boy" from the pharmacy comes to make a delivery: "He was a tall, very black boy in discolored white pants and a green nylon shirt. He was chewing gum slowly, as if to music. He set the tray down in the office opening next to the fern and stuck his head through to look for the secretary. . . . He rested his arms on the ledge and waited, his narrow bottom stuck out, swaying slowly to the left and right. He raised a hand over his head and scratched the base of his skull" (*ERMC*, 199–200). There is a reality and substance to this character that goes beyond the obviously effective details of his dress and his gum-chewing. His body is dramatically present in part because he acts upon it himself and because parts of it act on their own. He sticks his head through the office opening; he rests his arms on the ledge; he sticks his narrow bottom out; it sways left and right; he raises his hand; and he scratches his skull. One probably wouldn't want to argue that any of the body parts of this character are symbolic. They simply do not have enough space in the narrative, development, or intertextual significance to accumulate symbolic meaning. However, the body is an important element in all of O'Connor's fiction so that the accumulation of incarnational bodily details strongly supports, like the skeletal structure of a building, O'Connor's sacramental and grotesque themes, whether those body parts are, more specifically, say, sexually or epistemologically or even socially oriented.

The physicality of the deliveryman in "Revelation" sets the white characters off in trajectories of their own racism sometimes tempered with condescension. After he leaves the "white-trash" woman announces, "They ought to send all them niggers back to Africa." The pleasant lady and Mrs. Turpin agree that "there's a heap of things worse than a nigger" and that "it's all kinds of them just like it's all kinds of us." The physicality of O'Connor's characters frequently holds out the opportunity for change. Just after the pleasant lady and Ruby agree in their superior fashion that "it takes all kinds to make the world go round," Mary Grace, the violent instrument of Ruby's awakening, "snapped her teeth together. Her lower lip turned downwards and inside out, revealing the pale pink inside of her mouth" (*ERMC,* 200–201).

In "The Artificial Nigger" the focus of the story is on the physicality of blacks and the threat that such physicality poses to the white characters—Nelson and Mr. Head. Nelson, who has been taught to hate blacks by his grandfather, Mr. Head, doesn't even recognize a black man, even though that man's physicality is imposing: "One of his hands rested on his stomach which rode majestically under his buttoned coat, and in the other he held the head of a black walking stick that he picked up and set down with a deliberate outward motion each time he took a step" (*GM,* 109). The intense physicality of the descriptions of this man and the black woman to whom Nelson is attracted in the city are by no measure rare in O'Connor's fiction, although as Jeanne Perreault argues very effectively, the woman's sensuality is unrivaled. O'Connor's focus on the flesh, on the body, is a result not only of her artistic sensibilities but also of her deep immersion in the Catholic church. In a 1955 letter to Betty Hester she writes, "I am always astonished at the emphasis the Church puts on the body. It is not the soul she says that will rise but the body, glorified." That focus, O'Connor believed, belongs on the central mysteries of the life of Jesus: "the virgin birth, the Incarnation, the resurrection." She saw these as "the true laws of the flesh and the physical." For a secular audience it is no less astonishing that O'Connor believed that "death, decay, destruction are the suspension of these laws" (*HB,* 100).[26] That she saw death as a temporary state before the resurrection does not mean that death was not an important feature of the life that she represents in her fiction. In fact the deaths that she represents (those of Harry Ashfield, Mason Tarwater, the entire grandmother's family, Mrs. May, Bishop, Hazel, Solace Layfield, Tanner, Dudley, Mr. Guizac, General Sash, Julian's mother, Mr. Fortune, Mary Fortune Pitts, Thomas's mother, Norton) are frequently the most physically descriptive passages of the narratives.

In almost every O'Connor story there is a focus on a body part or on the entire body as symbol, but alongside those bright symbols there are also innumerable references to the body that might go unnoticed in the glare. Thus in "A Temple of the Holy Ghost" there is the hermaphrodite, who as the most obvious symbol in the story, helps the young girl realize or sense, as Miles Orvell puts it, that "the Word made flesh makes a temple of even the most grotesque of bodies." Parenthetically, Orvell points out that "the story is notable for the abundance of corporeal imagery it contains."[27] This corporeal imagery details not only the hermaphrodite but also Susan and Joanne, the girl's visiting cousins, and the imaginative birth of the baby rabbits, which the girl says the mother rabbit spit from its mouth. There is a great deal of nascent sexuality in the story. When the girl tells Susan and Joanne about Wendell and Cory, the boys who will visit them, Susan asks the girl a pointed question and subtly reveals in her body action a good deal about O'Connor's interest in the body[28]: "'How does a child like you know so much about these men?' Susan asked and pushed her face up close to the mirror to watch the pupils in her eyes dilate" (*GM,* 89–90). The self-absorption of the teenage girls is evident in their dress and their talk, but Susan's reflexive action here of pushing her own face up to the mirror to watch her eyes dilate reveals a character, or at least a narrator, who is intensely aware of the body. In "The Comforts of Home" rather obvious symbols stand in for body parts, as when Thomas tries to plant his pistol in Star Drake's "red pocketbook" because she had stolen it before and then put it back in his desk and also because he has arranged for Sheriff Farebrother to come to the house to arrest her for theft. However, he is caught in the act by the girl herself, Star Drake, the "nimpermaniac," as Thomas's mother sometimes sympathetically refers to her:

> "Tomsee put his pistol in my bag!" the girl shrieked.
>
> "Ridiculous," his mother said, yawning. "What would Thomas want to put his pistol in your bag for?" (*ERMC,* 140)

The pistol and the bag are appropriately ludicrous sexual symbols both in the context of Thomas's impotent rage that Star Drake has been taking advantage of his mother's charity and in the context of his repressed sexuality. However, there are more subtle indications in the story that the girl's body is important. When Thomas resentfully drives her back to her boardinghouse after a dinner at his house with his mother, he is so eager to get rid of her that he springs from the car and runs around to open her door: "She did not move from the car and Thomas was obliged to wait. After a moment one leg emerged, then her small white crooked face appeared and stared up at him. There was something about the look of it that suggested blindness but it was the blindness of those who don't know that they cannot see. Thomas was curiously sickened. The empty eyes moved over him" (*ERMC,* 125–26). Thomas might be partially, and ironically, "curiously sickened" by Star Drake's look of blindness, but he is also "curiously sickened" by her embodiment. The concentration on body parts and their actions here and throughout O'Connor's fiction is a constant and relatively subtle reminder of the embodiment of the human condition.

In *Wise Blood* there are rather obvious symbolic significances to both Asa Hawks's false self-blinding and Hazel's actual self-blinding. Thus, as is well recognized in the critical literature, the eye and sight in general are quite important as symbols for spiritual insight and blindness, knowledge and innocence. However, the eyes are simply one body part among many that are important in *Wise Blood.* Consider the failed seduction scene between Hazel and Sabbath Lily:

> He put his hat over his face and folded his arms across his chest. She lifted herself up on her hands and knees and crawled over to him and gazed at the top of his hat. Then she lifted it off like a lid and peered into his eyes. They stared straight upward. "It don't make any difference to me," she said softly, "how much you like me."
>
> He trained his eyes into her neck. Gradually she lowered her head until the tips of their noses almost touched but still he didn't look at her. (*WB*, 123).

Although Hazel has decided to seduce Sabbath as a way to prove to himself and to Asa Hawks that he "was in earnest when he said he preached The Church Without Christ" (*WB*, 110), he has little real interest in Sabbath. Hazel is stupidly convinced that it would take a while to seduce Sabbath, "considering her innocence. He felt it was too hard a job to be done in an afternoon" (*WB*, 121). Most of Hazel's body actions are entirely reflexive in the passage above (he puts his hat over his face and crosses his arms) or evasive (he trains his eyes on her neck or doesn't look at her at all). Sabbath looks him directly in the eyes and lowers her head to touch her nose to his, given that she is the real seducer. So, although the eyes are certainly symbolically important, other body parts (face, arms, chest, hands, knees, neck, head, noses) are heavily involved in signaling this inverted seduction scene. The eyes are also heavily symbolic in *The Violent Bear It Away.* Riding with Meeks, the copper flue salesman, into the city to meet his uncle Rayber, the schoolteacher, Francis Tarwater imagines his uncle's eyes: "He saw them dark grey, shadowed with knowledge, and the knowledge moved like tree reflections in a pond where far below the surface shadows a snake may glide and disappear" (*VBA*, 56). The symbolic significance of the eyes could hardly be more obvious in this passage.

However much O'Connor might have felt that for "the hard of hearing you shout, and for the almost-blind you draw large and startling figures" (*MM*, 34), a literature made exclusively of garish colors, loud noises, and obvious symbols would be, at best, aesthetically flawed. There are times when O'Connor whispers her sacramental message and traces ever so faint outlines of it, as in the description of Mason Tarwater eating his lunch in the city after unsuccessfully trying to have his father's will changed so that Rayber would not inherit his property: "The old man unbuttoned his coat and allowed his stomach to ease forward and rest on his lap while he ate. His face worked wrathfully; the skin between the pockmarks appeared to jump from one spot to another" (*VBA*, 30). There is no obvious symbolic significance to Mason's stomach or his pockmarked skin; however, the slow accumulation of such body-part details supports O'Connor's texts and meanings in ways that are indispensable, as I will demonstrate in the remainder of this book.

The investigative center of this book is the use of the body, body parts, and grammatical voice in O'Connor's exploration of sacramentalism, the incarnation, and the grotesque. The body, sacramentalism, the incarnation, and the grotesque have all to various degrees been well investigated within the methodology of literary criticism of various stripes—New Critical, structural, poststructural, feminist, and so on. *The Body in Flannery O'Connor's Fiction* is a new development in these discussions because it adds the methodologies of computational stylistics.

Grammatical Voice

If in this section we clarify how the term *grammatical voice* will be used in this book and how that differs significantly from the more usual literary understandings of *voice,* themselves frequently diverse and incompatible, we can avoid some potential serious confusion. There are two significantly frequent uses of the term *voice* in literary studies, one used from the perspective of narratology, the other from the perspective of Bakhtinian dialogism. Neither of these uses is the primary topic of this book; however, both will be occasionally referred to in the book. The narratological significance is illustrated by Gérard Genette's use of the term in his *Narrative Discourse.* There Genette defines *voice* as the manifestations of "the way in which the narrating itself is implicated in the narrative . . . and along with that its two protagonists: the narrator and his audience, real or implied." That is, in studying the voice of narratives, narratologists like Genette typically study questions such as who the narrator is and to whom the narrator is speaking or writing. In O'Connor's fiction one might ask from a narratological perspective about the voice of the narrator and the narrator's audience, meaning that one asks questions about, for example, whether the narrator is of the party of the devil, as John Hawkes would have us believe, or whether the audience is so deaf to O'Connor's sacramental message that it has to be shouted at, as O'Connor herself would have us believe.

As one might expect, even in narratology the term *voice* has more than one meaning. As Genette warns us, one confusion that is common in narratological study is that between voice and point of view. Point of view is, as Genette points out, primarily about "who 'sees'" in the narration, while voice is about "who 'speaks.'"[29] This is a distinction that will be useful to us. In "The River" the distinction between narratological voice and point of view is crucial for understanding the power of the narration. There is, of course, a distinction between the sophisticated narrator of the story and the major character, Harry Ashfield, who the narrator reports is "four or five" (*GM,* 31). In the following passage, which narrates the events that occur during and just after the Connin boys trick Harry into getting himself trampled by a hog, there are clear contrasts between narrative voice and point of view: "'Now you can lift up the board and put your face to the . . .' a quiet voice began. He had already done it and another face, gray, wet and sour, was pushing into his, knocking him down and back as it scraped out under the plank. Something snorted over him and charged back again, rolling him over and pushing him up from behind and then sending him forward, screaming through the yellow field, while it bounded behind. The three Connins watched from where they were. The one sitting on the pen held the loose board back with his dangling foot. Their stern faces didn't brighten any but they seemed to become less taut, as if some great need had been partly satisfied" (*GM*, 36). There are at least two, perhaps three, different points of view in this passage: that of Harry, who sees the face push into his and feels and hears "something" attacking him; that of the Connin boys, who see the hog bounding behind the fleeing Harry; and perhaps that of the narrator, who watches the faces of the Connin boys. The narrative voice of the passage is that of an ironic narrator who enjoys a good joke and understands the operation of psychological repression and scapegoating. Of particular interest in this passage is the use of the face as a body part. First, the Connin boys tell Harry to put his face to the opening in the pig pen; then, the hog's face appears to push into Harry's; finally, the slight emotional release of the abuse is registered in the Connin boys' faces. The narrator's voice is responsible for reporting all three uses; however, the point of view changes with each use.

The other common use of *voice* in literary theory is that of Bakhtinian multivoiced dialogism. In *The Dialogic Imagination* Bakhtin argues that the novel is differentiated from other language forms most consistently by its extreme dialogism, the mixture of separate "voices," *voice* referring to the utterances, thoughts, and contextual dynamics of individuals' language production.[30] One of the more familiar dialogic devices in literary prose is free indirect discourse, a mixture of direct discourse and indirect discourse. This mixture is commonly, but not exclusively, understood as a "dialogue" between the "voices" of characters and narrators. The following passage occurs in O'Connor's 1947 M.F.A. thesis story "The Turkey," a story typical of other early O'Connor short stories in having massive amounts of dialogism: "He [Ruller] remembered the minister had said young men were going to the devil by the dozens this day and age; forsaking gentle ways; walking in the tracks of Satan. They would rue the day, he said. There would be weeping and gnashing of teeth" (*CS*, 48). As I point out in my 1996 essay "The Dialogic Repetition of Free Indirect Discourse in Oral and Literary Narrative," the degree of dialogism in this passage is by no means rare across the entirety of O'Connor's fiction. Indirect discourse most recognizably occurs when a thought or instance of speech is reported in a dependent clause as the object of a verb of thought or speech, such as *remembered* above. In the first sentence there is an indirect discourse report of indirect discourse. The most imbedded discourse is that of the minister reported in a dependent clause ("young men were going to the devil by the dozens this day and age; forsaking gentle ways; walking in the tracks of Satan") as an object of the verb *said.* Then there is an indirect discourse report of that indirect discourse ("the minister had said young men were going to the devil by the dozens this day and age; forsaking gentle ways; walking in the tracks of Satan") as an object of the verb *remembered.* Thus in that first sentence the narrator's, Ruller's, and the minister's discourses are mixed. The second sentence is an indirect discourse report of the minister's speech; however, it is filtered through Ruller's consciousness and then reported by the narrator. So that sentence, too, is dialogically "multivoiced." Finally, the last sentence is the most multivoiced of the three. It is in the form of free indirect discourse, among the most dialogic of speech and thought representation modes. Free indirect discourse is so called because it is indirect discourse "free" of the reporting verb of speech or thought. To turn the last sentence into indirect discourse, one would simply have to subordinate it to a speech or thought verb as in, "He said that there would be weeping and gnashing of teeth." In this one multivoiced sentence, there occur the voices of Ruller, the minister, the narrator, and the Jesus of Luke 13:28.[31]

Grammatical voice, one of the central topics of this book, is not *voice* in the sense of the narrator's language in the context of the narrative nor in the sense of the author's, or narrator's, or character's unique voice, however multivoiced the narrative might be. Although, as we will see in chapter 6, some understandings of narratological voice are derived metaphorically from grammatical voice, the term *grammatical voice* most often refers to the complex interaction of grammatical subject, verb, and the semantics of both. It is not easy to find a simple definition of even *grammatical voice,* for the reasons that voice is complex and that linguists certainly do not agree on how to analyze voice, even in such a relatively well analyzed language as English. Gregory Ward, Betty Birner, and Rodney Huddleston's general definition of voice will serve us well as a beginning: "a system where the contrasting forms differ in the way semantic roles are aligned with syntactic functions, normally with some concomitant marking on the verb."[32] Specifically, *voice* normally refers to the affected/nonaffected semantic status of the subject of the verb. At least initially the clearest voice distinction in English is between the active and the passive. Consider the use of the verb *embarrass* in the following:

1. Her niece Sage embarrassed Meredith.
2. Meredith was embarrassed by her niece Sage.

In the active (1), the subject is the actor (controlling) participant while the object is the goal (noncontrolling, affected) participant. In the passive (2), the relationships among grammatical position and semantic roles are modified. The goal appears as subject, and the actor appears as object of the preposition *by.* The verb complex is also altered in occurring with a form of the verb *be*—here *was*—and the past participle form of the verb—here, *embarrassed.* A third voice distinction—the middle—will be of significant interest to us in this study. A common analysis of the middle voice argues that, although not syntactically unified in English, it is typologically a construction, or collection of constructions, that signals a subject that is affected by the action of the verb. In the passive (2), the subject is affected as the goal. Yet the passive is not exactly the middle because the middle further involves both formal and semantic distinctions that are not present in passives. As Huddleston argues, the middle voice "is in some sense intermediate between active and passive," as in (3):

3. Meredith embarrasses easily.

Note that the subject is the goal, as in the passive, but the verb complex does not contain *be* plus the past participle. Because the verb in the middle does not have an easily identifiable form, as does the passive, for example, there is quite a bit of disagreement not only on how to analyze the semantics of the middle in English but also on which constructions in English are actually middle, if any are. As Huddleston says of the term *middle,* "we put scare quotes around the term to signal that it is being used in an extended sense and is not to be interpreted as denoting a formal category in the voice system."[33]

I will be exploring these and other issues of terminology, analysis, and meaning in detail in chapter 2. However, now we can get a good sense of the range of constructions that will be analyzed in this book if we consider that among the many specific syntactic constructions that are typologically related to the middle voice are passives, body-action constructions, and reflexives. An example of a body-action construction from *Wise Blood* is "he saw the wild face turn," in which Enoch sees Hazel turn as Hazel is about to throw a rock at him (*WB,* 99). The verb *turn* here names a body action, and "the wild face" is both the actor and the goal, a unity of grammatical and semantic function that emphasizes (over the entirety of O'Connor's fiction) the problem of the spirit in the body, an essential incarnational, as opposed to Manichean, relation. And the isolation of the body part as grammatical subject serves O'Connor's celebrated exploration of the grotesque. Thus the present study tests the applicability of a cross-linguistic category (voice) in literary interpretation. James D. Benson, William S. Greaves, and Glenn Stillar have demonstrated that the use of transitivity, ergativity, and grammatical voice in Tennyson's "The Lotos-Eaters" creates dialogism, that is, a play of many worlds, one of which is middle in the sense that "its entities do not act on anything."[34] *The Body in Flannery O'Connor's Fiction* advances the discussion of the middle in literary interpretation in two ways. First, it expands the arena of the effect of the middle to the entire literary work of an author. Second, it examines the middle as it affects the interpretation of the literary functions of the body and actions by the body, the human body being a natural locus of middle-voice semantics since it is so frequently the actor or goal, or both.

Computation and Statistics

A stylistic analysis seeks to do at least one of the following: 1) advance linguistic and/or stylistic theory or methodology; 2) advance our understanding of the author(s) under discussion in a way that would not be possible without the methodology or theoretical apparatus of stylistics. By its very nature, computational literary stylistics makes possible an analysis that otherwise would be very difficult, even practically impossible, to perform. That is, in at least one variety, computational stylistics uses the computational power and convenience of the personal computer to search, re-search, calculate, and re-calculate linguistic patterns of interest in literary works. Ideally the analysis produces insight into the remarkably finely detailed formal level at which some literary meaning is produced.[35] The computer is of primary value in its searching and calculating capacities. One could theoretically, but not practically, search texts by hand, or eye, for the same patterns; however, the computer can find without error in seconds what it might take humans without computers days, weeks, or frequently months to find in much error-prone and tedious work. The same generalizations apply to the thousands of repetitive calculations for statistics, such as chi-square scores or log-likelihood scores, that are frequently indispensable in stylistic analysis.

The primary software tool for this study is my own text-analysis program Textant. The present study also introduces the reader to the use of the first-generation Brown Corpus in computational stylistics. I have electronically scanned O'Connor's texts for my study here and elsewhere. Body parts are interesting test cases for computational stylistics, first because the body has been treated extensively, although mostly nonstylistically, in the critical literature on O'Connor, and, second, because although body parts such as *eyes, face, head,* and *mouth* as tokens are extraordinarily easy to search for with text-analysis programs, the grammatical contexts in which they appear and produce literary significance are much more resistant to computational discovery. Although body parts are also extraordinarily easy to count using text-analysis programs, there are many complications with using probability tests with textual data. This thorny methodological problem will be discussed in some detail, using both the chi-square test and the log-likelihood test, the latter of which has been suggested as an alternative to the more problematic chi-square test. Once one has found all tokens of body parts of interest and has ranked the significance of the frequencies, one can then use the computer as a concordancer to find all tokens in context for a detailed qualitative analysis. However, with a frequently occurring word, such as *eyes,* the analyst is still, at this stage, faced with a bewildering variety of uses. *The Body in Flannery O'Connor's Fiction* will argue also for the use of collocational analysis as a methodology for discovering significantly frequent patterns at the sentence level that might then be analyzed at the grammatical level of voice. These collocational patterns (defined by John Sinclair as "the occurrence of two or more words within a short space of each other in a text") allow one to investigate the interesting grammatical context of texts above the level of individual words.[36] Inherent in a phrase such as "interesting grammatical context" is the inescapable qualitative core of most stylistic analysis, and most literary analysis, even that which is aided by computers. Thus, the present study will also include discussions of the grammatical context—voice—in which a large number of collocations with body parts is involved.

The Organization of *The Body in Flannery O'Connor's Fiction*

Chapter 2 explores the relationships between American (primarily T. Givón's and Suzanne Kemmer's) understandings of grammatical voice and Hallidayan systemic understanding of grammatical voice. There are advantages to using more than one approach in a stylistic analysis since where one stresses the syntactic nature of the English middle (e.g., Givón's), another stresses the typological connections among related constructions (e.g., Kemmer's), and still another stresses the lexical connections among verbs in English (e.g., Halliday's). Chapter 3 will demonstrate two statistical methods (chi-square and Dunning's log-likelihood) for determining significantly frequent words and collocations in one corpus as compared to another, specifically including those words and collocations that name or include body parts. Word frequency analysis and collocational tests such as chi-square and Dunning's log-likelihood help us to determine which words and combinations of words in any particular author's works are statistically unusual either because of frequent occurrence or infrequent occurrence. While the chi-square is the more commonly used statistic for discriminating frequency distributions, Dunning's log-likelihood is less sensitive to the sparse data (low frequencies) that one finds with some lexical items referring to body parts.[37] This chapter in particular will serve two purposes: 1) an exploration of the practical effects of choosing chi-square or Dunning's log-likelihood for statistical testing of frequency and collocation distributions in texts and 2) a consideration of dispersion calculations in order to determine how well distributed constructions might be in a text collection. Readers who have no interest in the statistical side of stylistics can skip chapter 3 entirely with no loss of understanding of the remainder of the book. Chapter 4 explores the distribution of body parts in O'Connor and the Brown texts and also explores the use of middle voice verbs and both non-body-part and body-part subjects to those verbs. Constructions with animate but non-body-part subjects indicate that the entire body is involved in the middle event (for example, "I'll roll"). Chapter 5 investigates both reflexives and body-part reflexives in O'Connor's fiction. In the concluding chapter 6, I discuss the differences in the use of the body and voice in linguistics and the interpretive humanities. This chapter makes the overall point that, contrary to the widespread belief that the interpretive humanities have long moved past linguistics, they continue to borrow and metaphorize terms and concepts from linguistics. Chapter 6 also contains discussions of 1) the importance of the body in current and recent literary theory, and 2) the differences in the treatment of body parts in literary theory and in stylistics.

There are significant disagreements among scholars on practically every issue of importance in *The Body in Flannery O'Connor's Fiction.* First, as we have seen in this chapter, there is disagreement about whether and how the concentration on the grotesque in O'Connor's fiction is a sacramental and incarnational concern. I believe that this question has been answered in general in this chapter. However, chapters 4 and 5 will return to the details of these arguments with further support in the voice and body-part patterns of O'Connor's fiction. There are vast differences in the ways in which various members and "schools" in the linguistic scholarly world analyze the middle voice. These issues lie at the foundations of verb argument structure, as in transitivity versus ergativity, foundations that will be developed in chapter 2 and further explored in chapters 4 and 5. Also there is a difference of opinion on the appropriateness of various statistical tests for analyzing the data patterns at issue in this book. Chapter 3 will consider some of the detail in questions that are important in this regard, in particular the appropriateness of chi-square and log-likelihood tests. And, finally, chapter 6 treats of the divide between the formalism of stylistic analysis and the nonformalism of poststructuralist and postmodernist theories as they are represented in writings on the middle voice, the body, and trauma.

The Body in Flannery O'Connor's Fiction is written with a general educated audience in mind; a general audience will find here not only a way to read O'Connor that gets at her "style" in the most basic sense (how her fiction is markedly unique even at the sentence level) but also detailed exploration of some of the fundamental theoretical issues of interest in literary studies today: the role of empirical evidence, the body, the persistence of religious significance. Those readers with academic specialties in linguistics, stylistics, text analysis, literature, and O'Connor's fiction in particular should also find it valuable. I have presented all linguistic, computational, and statistical information in ways that readers should find highly accessible, although again, readers may skip chapter 3, in which most of the statistical information is concentrated. The barriers between and among the interpretive humanities, linguistics, and stylistics are only partial, given that, as chapter 6 illustrates, there is plentiful borrowing that continues to this day, long after poststructuralism. The final barriers are in essence methodological rather than conceptual; however, works like this book—works that do connect the methodological and the conceptual—attempt to bridge the divide between the sciences and the humanities. Given that interdisciplinarity is a highly touted and sometimes even highly funded virtue today in higher education and given that computational stylistics combines literary analysis, computer programming, statistics, and linguistics, it seems highly likely, or at least desirable and reasonable, that stylistics will become popular once again, this time around in the specific form of computational stylistics. *The Body in Flannery O'Connor's Fiction* demonstrates that literary scholars need not abandon the qualitative and the fine-grained analysis of significance that they are used to in their field if they adopt some computational and stylistic methodology. In fact, as this book will demonstrate, it is the use of these methodologies that allows us to dig both deeper and wider into the significances that lie buried beneath the surface of O'Connor's fiction.

Grammatical Voice

The more you look at a sentence like that, the more you can learn from it.
Flannery O'Connor (*MM,* 69)

Quite aside from the interesting metaphorical uses of the middle voice in postmodern literary theory, grammatical voice in general is a site of much disagreement and competing descriptive and theoretical models in linguistics itself.[1] To engage in the issues in enough depth to make the whole arena of voice sufficiently clear and familiar for us to use in the analysis of voice in O'Connor's fiction, we will in this chapter explore a number of typological grammatical issues, not only in English but, very briefly, in other languages as well. However, we will be examining in this chapter a good number of interesting voice patterns in O'Connor's fiction as well so that this chapter, like all in the book, provides analysis of O'Connor's fiction, analysis that is crucial to the overall argument of the book. Perhaps the easiest entryway, with which probably most readers are familiar, is the active/passive distinction in English—touched on briefly in chapter 1. The following examples, the second from O'Connor's "The Displaced Person," the first a rewrite of the same passage for illustrative purposes, will begin further and more detailed consideration:

1. Over by the toolshed, about fifteen feet away, the two Negroes, Astor and Sulk, had stopped work to watch. The mulberry tree **hid** them but Mrs. Shortley knew they were there.
2. "Over by the toolshed, about fifteen feet away, the two Negroes, Astor and Sulk, had stopped work to watch. They **were hidden** by a mulberry tree but Mrs. Shortley knew they were there." (*GM,* 197)

Grammatical voice is most frequently, but not exclusively, understood to refer to the semantic relationship of the subject of the verb to the verb. Following the examples quoted above, in the active voice (1) the subject is roughly, for now, an "actor"—that is, the performer of the event. In the passive (2) the subject is prototypically a "goal"—that is, the noncontrolling affected participant of the event.[2] The active is formally marked by no extra morphology in the verb complex; however, the passive verb complex contains a form of the verb *be*—in (2), *were*—and the main verb in the past participial form—in (2), *hidden.* In the passive the actor appears in an optional prepositional phrase, in (2), "by a mulberry tree." As T. Givón argues, there are many functional motivations to use the passive, among them that the actor is unknown or unimportant, that the actor is contextually given, and that the goal is topically continuous.[3] These three motivations are illustrated in the following, as well as in (1) and (2) above:

3. "The army sent him halfway around the world and forgot him. He **was** wound**ed** and they remembered him long enough to take the shrapnel out of his chest." (*WB*, 24)
4. "'You go to hell,' a surly voice inside the ape-suit said, low but distinctly, and the hand **was** jerk**ed** away." (*WB*, 182)
5. "**He** felt that in the space between them, their spirits had broken the bonds of age and ignorance and were mingling in some unheard of knowledge of each other. **He was** transfix**ed** by the child's silence." (*VBA*, 134)

In (3) it is unknown or perhaps even unimportant who the actor was who wounded Hazel Motes in the war. In (4) it is clear from context that it is the man in the ape-suit who jerks his hand away from Enoch. And in (5) the "he" of the second, passive sentence—Rayber of *The Violent Bear It Away*—is topically continuous with the "he" of the first sentence. The importance of topic continuity is revealed in (1) and (2) especially clearly. In the altered (1) there is an unmotivated topic shift between the first and second sentence. In the first sentence of (1) the subject-topic is "the two Negroes," but in the second sentence the topic-subject shifts to "the mulberry tree." In O'Connor's (2), the subject-topic of the second, passive sentence, "they," is topically continuous with the subject-topic of the first sentence, "the two Negroes."

Languages with a Morphological Middle Voice

In languages that do formally mark the middle voice, there is typically a morphological marker of some sort on the verb complex. The following examples of classical Greek from Suzanne Kemmer demonstrate two well-recognized uses of the middle voice:

6. loúo-**mai** tâs cheîras
   "I wash my hands."
7. hállo-**mai**
   "I leap."

Example (6) illustrates the use of the Classical Greek morphological middle inflection *mai* for what Kemmer terms "body care" and (7) that for "translational motion,"[4] that is, motion that results in the subject changing location. As noted in chapter 1, the term *middle voice* most generally refers to a formal/semantic categorization of a verb whose subject is affected by the action of the verb without being an explicit passive goal.[5] Morphologically marked middle voice is not restricted to ancient languages. Many modern American Indian languages, for example, have robust explicitly marked middle systems.

The middle voice is particularly problematic in English because it is not grammatically realized in English with consistent morphological or syntactic patterns.[6] Thus there are no signals for the middle voice in English like the presence of a form of the *be* verb and the past participle, which relatively unambiguously mark the passive voice in English. Note, then, that there are no morphological or syntactic signals of the middle voice in the English glosses for (6) and (7). The lack of consistent morphological and syntactic signals for the middle voice does not mean, as we will see, that there are no middle voice constructions in English. Rather than identifying them solely with form, we will instead rely primarily on semantics.

Because many of the middle voice constructions in O'Connor's fiction are prototypical in their middle voicedness, and because, as we will see in chapter 6, poststructuralist literary theory has made much out of the construction, however metaphorized it might be in those uses, it will be useful to consider a few examples from a contemporary language with an explicitly marked and robust middle voice. The existence of the middle voice among many modern American Indian languages whose diversity and linguistic richness equal and frequently exceed that of Indo-European languages seems especially worth pointing out, at least briefly, given the remarkable generalizations of some postmodern writers on the middle voice. Dominick LaCapra, for example, writes, "Modern languages do not have a middle voice in grammar but may at best allow for a discursive analogue of it," this startling overgeneralization made in the context of his discussion of Roland Barthes's metaphorical extension of the grammatical middle voice to the discursive middle-voicedness of "intransitive writing." I will return in detail to this postmodern nostalgia in chapter 6.[7] For now, however, consider the following examples from Creek, an American Indian language currently spoken in Oklahoma:

8a. ca-tonoof-k-itooms
I-bruise-MID-be
"I'm being bruised."

b. *iimoomiit ca-tonoof-k-itooms
on purpose I-bruise-MID-be
"I'm being bruised on purpose."

These Creek examples have been simplified in their morphological divisions to make the presentation of the crucial details a bit clearer.[8] The verb *tonofita,* "to bruise," is an inherently transitive verb, meaning that it takes in its "active" form an actor subject and a goal object. In (8a) the subject is marked by *ca-*, "I." The verb is signaled as being in the middle voice by the inclusion of the *-k(a)* suffix. Although (8a) might look very much like a passive, at least in its English translation, it is not, for two reasons: 1) it is impossible to express the actor, as it is possible to do in, for example, an English passive ("I'm being bruised by you"); and 2), as (8b) illustrates by its ungrammaticality, there is not even an implied actor in the Creek middle, here attempted by the addition *iimoomiit,* "on purpose." Note that the addition of that adverbial is possible in the English translation, indicating that the English translation of the Creek middle is a passive. The middle in (8a) is termed a "resultative" because it communicates the result of the action on the goal subject. Given the lack of an explicit morphological marker of the middle voice in English, it is important to stress the productivity of this pattern in Creek. Among the verbs that pattern like *tonofita* in (8) are those in the following very small selection:

9\.

ACTIVE		MIDDLE	
apallayita	"wrap"	apalla*k*ita	"wrapped"
awanayita	"tie up"	awana*k*ita	"tied up"
pooyita	"finish"	poo*k*ita	"finished"
kacita	"break"	kac*k*ita	"broken"

There are many historical and phonological complications in the realization of the middle in Creek, but it is a productive system in the contemporary language.

Other Creek middle construction types, whose English semantic equivalents will be discussed as they appear in O'Connor's fiction, are represented by the following:

10\. ca-tonoof-k-os-ii-tooms
I-bruise-MID-DIM-ST-be
"I bruise easily."

11\. iimoomiit łakpal-k-ey-s
on purpose turn-MID-I-DEC
"I'm turning on purpose."

In (10) the combination of the middle marker *-k(a),* the diminutive morpheme *-os(i),* and the stative morpheme *-ii* produces what is termed the "facilitative middle," so called because what is communicated is that there is some quality of the subject-goal that facilitates its being acted upon in the way that the verb indicates, here "to bruise." In (11) we have what is called a "body action" middle construction, in which the actor acts on itself.[9] Note the presence of both the adverbial adjunct *iimoomiit* and the middle *-k(a).* There is another indicator of an actor subject in this construction—the controlling actor agreement suffix *-ey* rather than the noncontrolling goal agreement prefix *ca-* for first person, which we saw in (8) and (10). The construction type in example (11) illustrates very clearly the disjunction of the middle and the passive in Creek, in that the only participant is an actor rather than a goal. Like the resultative middle verbs in (9), the body-action middle verbs in Creek are numerous and include the following small sample:

12.

ACTIVE		MIDDLE	
accaayita	"lean"	accaakita	"leaned, lean"
takhayita	"line up"	takhakita	"lined up, line up"
folotita	"turn"	folotkita	"turned, turn"
akoyyita	"move"	akoykita	"moved, move"

Again, the commonality in all of the middle constructions is that there is a subject that is affected by the action of the verb, whether that subject is a goal or an actor.

Transitive and Ergative Approaches to the Middle

In part because of the absence of any consistent formal signal of the middle voice in English, there are substantial disagreements among linguists on just how to analyze or even what to analyze as the English middle voice. There are two historically popular ways of approaching the middle voice, which can be termed the transitive approach and the ergative approach. I will explain those two ways here, with greater attention given to the second of them. A third approach can be termed typological; that approach, represented in Kemmer's work and compatible with the ergative approach, will allow us to highlight some elements of the middle and especially related constructions that would otherwise escape our notice. These three approaches to the middle voice are important at least in part because it is highly unlikely that any one of them provides the whole and final truth about the English middle and because each foregrounds elements that the other two do not.

Givón's approach can be typified as the "transitive approach" to the middle. The term *transitive approach* is used by Kristin Davidse and Leisbet Heyvaert in a similar but slightly different way. Here I borrow it to characterize Givón's approach to the middle because 1) it stresses the importance of the middle verb being inherently transitive, and 2) it stresses that the subject is a goal. Givón lists the following four criteria for classifying a construction as a middle-voice one in English:

a. The verb involved is inherently a *transitive* verb.
b. The grammatical subject is a *patient* [our *goal*].
c. There is no clearly discernible *responsible agent* [our *actor*], and thus no *action.*
d. While a discernible agent [actor] is absent, the construction is *not* used primarily as an *agent-demoting* [*actor-demoting*] device.[10]

Consider the examples, then, in (13):

13a. The book is selling well.
b. *The book is selling well by the bookstore.

The example in (13a) fulfils the (a) and (b) requirements. The word *inherently* is difficult to define operationally in the phrase "inherently a *transitive* verb," but one could safely specify that a particular verb in a particular sentence cannot be middle in Givón's sense unless the verb could act as a transitive verb with its subject as an object. In (13a) the verb *sell* can be transitive (one can sell a book). In (13a) the subject is a goal as one can demonstrate in a nearly synonymous sentence in which the book occurs as a direct object: "The bookstore is selling the book well." Sentence (13b) indicates that there is no actor in the middle (requirement c) and that therefore the middle is not an actor-demoting device (requirement d). Sentence (14a), below, is not a middle in Givón's sense:

14a. The book just sits on the shelf.
  b. *She is sitting the book on the shelf.

The subject of (14a) is not a goal; furthermore, the verb *to sit* in the sense in which it is used in (14a) is intransitive as is demonstrated by the ungrammatical sentence in (14b).

Another tradition, more common in systemic linguistics, can be labeled the "ergative approach." I also borrow this term with some modification in my application from Davidse and Heyvaert. In order to understand the significance of the ergative approach, it is necessary to consider very briefly what are classified as "nominative/accusative" languages and "ergative/absolutive" languages, in the most restrictive sense. Ergative/absolutive languages generally pattern at least morphologically in a different way from nominative/accusative languages such as English. Consider, first, the following English examples:

15a. She hired her. b. She celebrated.

Theoretically, as Lindsay J. Whaley points out, the subject of the transitive and the object of the transitive within the same clause, that is, in (15a) *she* and *her*, must be distinguishable because otherwise "their grammatical relations [could not] be recovered from the morphosyntax." The subject of the intransitive, in (15b), could logically look like either the subject of the transitive (*she*) or the object of the transitive (*her*) because the one argument in an intransitive cannot be confused with either the subject of the transitive or the object of the transitive: they simply do not occur together in the same clause.[11] In English the subject of the intransitive patterns like the subject of the transitive, the *she* of (15b) and (15a), respectively. The subject of the transitive and the subject of the intransitive are the nominative arguments (for example, *she*), and the object of the transitive is the accusative argument, the *her* of (15a). Thus English is called a nominative/accusative language.

Thoroughgoing ergative languages are common in Australia and the Philippines. The defining difference for an ergative/absolutive language is the treatment of the subject of the intransitive verb. Consider for instance the following examples from Dyirbal, an Australian language (data and analysis from R. M. W. Dixon):

16.	ŋuma	banaga-n^{y}u	
	father + ABS	return-NON-FUTURE	
	"Father returned."		
17.	ŋuma	yabu-ŋgu	buṛa-n
	father + ABS	mother-ERG	see-NON-FUTURE
	"Mother saw father."		

We can think of *ŋuma*, "father," in (16) as a subject of an intransitive verb. It is marked morphologically as an absolutive argument in Dyirbal by the presence of a zero suffix. In (17) the object of the transitive verb is also marked by the zero ABSOLUTIVE suffix. However, note that the subject of the transitive, *yabu*, "mother" in (17) is marked by the *ŋgu* ERGATIVE suffix. Thus in ergative languages the "subject of the intransitive" and the "object of the transitive" are treated the same, as "absolutives," while the "subject of the transitive" is treated differently, as the "ergative." A bifurcation of Dixon's figure for illustrating the fundamental argument grouping difference between a nominative/accusative language and an ergative/absolutive language occurs in figures 1 and 2.[12]

FIGURE 1: **Nominative/accusative structure**

NOMINATIVE	{ Subject of the Transitive Subject of the Intransitive
ACCUSATIVE	{ Object of the Transitive

FIGURE 2: **Ergative/absolutive structure**

ERGATIVE	{ Subject of the Transitive
ABSOLUTIVE	{ Subject of the Intransitive Object of the Transitive

Thus, again, the real question is the patterning of the subject of the intransitive. Does it pattern with the subject of the transitive, in which case the language is nominative/accusative, or does it pattern with the object of the transitive, in which case the language is ergative/absolutive?

In the systemic tradition, especially that represented by M. A. K. Halliday's work, ergativity is at the core of the English verb lexicon, even though the English case system, as we have seen, is nominative/accusative. The addition of ergativity as an analytic frame, especially within lexical analysis, allows us to see a great deal more detail in the middle verb system of English than we could otherwise see. Halliday and Christian M. I. M. Matthiessen argue that ergativity is a thoroughgoing part of the entire transitivity system of English, but we will concentrate on its role in the lexicon. As Halliday and Matthiessen, and also Davidse, point out, there are two systems of transitivity in English, with "transitivity" broadly understood as the organization of arguments around a verb. These two systems are referred to as the narrow "transitive system" and the "ergative system." Consider the following examples illustrating the "transitive system" narrowly understood:

18a. The dog is barking. b. The dog is disturbing the neighborhood.

19a. The child is coughing. b. The child is spreading its germs.

20a. The painter is working. b. The painter is painting the wall.

These pairs of sentences are actor centered since referentially identical subjects can be assumed in both the (a) and (b) sentences of each pair. Another way to think about these sentences is that they are nominative centered since the subjects of the intransitive and the transitive are the same, both formally and semantically. As Halliday and Matthiessen and Davidse explain, transitive sentences, like those in (18b), (19b), and (20b), expand the clause to include the goal explictly. Davidse points out that intransitive and transitive related sentences, like those in (18)–(20), almost always include different verb lexemes. However, perhaps even clearer examples of the actor-centeredness of the "transitive system" in English are the following, in which the verb lexemes are the same:

21a. The child is eating. b. The child is eating the food.

22a. The students are learning. b. The students are learning the material.

Although, as Davidse argues, the goals might be implied even in the (a) sentences, the (a) and (b) sentences are minimally different simply by the explicit addition of the goals in the (b) sentences.

Verbs do not have to be actor centered in English. They can, as Halliday and Matthiessen and Davidse argue, be medium centered. The *medium* in systemic grammar is the entity in the sentence through "which the process comes into existence."[13] It is the central participant of the ergative verb in that it is the only required participant. In the case of the medium-centered verb, one has evidence of an "ergative system" in the verb lexicon of English:

23a. The window shattered.
b. The man shattered the window.
c. The ball shattered the window.

24a. The curtain moved.
b. The woman moved the curtain.
c. The wind moved the curtain.

These sets of sentences are medium centered. Given that we now know the simple basics of what constitutes a thoroughgoing ergative language such as Dyirbal, a way to understand the use of the term *ergative* to refer to "ergative verbs" in English is to look at the medium analogously as the absolutive argument. That is, the subject of the intransitive and the object of the transitive are central to the ergative English verb in the same way that they are treated similarly in ergative languages such as Dyirbal. Note in (23) and (24) that the subjects of the intransitives in the (a) sentences are identical to the objects of the transitives in the (b) and (c) sentences. Halliday and Matthiessen and Davidse explain that the ergative verb expands not to the goal but to the agent, the instigator of the event. As the (b) and (c) sentences show in (23) and (24), the agent can be human or not. Davidse argues that it is the identity of the verbs in ergative constructions that allows us to understand the subject of verbs such as *shatter* and *move* in (23a) and (24a) as mediums rather than actors as in the intransitive constructions of the (a) sentences of (18)–(22).

The ergative lexical pattern in English is very common. Halliday and Matthiessen found in a random sample of dictionary verb entries that 60 percent were of the ergative pattern.[14] Verbs that pattern ergatively are those in table 1, in addition to those mentioned above.

TABLE 1: **English ergative verbs**

cook	boil	blend	raise	swing	unravel
simmer	melt	bend	lift	close	tangle
open	turn	focus	rush	tire	zip
shut	sail	roll	shrug	button	wake
break	attach	jerk	sink	latch	weather

Many of these verbs occur in Halliday and Matthiessen's illustrations of ergativity. In order to demonstrate the ergative patterning of any verb in table 1, one needs simply to use the frames "Subject$_i$ is verbing" and "Subject$_j$ is verbing Object$_i$" where Subject$_i$ and Object$_i$ are coreferential and the verbs are the same. Thus, one can say, "It is shutting" and "I am shutting it," where *it* refers to a door that I am shutting and that is therefore shutting, or "It is melting" and "I am melting it," where *it* refers to butter that I am melting and that is therefore melting, or "It is simmering" and "I am simmering it," where *it* refers to a sauce that I am simmering and that is therefore simmering. Note that nonergative verbs cannot participate in this patterning. Thus in "It is eating" and "I am eating it," *it* cannot naturally have the same referent in the two sentences so that I am eating something and that something is therefore eating.[15]

For the interaction of the body, voice, and literary thematics, a second, and even more important, pattern is a semantic difference between the transitive paradigm and the ergative paradigm: as Davidse argues, the medium in the ergative participates in the process in a fundamental and indispensable way in which the goal in the transitive does not participate. Consider, then, the following sentences:

25a. The boy shattered the window.
 b. What the boy did was shatter the window.
 c. What the window did was shatter.
26a. The students learned the material.
 b. What the students did was learn the material.
 c. *What the material did was learn.

As Davidse points out, the "do-probe" (the frame "what the ____ did was ____"), can be applied to ergative forms such as (25a) to show in (25b) that the instigator-agent participates in the event and crucially in (25c) that the medium also participates in the event. She also argues that the success of the do-probe in (26b) and its failure in (26c) illustrate that in the nonergative transitive (26a), the actor participates in the event but the goal, "the material," does not: "Within the ergative system, something is being done to the Medium AS WELL AS the Medium itself 'doing' the process. It is characteristic of the central ergative participant that it co-participates in the process; the ergative middle allows one to isolate the Medium in its 'doing' relation to the process."[16]

Davidse and Heyvaert point out that a good number of analysts have argued that the middle voice is isomorphic with the one-participant ergative construction. One problem is, according to Davidse and Heyvaert, that the middle is not necessarily ergative, as we saw above in the so-called transitive analysis of the middle as exemplified by Givón. To review, consider the following:

27a. The machine bent the metal strip.
 b. The metal strip is bending.
 c. What the metal strip did is bend.

28a. He read the book.
 b. The book reads quickly.
 c. *What the book did was read.

The examples in (27) illustrate the ergative pattern. Example (27a) illustrates the two-participant ergative with an agent and a medium; (27b) illustrates the medium alone in the middle-voice structure; and (27c) illustrates the do-probe to demonstrate the participation of the medium in the event as a source for "energy input," as Davidse terms that participation. In (28a) we have the verb *read* used transitively. In (28b) we have an example of *read* used in the middle voice. The subject "the book" is the goal of the event not the actor. Example (28c) demonstrates that *read* is not an ergative verb; that is, the goal does not participate as an energy source in the event in the way that an ergative medium does. For these and other reasons, Davidse and Heyvaert conclude that the core of the meaning of the middle voice is that the subject "is—or is not— conducive to the Actor [or Agent] carrying out the process."[17] Thus in Davidse and Heyvaert's analysis of the middle, whether the verb is ergative or transitive, there must be a construed actor or agent that the middle subject either allows or doesn't allow by nature to perform the event. So, for example, according to them it is possible, using the "all by itself" test, to distinguish a middle and nonmiddle use of the one-participant ergative. Consider the following:

29a.	He thawed the meat.	30a.	He steered the new car.
b.	The meat thawed quickly.	b.	The new car steers easily.
c.	The meat thawed all by itself.	c.	*The new car steers all by itself.

The ergative (29b) can be interpreted, then, in two ways if one follows Davidse and Heyvaert's analysis. First, it can be considered simply as a one-participant ergative if one interprets the meat as thawing all by itself, as is explicitly signaled in (29c). Or it can be interpreted as a middle if one interprets the meat as somehow allowing the agent to thaw it. The ungrammaticality of (30c), then, demonstrates the thoroughgoing middle nature of (30b). There must be an agent conceptualized in (30b).[18]

Davidse and Heyvaert's "conducive" analysis of the middle is what we might see as a strict and narrow interpretation of the middle voice. However, we must not overreact and simply toss out the one-participant ergative, at least in stylistic analysis, for the reason that it is almost always ambiguously middle, even in the sense of Davidse and Heyvaert's strict analysis of the middle. Thus, consider the following examples from O'Connor:

31. "The man leaned off his platform and **his dried-up face** drew into a glare." (*WB*, 61)
32. "**Their hands** were resting on the table, red-speared at the tips." (*WB*, 15–16)
33. "**Her lower lip** turned downwards and inside out, revealing the pale pink inside of her mouth." (*ERMC*, 201)
34. "**Her eyebrows,** thin and fierce as a spider's leg, had drawn together ominously." (*GM*, 233)

In each of the examples in (31)–(34), the body-part terms in bold type serve as the subject of ergative verbs. The question is, then, whether these verbs are used in a purely middle sense or whether they are simply one-participant ergative verbs. If the difference is whether the subjects are perceived to act on their own, one cannot tell. Thus, one can say, "his dried-up face drew into a glare all by itself," "their hands were resting on the table all by themselves," "her lower lip turned downwards and inside out all by itself," and "her eyebrows had drawn together ominously all by themselves." These examples would seem to indicate that the verbs are used simply as one-participant ergatives. However, one can also imagine that there are agents, that is the owners of these body parts, manipulating them and thereby making these sentences exemplars of the prototypical middle voice.

The Aesthetic Ambiguity of the Ergative Middle

The ambiguity of one-participant ergative verbs, between internally and externally caused, is their essential value in signaling literary explorations of the body versus the mind. As Davidse argues, the one-participant ergative "neutralizes the features 'self-instigated' and 'externally instigated.'"[19] Only rarely does the context make clear that the ergative verbs are being used with external agents; in such cases the ergatives are sometimes used as participles, as in the following: "**She shut her eyes** and saw the pin point of light but so far away that she could not hold it steady in her mind. She felt as if she were blocked at the entrance of something. She sat staring with **her eyes shut,** into his eyes" (*WB*, 231–32). Here, Mrs. Flood, Hazel's landlady, shuts her own eyes. The participial use of the ergative verb *shut* in the next sentence is then unambiguously externally instigated. Even when context makes clear that there is an external instigator, that instigator may not be fully causative but instead may be permissive, as Davidse and Heyvaert argue. Consider the following: "He tried when possible to pass over these thoughts, to keep his vision located on an even level, to see no more than what was in front of his face and to **let his eyes stop** at the surface of that. It was as if he were afraid that if he **let his eye rest** for an instant longer than was needed to place something—a spade, a hoe, the mule's hind quarters before his plow, the red furrow under him—that the thing would suddenly stand before him, strange and terrifying, demanding that he name it and name it justly and be judged for the name he gave it" (*VBA*, 21–22).In this passage the thoughts that Francis Tarwater is trying to avoid are that he might become like his great-uncle in being obsessed with a "hunger" for Jesus, "the bread of life." This passage is one of the clearest statements of O'Connor's incarnational and anti-Manichean viewpoint. As I pointed out in chapter 1, Francis's notion of what it means to be called by God demonstrates his fundamentally Manichean views, views that O'Connor clearly ridicules: "When the Lord's call came, he wished it to be a voice from out of a clear and empty sky, the trumpet of the Lord God Almighty, untouched by any fleshly hand or breath" (*VBA*, 22). As readers of O'Connor know, Francis's first mission is to baptize a representation of the very real and very earthly human: his mentally retarded cousin, Bishop. Consistent with Davidse and Heyvaert's analysis of the middle as a "letting-construction" (that is, conducive construction), the constructions "let his eyes stop" and "let his eye rest," such types labeled by Leonard Talmy as "ENABLING causation," both demonstrate a fundamental fact of the body in O'Connor's fiction—that it frequently knows better than the agentive mind. As the examples below indicate, the ENABLING causative "let X verb" indicates a degree of volition on the part of the medium-subject of the embedded ergative verb (35) that is not present in the direct ergative causative (36) or the periphrastic "make X verb" causative (37):

35. Mary let the dog stop when he wanted to.
36. ?Mary stopped the dog when he wanted to.
37. ?Mary made the dog stop when he wanted to.

As Givón says of the "let" construction illustrated in (35), the "manipulee" ("the dog") "must retain a degree of agentiveness" for us, meaning that it must maintain the participation that is typical of the ergative medium. Note that (35) demonstrates that the adverbial "when he wanted to," ascribing volition to the dog, is compatible with the volition of "let X verb" and that (36) and (37) demonstrate that that volition is not compatible with the lack of ascribed volition in either the direct ergative causative or the periphrastic "make X verb" causative. As Davidse and Heyvaert argue, using a nonergative example, "*The ladder fixes quickly and easily under the window ledge* conveys that the ladder is designed in such a way that it *lets* one fix it quickly and easily to the window ledge."

The issue of causation, or instigation, in the ergative/middle is far more complex and context-dependent than even my discussion has so far indicated. Eric Buyssens points out in one of the relatively few middle-voice studies besides Davidse and Heyvaert's using corpus data that the agent of a middle may be unambiguously indicated by adjuncts:

38. The reaction gradually diminishes or habituates over repeated presentation of this standard sound.
39. The body twisted **in a violent effort to free itself of the dangerlike teeth.**[20]

Thus in (38) the reaction diminishes or habituates from agentive sheer repetition. And in (39) the body twists from its own effort. One might argue that at least in example (39) the ultimate cause may be perceived to lie with the subject, especially because of the presence of the reflexive *itself* in the prepositional phrase. Our next example, (40), occurs as part of the description of Francis Tarwater waking up after his rape by the man in the panama hat who gives him a ride in his car and drugs him as well.

40. "The boy's mouth **twisted** open and to the side as if it were going to displace itself permanently." (*VBA*, 232)

The reflexive in the *as if* quasi-simile adjunct implies a degree of agency for Francis's mouth, that agency emphasizing the reaction of his body to the rape. The ascription of partial agency to body parts and even inanimate objects in middle constructions is part of the stylistics of O'Connor's aesthetically grotesque writing:

41. "The pick-up truck slowed even more **as if** it were reading the sign and Haze pounded his empty horn. . . . In a second a red square face was at his car window. It watched the back of his neck and hat for a minute and then a hand came in and sat on his shoulder." (*WB*, 75–76)

In (41), the *as-if* quasi simile ascribes hypothetical agency to a "reading" pick-up; however, world knowledge tells us that pick-up trucks slow through human agency. As Buyssens argues using the example in (42), below, the absence of explicit mention of the agent does not mean "that the locutor is not thinking of it":

42. The curtains blew in.

Buyssens points out that the writer of (42) knows very well that the wind is the instigator.[21] Thus, just as world knowledge tells us what the agent of the verb is in (41) and (42), it also tells us that it is the bus driver who opens the door to the bus in the following example from "Everything That Rises Must Converge":

43. "The door **opened** with a sucking hiss and out of the dark a large, gaily dressed, sullen-looking colored woman got on with a little boy." (*ERMC*, 15–16)

As I will discuss in detail later in this chapter, when the subject of the ergative verb is a body part, the agency of that subject is in one sense perfectly clear but on the other hand ambiguous. Thus compare (43) with (44), below. In (43) there is no question that the bus driver opens the door. In (44), though, there is some ambiguity about the agent that opens his mouth.

44. "Sitting upright and rigid in the cab of the truck, his muscles **began to jerk,** his arms **flailed,** his mouth **opened** to make way for cries that would not come. His pale face **twitched** and grimaced." (*VBA*, 216)

In (44) Francis Tarwater reacts to his horrifying memories of drowning his mentally retarded cousin Bishop. The question is of course whether he controls the body parts that act in these sentences. As he sits in a parked truck it is ambiguous even whether he is sleeping or at least dozing. These ambiguities are of aesthetic importance since the questions of who controls whom in *The Violent Bear It Away,* whether Francis controls himself, whether he is fated to do as his great-uncle wished, are primary narrative puzzles.

The Typological Approach to the Middle Voice

In the hunt for ever narrower and more operationalized definitions of the middle voice, what we have seen in Davidse and Heyvaert's approach is the ultimate restriction of the term *middle voice* to what is sometimes called the "facilitative middle," or in Davidse and Heyvaert's terms, the "conducive middle." It is indeed true that one can at least try to limit operationally the definition of the middle to the facilitative if one is willing to accept the requirement that there be a conceptualized agent in the event and that the subject be understood as "conducive." However, one explanation for the motivation to find ever narrower operational definitions of the middle voice in English is the very lack of middle voice morphology, or consistent form, in English. If there is no consistent form and if there are only diagnostics such as the inability to occur in the frame "it verbed all by itself," one has to question, at least in a stylistics study in which we are interested in semantics at least as much as in form, the value of limiting the middle to what is effectively only one small corner of the typological middle. In spite of its formal inconsistency, the middle helps to provide a semantic coherency to a number of different constructions in English and helps us to consider the semantics of O'Connor's use of body parts within an explanatory framework motivated by a crosslinguistic (typological) theory of grammatical voice. That range of constructions is larger than the one-participant ergative and one-participant transitive middles that we have explored thus far, although those constructions are at the core of even the typological middle. As Givón says, the middle is "likely to involve a *family* of constructions" and those constructions "are often a *transitional diachronic* phenomenon, rather than a stable synchronic one."[22] To account for the full subtleties and range of both form and semantics in O'Connor's middle constructions, we can widen our working definition of *middle voice* on the basis of Kemmer's typological exploration of the middle as a voice which is defined (1) by identity between the "initiator" (roughly, agent or actor) of the event and "endpoint" (roughly, medium or goal of the action) and (2) by relatively low elaboration of the event (in part, for our purposes, the syntactic expression or not of reflexive objects).[23] Kemmer's more typological view of middle constructions allows us to widen the scope of what we consider middle and middle-related constructions in English, especially to the reflexive, which we will find of enormous interest in chapter 5.

In Kemmer's account of the middle the primary determinant of the prototypicality of a middle construction is its lack of formal and semantic separation of the initiator and endpoint. The remaining figures in this chapter, which are designed to demonstrate the semantic roles of participants and the relative distinguishability of initiator and endpoint, are inspired by, but not the same as, Kemmer's "event schemas." Figure 3 illustrates an active clause.

FIGURE 3: **The active**

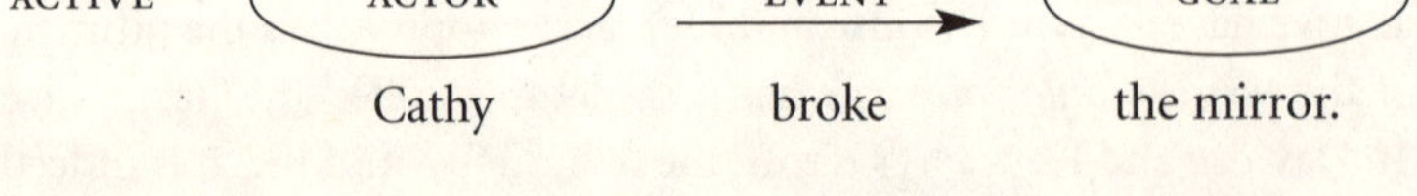

In figure 3 the sentence "Cathy broke the mirror" is prototypically active. The subject is an actor, and there is a clearly separate endpoint-goal, which is acted on by the initiator-actor through the event. Figure 4 illustrates a passive clause.

FIGURE 4: **The passive**

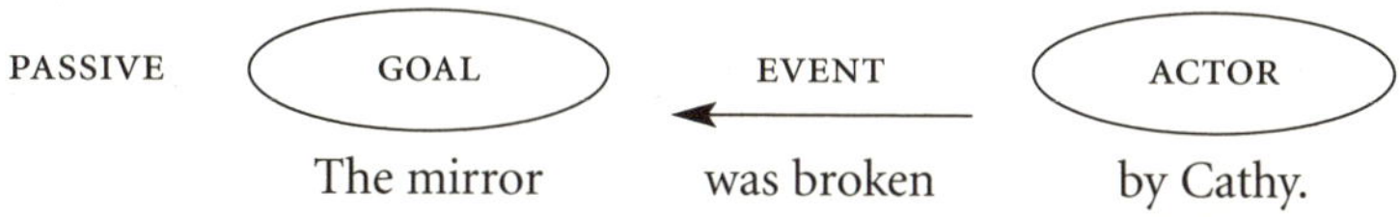

As Kemmer details, the passive is frequently diachronically related to the middle; yet they are synchronically distinct in English. Like the middle, the passive contains an affected subject, "the mirror" in figure 4. However, like the active, the passive contains a clearly separated endpoint-goal and initiator-actor. Figure 5 illustrates the prototypical middle voice, in particular, the resultative or facilitative middles.

FIGURE 5: **The resultative or facilitative middles**

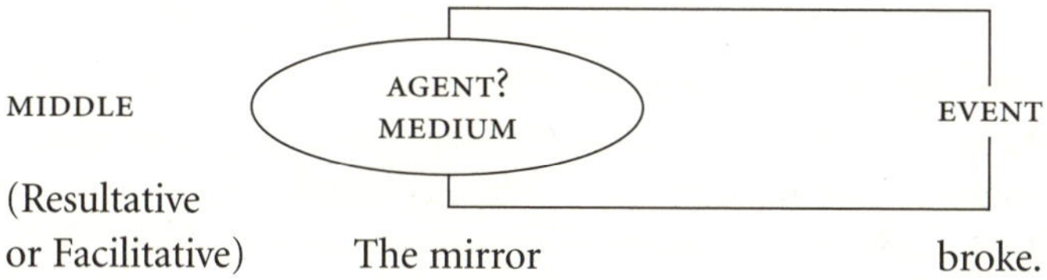

In "The mirror broke" the subject is the medium, the verb may be used transitively (although it is not here), and there is no clearly discernable separate agent. The sentence in figure 5, "The mirror broke," may ambiguously signal either a resultative middle or a facilitative middle. A resultative middle focuses on the effect of the verb on the medium, and in the facilitative middle the medium is somehow at least partially responsible for the action.[24] Thus in the facilitative the mirror may have broken because it was old, as might be implied in the sentences "The mirror broke easily" or "The mirror just broke."

Another core middle, like the facilitative and the resultative, is the body-action construction. These middles, as Kemmer argues, help to signal "actions carried out on or through one's own body." The body-action middle is illustrated in Figure 6.

FIGURE 6: **The body-action middle**

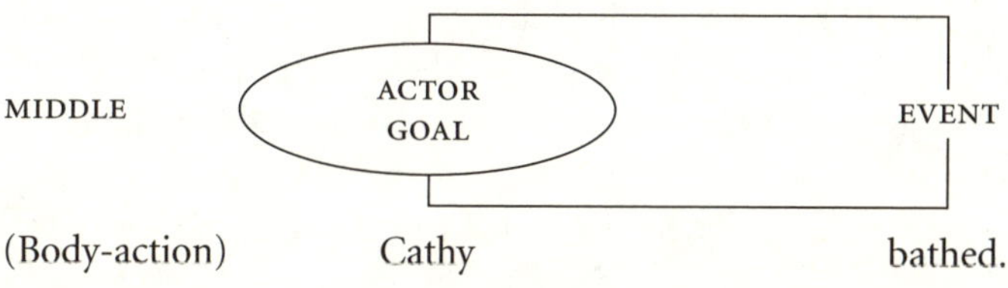

In "Cathy bathed" the actor and goal are identical, and there is low elaboration in that there is no separate grammatical object, just as in figure 5's "The mirror broke." In the body-action middle, as Kemmer points out, "one acts in a sense *through* the body; the body, since it is under the control of the person moving [or bathing], is participating in the action."

Kemmer argues that it is the low elaboration of events, in part the indistinguishability of subject and object, that most characterizes the middle cross-linguistically. She explains that constructions closely related to but yet separate from the middle, such as reflexives, may also be understood in part by their relative elaboration of events.[25] Thus figure 7 illustrates the English reflexive.

FIGURE 7: **The reflexive**

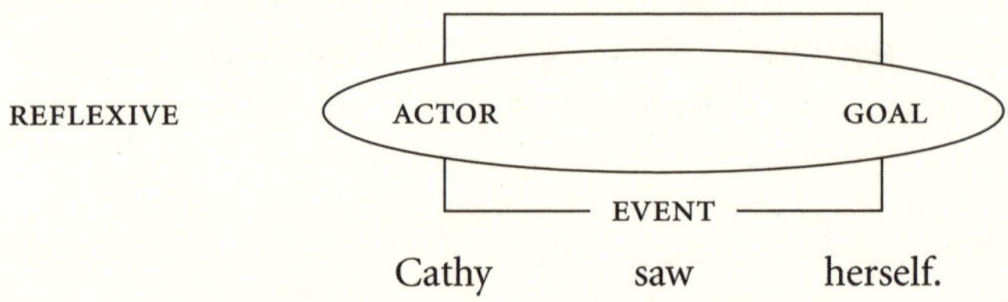

In "Cathy saw herself" there is a goal that is grammatically but not semantically separate from the actor. Thus, in contrast to the core middle illustrated in figures 5 and 6, the reflexive is more syntactically elaborated. However, like the middle, the reflexive initiator is semantically identical to the endpoint. In figure 7 that semantic unity is indicated by the oval, which encircles both the goal and the actor as separate grammatical entities.

Figure 8 represents a summary cline of Kemmer's theory of the semantic and formal separation of initiator and endpoint.

FIGURE 8: **Semantic and formal separation of the initiator and the endpoint**

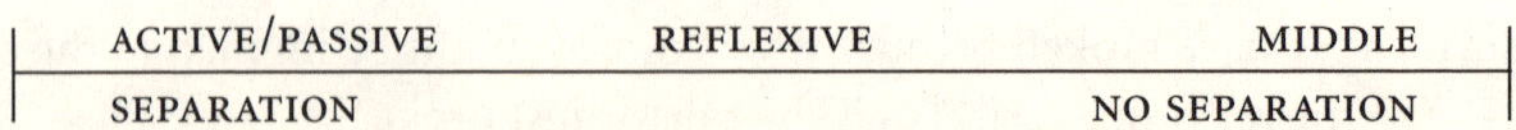

See a similar but more complex diagram in Kemmer. As Kemmer explains, in the transitive active or the passive sentence, there is maximum separation of the initiator and endpoint, both semantically and syntactically. There is a grammatical subject representing either the initiator or the endpoint, respectively, in the transitive active and the passive. In the transitive active there is a grammatically and semantically separate endpoint, and in the passive there is a potentially grammatically and semantically separate initiator in a prepositional phrase. In the reflexive there is a grammatically separate initiator and endpoint, yet the initiator and endpoint are semantically co-referential. In the core middle, whether of the resultative or facilitative or body-action types, there is no grammatical separation of the initiator and endpoint, and semantically the initiator and endpoint are also merged.[26]

While those in the systemic tradition write of the "self-engendered" nature of the ergative middle or the merger of "the features 'self-instigated' and 'externally instigated'" in the ergative middle, Kemmer writes of low elaboration and merger of initiator and endpoint in the middle.[27] Thus, consider the two sentences that follow from O'Connor's *The Violent Bear It Away:*

45. "You can **roll** me to it if nothing else." (*VBA,* 14)
46. "I'll **roll.**" (*VBA,* 14)

In these two sentences Mason Tarwater instructs his great-nephew Francis Tarwater on how to get his body from their house to his grave (*it*) outside when he dies. Example (45) has active voice semantics since the initiator (*you*) is both formally and semantically separate from the endpoint (*me*). However, example (46) has middle-voice semantics since there is a merger in *I* of the initiator and the endpoint. Thus in (46) Mason Tarwater implies that there is something about him that makes him easy to roll. In a facilitative middle such as "I'll roll" there is little conceptual or formal differentiation of the initiator (referentially, in part, Mason) and the endpoint (referentially, in part, Mason's body). The facilitative is a subtype of the more general middle body-action constructions like that in (47), below.

47. "Suddenly he threw himself on the ground and began to **roll** like a man on fire." (*ERMC,* 79)

In (47), engaged in his struggle to the death with his granddaughter, Mary Fortune Pitts, Mr. Fortune of "A View of the Woods" reacts to the pain of being bitten and kicked mercilessly. The construction "began to roll like a man on fire" encodes a body-action middle since Mr. Fortune is acting on his own body here. That is, the initiator and endpoint are the same.

The middle "He rolled" is, then, less grammatically elaborated than the reflexive although both signal a semantically reflexive event. Note that *roll* is an inherently middle (or ergative middle) verb since in its intransitive form it communicates the identity (or neutralization) of initiator and endpoint. In (47) contrast *roll* with *threw,* the latter of which, not being an inherently middle verb, requires the reflexive "threw himself" to signal identity of initiator and endpoint.

Body Parts and the Middle

In later chapters, we will consider in some detail two constructions in which body parts themselves serve as the initiator or endpoint of the body-action verb, as in (48) and (49), below.

48. "The driver's **head** was beginning to **roll.**" (*VBA*, 212)
49. "All his teeth were backed with gold and he would **roll** his **eyes** at Miss Kirby in an impish way and say, 'Haw haw,' sitting in their porch swing with his legs spread apart and his hightopped shoes pointing in opposite directions on the floor." (*GM*, 87)

In (48) when the truck driver who picks up Francis Tarwater begins to nod off in sleep, the initiator and endpoint are conceptually the same, as in "he rolled"; the formal difference between (47) and (48) is the use of a body part in (48) rather than a pronoun referring to the entire initiator/endpoint. In (49), in which part of Mr. Cheatam's romance with Miss Kirby in "A Temple of the Holy Ghost" is reported, we have an example of a construction similar but not identical to what Barbara Fox calls "the body-part reflexive," the difference being that in the languages that Fox examines there are reflexive morphological signals specific to the body-part reflexive. Fox argues: "Given that reflexives signal the repeated mention of a participant it follows that any action a participant performs on his body will qualify for the status of reflexive, since a person is essentially, at least in space, equivalent to his body."[28] Mr. Cheatam does not roll his entire body; he rolls his eyes. Example (49) is quite typical in the context of O'Connor's unrelenting concentration on the human body as a site of both the grotesque and the incarnational. "A Temple of the Holy Ghost" ends in one of O'Connor's frequent nascent revelations for the focalized character, this time "the child." During the benediction at the convent the child thinks of the hermaphrodite as the "priest rais[es] the monstrance with the Host shining ivory-colored in the center of it." In the course of the story the child has recognized herself, her two cousins, and Miss Kirby as "temples of the Holy Ghost." At the end of the story, as she continues to receive the sacramental gift of this revelation, she notices the details of another character's body: "The child observed three folds of fat in the back of his neck and noted that his ears were pointed almost like a pig's" (*GM*, 100). We will return to the connections among the grotesque, the sacramental, and the body in the next section, after we examine in more detail the interrelations of the body and the middle voice.

An issue of crucial importance in this book is the patterning of body parts, the middle, and agency. Thus it is not really sufficient to say that middles have an implied agent while some one-participant ergatives do not. Of more interest is the question of why some verbs imply the agent and why some do not. Thus consider the following, in which I use Davidse's do-probe, the "all by itself" test, as in Davidse and Heyvaert and Samuel J. Keyser and Thomas Roeper, and the facilitative adverbial test, as in Leonard Faltz, Kemmer, Davidse, and many other sources.[29]

50a. He shrugged his shoulders.
b. His shoulders shrugged.

c. ?What his shoulders did was shrug.
d. ?His shoulders shrugged all by themselves.
e. ?His shoulders shrug easily/nicely/authoritatively.

In (50a) and (50b) it appears that the event *shrug* is ergative. Yet it does not allow the do-probe in (50c), and it appears from (50d) to require an agent external to the medium. Note that it also does not appear that the verb is middle in the sense that its subject is facilitative. If we attempt to create a facilitative middle in (50e), we end up with an exceedingly odd sentence, no matter what facilitative adverbial we try to use (*easily, nicely, authoritatively*). One can argue that ergative verbs are ambiguous between being ergative and middle. However, verbs like *shrug* are problematic because it appears that the shoulders do indeed shrug, like subjects to one-participant ergative verbs, but it sounds odd to isolate them with the do-probe, as in (50c), or to ascribe sole agency to them, as in (50d). Another verb that works very much like *shrug* is *furrow.* It is instructive to contrast *shrug* and *furrow* with *read,* the last of which may be used in prototypical facilitative middles:

51a. He furrowed his brow.
b. His brow furrowed.
c. ?What his brow did was furrow.
d. ?His brow furrowed all by itself.
e. ?His brow furrows easily.

52a. I read this book.
b. *This book read.
c. *What the book did was read.
d. *The book read all by itself.
e. The book reads quickly.

Furrow is like *shrug:* it appears at first to be ergative in that (51b) is possible. Note that *read* is clearly not ergative in that (52b) is ungrammatical. Oddly, *furrow* also patterns like *shrug* in that it is at least questionably ergative in not clearly allowing either the do-probe in (51c) or the assignment of agenthood to its one participant as in (51d). And note that *furrow,* also like *shrug* but unlike *read,* cannot occur in the facilitative middle.

We are now in the position of having clearly ergative verbs, like *thaw* and *bend,* clearly facilitative middle verbs like *steer* and *read,* and verbs that appear to a be little of both, or neither, like *shrug* and *furrow.* In the case of the clearly middle verbs like *steer* and *read,* it is as Davidse and Heyvaert say: the subjects provide a "conducive," or facilitative, semantics for the operation of the event named by the verb. The subjects do not in any sense perform the event.[30] Thus the car does not steer in "The car steers easily." Instead the car allows the actor to perform the event, is conducive to that performance. In the case of clearly ergative verbs like *thaw* and *bend,* the ergative medium performs the event. Then there is the curious class of verbs like *shrug* and *furrow,* which appear to be ergative but do not allow the do-probe, do not allow agentivity in the ergative subject, and do not allow a facilitative middle. Other verbs that appear to work in this way are the following:

53a. He lowered his eyes.
b. His eyes lowered.
c. ?What his eyes did was lower.
d. ?His eyes lowered all by themselves.
e. ?His eyes lower easily.

54a. He turned his face.
b. His face turned.
c. ?What his face did was turn.
d. ?His face turned all by itself.
e. ?His face turns easily.

The first mystery to solve here is the fact that these verbs—*lower, turn, shrug,* and *furrow*—allow the one-participant ergative construction in the (b) sentences but not the do-probe in the (c) sentences. If we compare the questionable acceptability of (53c) and (54c) with the ungrammaticality of a facilitative middle verb like *read,* as in *"What the book did was read," we can see that the questionable acceptability of a sentence such as "What his eyes did was lower" is probably a pragmatic issue rather than a semantic one. That is, when we say something like "What the window did was break," we are providing new information typically to comment on the topic of what the window did, perhaps topic-worthy because someone threw a ball at the window or the window is missing, or something similar. It is hard to imagine a situation in which what his shoulders did, or what his eyes did, or what his face did, or what his brow did, especially if those events are *shrug, lower, turn,* or *furrow,* would be newsworthy. However, consider the ergative verbs *lower* and *turn* with a different objects and subjects:

55a. We lowered his temperature.
b. His temperature lowered.
c. What his temperature did was lower.
d. His temperature lowered all by itself.
e. His temperature lowers quickly.

56a. He turned the car.
b. The car turned.
c. What the car did was turn.
d. The car turned all by itself.
e. The car turns easily.

In (55) and (56) it suddenly appears as if *lower* and *turn* are fully ergative with the possibility of a facilitative middle as in the (e) sentences. If we ignore the do-probe sentences in (c) because they are as sensitive to pragmatic issues as to semantic ones and instead concentrate on the acceptability, near acceptability, and unacceptability of the (d) and (e) sentences that ascribe agency respectively either to the ergative subject or the implied instigator, we can begin to understand the importance of the body for grammatical voice. In (53a) the object of *lower* is *eyes;* in (54a) the object of *turn* is *face.* In (55) and (56) neither *temperature* nor *car* are body parts although *temperature* is a body function in (55). The non-body parts are acceptable in the (d) sentences of (55) and (56) because we can imagine both one's temperature and a car lowering and turning independently of human control. That is, one can, on the one hand, imagine their containing all of the agency in the semantic representation of those sentences. The non-body parts are acceptable, on the other hand, in the (e) facilitative middle sentences of (55) and (56) because we can just as easily imagine one's temperature and a car being operated on by controlling human agents. Thus physicians and nurses might say of one's temperature that it lowers easily; someone test driving a car might also say that it turns easily.

The essential problem in all linguistic analysis, or analysis of any natural phenomena, is that the finer the gradation of analysis, the finer the gradation of phenomena that one finds. Thus if a particular construction takes a body part, for example, as its subject, it is frequently unclear exactly how much agency lies within that body part and how much agency lies outside of it. Do we shrug our shoulders or do our shoulders shrug themselves; do we turn our heads or do they turn themselves; do we lower our eyes or do they lower themselves? If we look again at the examples in (50), (51), (53), and (54) it appears that the (d) and (e) sentences highlight the special nature of these verbs and their body-part subjects. Thus, for example, even though we can say "His shoulders shrugged," the shoulders do not have enough agency to make the sentence "His shoulders shrugged all by themselves" sound natural. That is, the mind that controls the shoulders maintains too much agency for the body part to act on its own. At the same time his shoulders appear not to have any kind of semantics that make them conducive to being shrugged in a facilitative middle such as "His shoulders shrug nicely." This same control issue is at work in the body-part subjects of *furrow, lower,* and *turn* in (51), (53), and (54). Thus with verbs such as *lower* and *turn,* the body parts are neither agentive nor facilitative. Although the body parts may function as ergative subjects, one cannot stress their agentivity with "all by themselves" or stress their conducive nature with facilitative middles. What this demonstrates at least about some body parts is that there is no clear demarcation between the body parts and the human mind "behind" them. The inability of these body part subjects to be isolated either as fully agentive subjects or fully facilitative subjects supports an analysis of them as central middle subjects in Kemmer's sense that the middle is characterized by low elaboration, particularly the low elaboration of the difference between the initiator and the endpoint. In the case of a body part that can act independently of human control, like the non-body-part temperature in the example above, one can get both ergative and facilitative middles, as in the following:

57a. She curled her hair.
b. Her hair curled.
c. What her hair did was curl.
d. Her hair curled all by itself.
e. Her hair curls easily.

58a. She splintered her fingernails.
b. Her fingernails splintered.
c. What her fingernails did was splinter.
d. Her fingernails splintered all by themselves.
e. Her fingernails splinter easily.

Unlike such body parts as shoulders, eyes, brows, and faces, hair and fingernails are potentially independent of human agency and thus can be given the agency of the ergative (in the d sentences of [57] and [58]) or be given the conduciveness of the facilitative middle (in the e sentences of [57] and [58]).[31]

The Grotesque, the Body Part, and Agency

What is grotesque about body parts that act with agency is that they act independently of the human agency that is understood to normally control them.

59. "His **hand** was moving along the edge of the ditch as if it were hunting something to grip." (*WB*, 230)
60. "At the moment of his death, he sat down to his breakfast and lifted his knife in one square red hand halfway to his mouth, and then with a look of complete astonishment, he lowered it until the **hand** rested on the edge of the plate and tilted it up off the table." (*VBA*, 10)
61. "He made such a desperate effort to see over it and find out what comes after the past that his **hand** clenched the sword until the blade touched bone." (*GM*, 167)
62. "A numbness developed in one of her legs and her **hands** and head began to jiggle and eventually she had to stay in bed all the time with only a colored woman to wait on her." (*GM*, 251)

Each of these examples contains either *hand* or *hands* as subject of an ergative middle verb. Each of the constructions could be rewritten with *hand* or *hands* as the ergative object, as in "he moved his hand," "he rested his hand," "he clenched his hand on the sword," and "she jiggled her hands." However, in (59)–(62), the ergative middle subjects instead act on their own. One of the reasons that they act on their own is the absence or near absence of agentivity on the part of their owners. Example (59) occurs near the end of *Wise Blood* as Hazel Motes lies, probably dying, in a drainage ditch. Thus his hand moves as if it has a will of its own. In example (60) Tarwater the elder dies at the breakfast table. And part of the effective style of this passage is the use of the referent *hand* as the ergative object of *lowered,* then as the ergative intransitive subject of *rested,* and then as the ergative transitive subject of *tilted.* That is, as Tarwater dies, his hand takes on more and more agency. And in (61) at the moment of General Sash's death, at the age of 104, his hand occurs as the ergative subject of the verb *clenched.* Finally, consider example (62), in which Mrs. McIntyre of "The Displaced Person" is described in her weakened condition at the end of the story. Here she appears to be losing control of her entire body, as both her head and her hands occur as one-participant ergative subjects.

It is not necessary that a character die or even be near death for the occurrence of a body part in the ergative subject position. Consider the following example:

63. "His **hand** tightened on the boy's shoulder and his mouth stretched painfully." (*VBA*, 92)

In (63), from *The Violent Bear It Away,* Rayber's hand is described as gripping Francis's shoulder. In itself that action has no special significance. However, as we will see in chapters 4 and 5, the cumulative effect of such a concentration on body parts and middle or ergative verbs in O'Connor's fiction clearly supports her thematic interest in the sacramental and the grotesque. As a qualitative example of this concentration, consider even the remainder of example (63). There, Rayber's mouth is the ergative middle subject of the verb *stretched.* Note the qualitative alienation, or formalist defamiliarization, of such an expression compared to "He grimaced" or "He smiled." The verb *stretch,* like a good number of other ergative verbs, is frequently used by O'Connor to grotesque effect.

64. "His eyes glinted through his tears and his face **stretched** in an evil crooked grin." (*WB*, 59)
65. "Sheppard's mouth **stretched** in disgust. . . . Sheppard's mouth **stretched** wryly." (*ERMC*, 145, 158)

In (64) Enoch Emery is described as he is taunting Hazel with his supposed knowledge of where Sabbath and her father live. In (65) Sheppard of "The Lame Shall Enter First" is described twice with his mouth as the ergative subject of the verb *stretched.* In the first Sheppard demonstrates self-satisfied disgust at his own son's "selfishness"; in the second he demonstrates self-satisfied superiority at the news that Johnson's grandfather has "abandoned" him to go off into the hills to wait for the apocalypse.

What we have discovered in this chapter is that ergative/middle verbs are especially revealing of a split in the semantics/pragmatics of a person. It is not surprising at all that a thematics of the body-mind split as is intimately involved in the incarnational and the grotesque would find itself manifested in the minutiae of grammatical voice and body parts. No one can write effectively with only large scale symbols. However, it is remarkable that linguistics has the analytic frameworks to explore this fine-grained meaning in O'Connor's fiction. In chapter 3 we will explore in detail the next and final set of tools—statistics—that we need to examine the patterning of verbs and body parts in O'Connor's fiction within the specific framework of computational stylistics.

CHAPTER 3

The Statistical Body

It may be that on the page proofs I can get rid of some more of the as-if and seems.
Flannery O'Connor (*CW*, 1109)

Chapter 2 set the linguistic stage for the analysis of the middle voice in this study and carried through on some of that analysis. This chapter will set the computational and linguistic stage for analyses in chapters 4 and 5 and will also in its demonstrations perform a fair amount of interesting stylistic analysis itself. The arguments that have been made in chapters 1 and 2 do not depend on computer technology, but this chapter concentrates on the basics of both computer concordancing and textual statistics. Thus this chapter begins with a description of the Brown Corpus and its use as a contrast for O'Connor's texts. Next I describe the concordancing package that I use for the remainder of the work of the book and the details of the statistics that are used as well. In particular, the concordancing topics include the structure and motivation for my own concordancing program—Textant (TEXT ANalysis Tools)—which is similar to programs commercially available, such as WordSmith and MonoConc. Among the procedures that a concordancing program makes possible are frequency counts, word and phrase searches, keyword analysis, and collocation analysis. Statistical procedures and tests that may be performed on the numerical results of the concordancing program include chi-square, log-likelihood, t-scores, and mutual information.[1] Among the topics dealt with in this chapter is the advisability of tests such as these to make conclusions based on probability. As I indicated in chapter 1, this chapter may be skipped by readers not interested in the technical issues covered.

Corpora

One of the dramatically effective methodologies that the personal computer makes possible in modern literary analysis is the use of comparative text collections in the demonstrable proof of the stylistics of a literary author. A corpus is simply a collection of texts for empirical study. That corpus is sometimes as small as in the tens of thousands of word tokens; it is sometimes as large as a half billion word tokens. Corpus linguistics is now one of the most exciting "new" methodological areas of linguistics; however, the "newness" of the field is largely the result of the relatively newly widely available corpora, personal computers, and concordancing programs that facilitate the work of the field. The Brown Corpus, originally made available in 1964, contains one million words of written American English in excerpts of around two thousand words. Although not the first corpus, it was the first computerized corpus. Even more significantly, it is American in origin, an ironic fact given that, as Graeme Kennedy points out, Noam Chomsky's decidedly anticorpus and antiempiricist theories were first coming into prominence around the time that the Brown Corpus was being assembled and distributed. Empirical linguistics is thankfully now recovering from Chomskian rationalist domination. Among the larger British corpora are the British National Corpus (BNC; 100 million words) and the COBUILD Bank of English (over 500 million words). American linguistics is now playing catch-up with European corpus linguistics. The American National Corpus (ANC), modeled on the BNC, released its first 10 million words in 2003 and its second version, with over 20 million words, in 2005.[2]

Most of the texts of the Brown Corpus were randomly sampled from the Brown University Library and the Providence Athenaeum. The Brown fiction subcorpora, used here for comparative purposes, are collections of excerpts from American English fiction, all originally published in 1960 and 1961. The subcorpora contain the genres of general fiction, mystery, science fiction, westerns, and romance. I do not use the entire Brown Corpus, just the Brown fiction subcorpora (hereafter "the Brown texts"), containing 235,431 words in 117 excerpts. The Brown texts are ideal for comparison with O'Connor's fiction since she was American and was writing in and around the time of 1960 and 1961. Thus the Brown texts may be used to get a generalized snapshot of the form of American fiction around the time of the publication of O'Connor's fiction. The fiction texts in the British English Lancaster Oslo/Bergen Corpus (LOB), which is nearly identical in general structure to the Brown Corpus, may be used for specific comparison with British fiction of the same period.[3] The date-specific and nationality-specific nature of the Brown and LOB corpora and their consequent close fit for comparison with American or British writers of the same period demonstrate, in the ongoing rush to create ever larger and ever newer corpora, that older and smaller corpora have specific and evolving uses that the newer and larger corpora may not have.

Concordancing Packages

Even corpora as relatively small as the Brown texts from the Brown Corpus are most efficiently used by means of a computerized concordancing package. There are a number of inexpensive concordancing packages currently available for purchase through the Web. Two of the best state-of-the-art concordancers are MonoConc and WordSmith. For reasons of convenience, flexibility, and self-designed multiple and redundant tests of reliability, many linguists who work in corpus linguistics write their own concordance software. For these reasons and others (for example, cost control in pedagogy), I wrote and use my own concordancer—Textant—for text analysis.[4] Textant produces the standard frequency counts, word lists, and statistics that one finds in most text-analysis programs. It provides total word counts for each corpus. It can produce both alphabetically sorted and frequency-sorted type/token counts; these windows also provide ratios. In either of the type/token count windows, users may create, save, retrieve, and modify lexical groups for the purposes of efficient group searching in the search window. A separate collocations window provides both fixed-phrase and variable-phrase collocations along with frequency counts, t-scores, mutual-information, chi-square, and log-likelihood scores. The fixed-phrase collocations may vary in length from two to eight words. The distance for the variable-phrase collocations may vary from one to four words on either side of the optional target word. If a target word is specified, only those collocations with the target word are listed by the program. There are separate stoplist files for personal pronouns, reflexive pronouns, auxiliary verbs, modal verbs, determiners, coordinating conjunctions, subordinating conjunctions, and prepositions, which may be selected in any combination or alone. The stoplists may be applied to both collocation windows and the total word token count. The option of using the stoplists allows users to choose, for example, whether to include prepositions and determiners in the lists of collocations since collocations of the sort "of the" are common but of no interest to most researchers. Of central importance in this book, Textant also produces keywords and lexical comparisons with both chi-square and log-likelihood figures.[5] Besides the statistics that are generated in the type/token pages and the collocation pages, Textant produces tables in which users may enter data for statistical processing, especially in cases in which figures need to be rechecked because of winnowing the data for false hits. A false hit for a body part would include the token *Head* in "Mr. Head" of "The Artificial Nigger." The descriptive statistics that may be produced are minimum, maximum, sum, count, mean, median, mode, variance, and standard deviation. Both chi-square and log-likelihood may also be produced individually.

Probability and Randomness

Adam Kilgarriff begins an essay entitled "Comparing Corpora" with a stunning declaration: "There is a void at the heart of corpus linguistics." That void is created, Kilgarriff notes, by the lack of reliable ways of measuring the differences between and among corpora. Thus, he argues, if a grammatical description or a set of computerized tools is developed for one corpus, we have no way of predicting on the basis of probability whether a new corpus can be described by the same grammar or manipulated in similar ways by the same computerized tools.[6]

Although he does not discuss the discipline of stylistics, the lack of a set of such measures would make impossible the kind of stylistics work that is described in this book. The primary issue at the heart of the question of the use of probability tests to determine differences among and between corpora is randomness. Statistical hypothesis testing of the sort that one normally sees with chi-square tests, log-likelihood tests, and t-tests, for example, is specifically designed to test the null hypothesis, for example, that there is no difference between the corpora with regard to the frequency of the counted items. In comparing two corpora, Michael P. Oakes argues, one normally tests the hypothesis that the two corpora are generated randomly based on the frequencies that result when the corpora are combined. Thus, one asks, for example, whether the distributions of the word *know* are those that would result from the two corpora combining to form one corpus and the two individual corpora being constructed from randomly sampling from the combined corpus. There are numerous corpus studies that use chi-square and other of these statistical formulas to test the probability of the null hypothesis for such differences. Kay Wikberg uses chi-square to test statistical independence of the Brown Corpus and the LOB Corpus internally for differences between informative prose and imaginary prose in the frequencies of *as if* and *as though.* Randolph Quirk uses chi-square and probability testing to determine the various phrasal distributions of constructions such as "have a swim" and "take a swim." Charles F. Meyer uses chi-square and probability testing to determine the significance levels of differing distributions of pseudotitles (for example, "former assistant to the director John Bowie") in several subcorpora of the International Corpus of English. I use chi-square in my 2003 *Narrating Knowledge in Flannery O'Connor's Fiction* to test the statistical independence of several linguistic signals: for example, analytic negation, cognition verbs, speaker changes in dialogue. And the widely used program WordSmith provides statistical probabilities along with log-likelihood scores in the analysis of collocations.[7] In all of these studies and concordancing programs and many more, one operating assumption, or at least possibility, is that words are distributed randomly in what is sometimes referred to as a "bag of words," as A. De Roeck, A. Sarkar, and P. H. Garthwaite point out. Regardless of the fact that hypothetical randomness in text construction is untenable, we can learn a great deal about texts through the investigation of the failure of randomness. Textant provides probability figures for chi-square, log-likelihood, and t-score collocation, keyword, and word frequency scores, although we will generally not rely on those probability figures in this book.

There are at least three ways in which a text is not simply a "bag of words," those three patterns referred to by John Burrows as "transitional probabilities," "contextual or semantic probabilities," and "recursive probabilities."[8] First, regarding the syntagmatic order of words, there are what Burrows calls "transitional probabilities." If one posited a very small bag of words with only three words in it (for example, *the, cat, slept*), there are six random possibilities if one chose the words simply by reaching in and pulling them out one by one and placing them in that chance order: "the cat slept," "cat the slept," "slept the cat," "slept cat the," "the slept cat," "cat slept the." As we will see below, one of the more interesting collocations in O'Connor's texts is the "as if" quasi simile; the construction is widely recognized as a stylistic feature of O'Connor's writing, even without quantitative analysis. If texts were constructed by randomly choosing words from a bag of words, the collocation "if as" would be just as likely as "as if." In fact, the sequence "if as" occurs only three times each in O'Connor's fiction and the Brown texts while "as if" occurs 739 times in O'Connor and 96 times in Brown. Thus the choice of the order of the words is certainly not due simply to chance. John Sinclair refers to the mistaken assumption that any one word is just as likely to follow a particular word as another "the open-choice principle." Sinclair opposes this principle to what he calls "the idiom principle": "that a language user has available to him or her a large number of semi-preconstructed phrases that constitute single choices, even though they might appear to be analysable into segments."[9] A second way in which a text is not a "bag of words" is paradigmatic choice. Thus, as Burrows argues, there are "contextual or semantic probabilities." Once words like *dog* and *pet* and *veterinarian* are introduced into a text, it is likely that the word *cat* will be introduced as well. Thus, because the word *Jesus* occurs 226 times in O'Connor, one expects the word *Christ* (occurring 83 times), and *Lord* (147 times). All of these words occur in the Brown texts as well, so one might argue that these words do not occur simply because of semantic probabilities but because they are likely to occur in any literary text corpus. However, the word *baptize* occurs in O'Connor's texts 33 times but does not occur at all in the Brown texts. Other words in the same semantic field that occur only in O'Connor's text are *baptismal* and *baptism.* Third, Burrows points out the existence of "recursive probabilities." Once any particular word is introduced, such as *veterinarian,* it is likely that that word will occur at least once again. This last probability leads to the further complication of what is called "burstiness" or "clumpiness" in corpora, the repetition of a word in a relatively small segment of text.[10] Thus the word *Mammadoll* first occurs in O'Connor's texts in chapter 1 of *Wise Blood,* in the dialogue of Mrs. Hitchcock. It occurs for its second and last time in the very next sentence of her dialogue. Other words that occur more than once in O'Connor on account of "recursive probabilities" but do not occur in the Brown texts are, with their frequencies, *valise* (15), *crowbar* (3), *extinct* (5), *dissatisfaction* (7), *wart* (5), *burnt* (19), *Chrustian* (4). The last two examples illustrate the importance of dialect and accent representation in such recursive probabilities. Perhaps the area of the lexicon in which clumpiness and recursive probabilities are most evident is in names of characters. For example, the following names occur only in O'Connor's texts and with a high degree of clumpiness: *Pritchard* (58), *Asbury* (83), *Obadiah* (6), *Teagarden* (3), *Rayber* (269), *Farebrother* (13), *Melsy* (7). Of course, there are many words, including names, that occur in Brown but do not occur in O'Connor. The fact that tokens of a word tend to cluster together sometimes gives a false impression of the overall dispersion or generalization of the use of the word type. We will further consider these issues of dispersion later in this chapter, but for now consider a typical small burst of tokens of a word in the following passage from "Good Country People." Here, as Mrs. Hopewell and Hulga are eating their breakfast, Mrs. Freeman is telling of her daughter Glynese's date with Harvey Hill: "'Glynese gone out with Harvey Hill again last night,' she said. 'She had this **sty**.' 'Hill,' Mrs. Hopewell said absently, 'is that the one who works in the garage?' 'Nome, he's the one that goes to chiropracter school,' Mrs. Freeman said. 'She had this **sty**. Been had it two days. So she says when he brought her in the other night he says, "Lemme get rid of that **sty** for you," and she says, "How?" and he says, "You just lay yourself down acrost the seat of that car and I'll show you." So she done it and he popped her neck. Kept on apopping it several times until she made him quit. This morning,' Mrs. Freeman said, 'she ain't got no **sty**. She ain't got no traces of a **sty**'" (*GM*, 182). This short passage contains every single one of the five occurrences of the word *sty* in the entirety of O'Connor's fiction. And although the word does not occur in the Brown texts even once, we would not want to argue that somehow O'Connor stylistically favors the word *sty,* although we might want to argue that the comic repetition of the word in Mrs. Freeman's story indicates her own inclination towards the word. It is Mrs. Freeman who, the narrator says, "had a special fondness for the details of secret infections, hidden deformities, assaults upon children. Of diseases, she preferred the lingering or incurable" (*GM,* 174). A similar but not quite so extreme clumpiness occurs with the word *wart,* which occurs five times in O'Connor but not at all in the Brown texts. All five of its tokens occur in the story "Revelation" in combination with *hog.* Mary Grace introduces the word in the phrase: "Go back to hell where you came from, you old wart hog" (*ERMC,* 207). There is a memorable use of the plural *warts* in "The River": "Behind, in the distance, the city rose like a cluster of warts on the side of the mountain" (*GM,* 41). Again, the symbolic significance of this use of *warts* makes it memorable, but one would not want to argue that the words *wart* and *warts* are stylistically typical of O'Connor in the sense of high frequency.

There is at least one important way in which the argument against null hypothesis testing in corpus linguistics can be overstated. As Burrows argues, it is not the case that we are expecting two texts that we compare to behave in a completely random fashion. Instead we are comparing the texts, asking whether we can reject the null hypothesis that if the texts came from one population they are constructed randomly from that population.[11] Thus in that population the words *the, cat,* and *slept* almost always would occur in that order. Even so, because the probability testing of the null hypothesis depends on the assumption of absolute independence between tokens that are counted, it is then theoretically more sound not to rely on probability testing in determining differences among texts. There are several alternative methods for determining differences, many of them reliant on the same statistical measures that are normally subjected to probability testing. It is widely accepted in corpus linguistics, even among those who criticize the use of hypothesis testing, that one may still use tests such as chi-square and log-likelihood to rank frequency differences of words between corpora. Paul Rayson and Roger Garside, as well as Geoffrey Leech, Paul Rayson, and Andrew Wilson, after Ted Dunning, use log-likelihood rather than chi-square to protect against unreliable results with low-frequency words. Rayson and Garside also eschew the use of probability figures to determine significance, arguing along with Kilgarriff and Tony Rose that those statistics are unreliable since words that appear in a text do occur non-randomly.[12] Even though I will not use probability testing to determine significance but instead will use log-likelihood to rank word frequencies and collocations, as in Rayson and Garside, it will be convenient to have a log-likelihood cutoff point below which we will not go in detailed discussion of word and collocation frequencies. That cutoff will be 6.635 for the reason that it is the required .01 probability figure. The cutoff of 6.635 is not a matter of having one's probability and one's rejection of probability at the same time. I will not make much of the figure other than using it as a cutoff. In fact there will be both body-part terms and collocations that score above 6.635 but that I do not discuss in depth or even sometimes at all because I will instead be most interested in the very highest scoring body-part terms and collocations or most interested in highly scoring body-part terms that fall into a more restrictive semantic class. Although *The Body in Flannery O'Connor's Fiction* is more quantitatively slanted than most literary analysis, it is not purely quantitatively driven. I will also occasionally discuss words and collocations that fall below the 6.635 cutoff, mostly to illustrate patterns that escape quantitative analysis.

Frequency and Stylistic Significance

Before we dive into the details of the various possible measures of frequency with an eye towards justifying our ultimate reliance on what is called the log-likelihood measure, it is worth pausing for a moment to consider the justifications for frequency counts in the first place. The importance of them in stylistics can certainly be overstated, not least in so far as words that occur with the total frequency of one, what are technically called *hapax legomena* in corpus linguistics, can be of enormous significance in an author's work.[13] To take just a few from O'Connor's texts, for those readers relatively familiar with her stories and novels, the following small section of such words in O'Connor's texts have heavy significance, even though they each occur only once: *ddbirrrttdt, Byzantine, Vapex,* and the number *55890.* Each of these words (or the number) takes special significance through becoming symbolic of some complex of emotion and/or thought in each story that it occurs in.The word *ddbirrrttdt* (a mispronunciation of the word *bird)* is the only word spoken by Lucynell Crater the junior and is taught to her by her future husband, Tom T. Shiftlet, who will abandon her at a diner on their honeymoon (*GM,* 59). She says the word four times during the story: *burrttddt, ddbirrrttdt, burrddttt, bddurrddtttt,* each time differently, but the simplemindness of the pronunciations and the innocence and incarnation symbolized by the use of any bird in O'Connor's fiction give even the one word *ddbirrrttdt* significance that far outstrips its frequency. The only other "nonstandard" pronunciation of the word *bird* is that of the priest in "The Displaced Person," who sees in Mrs. McIntyre's peacock the image of Christ as he will return: "What a beauti-ful birdrrrd!" (*GM,* 202). The word *Byzantine* occurs in O'Connor's "Parker's Back" and is symbolically and literally the representation of Parker's hunger for Christ since it is the complicated, expensive, and painful tattoo of the Byzantine Christ with the "all-demanding eyes" that leads him to the suffering at the hands of the tattooist, his friends in the pool hall who mock him, and his wife, Sarah Ruth, who beats him for his "idolatry" (*ERMC,* 235). The word *Vapex* occurs only once, in "Good Country People," but memorably because Hulga Hopewell puts some on the collar of her "dirty white shirt" that she wears on her date with Manley Pointer. The text tells us that "she did not own any perfume," which itself is not especially odd. What is odd but yet consistent with the character of the overly educated, but yet naïve and childlike Hulga is that she would use Vapex instead of perhaps her mother's perfume or going without anything (*GM,* 187). Even a number that occurs only once, such as *55890* in "A Good Man Is Hard to Find," can take on literary significance if it functions symbolically to encode character traits or story atmosphere, as this one does, indicating the grandmother's busybody nature and the family's ordinariness. The narrator reports the grandmother's notation of the details of the beginning of the family's trip: "Bailey and the children's mother and the baby sat in front and they left Atlanta at eight forty-five with the mileage on the car at 55890" (*GM,* 10). Of course, there are many, many hapax legomena in O'Connor's texts that do not take on special significance for most readers: for example, *firewood, happiest, empire, exertion, saucer.*

Thus if hapax legomena can take on literary significance in the way that I discuss here, what might be the purpose of frequency counts? As we will see below and in chapter 4, the body part *face* occurs with even greater relative frequency than the body part *eye* in O'Connor's fiction, yet the critical literature recognizes the literary significance of the eye much more frequently and in depth than the significance of the face. The likely causes of this differential attention in the literature, and probably on the part of the average reader of O'Connor, are perfectly understandable. First, the eye has greater potential local and global literary significance. For example, O'Connor's *Wise Blood* takes its overarching plot from the self-blinding of Oedipus.[14] Second, one of the primary human senses, if not the most important one, takes as its conduit the eye. Third, as I point out in *Narrating Knowledge in Flannery O'Connor's Fiction,* vision, as it is reflected especially in the frequency and use of the verb *see,* is at the center of O'Connor's aesthetic theory and practice.[15] The discovery that *face* is at least with regard to frequency as important as *eye* leads us deeper into those aesthetics in the sense that the frequency counts allow us to widen our understanding of the significance of body parts in O'Connor's fiction, beyond those to which she herself or our culture draw especial attention. More sophisticated frequency calculations, to be structurally explored below, allow us to widen the scope of significance even more broadly.

Frequency counts will be of importance to us as well in analyzing the combinatory possibilities and patterns in O'Connor's fiction, particularly in collocations—"the occurrence of two or more words within a short space of each other in a text."[16] Thus there is O'Connor's *as-if* quasi simile that has been written about extensively, not only from traditional literary perspectives but also from stylistic ones. That extensive commentary is a result of at least two patterns. First, as we saw in the epigraph to this chapter, O'Connor herself was aware of and commented on the high frequency of the collocation *as if* in her writing, even to the point of complaining that she had a difficult time reducing its frequency of occurrence, as if it were a stylistic flaw. Second, *as if* has multitentacled connections to O'Connor's central and most important themes. When Mason Tarwater first meets Bishop, the retarded child of his nephew Rayber, Francis Tarwater focalizes the meeting: the elder Tarwater "looked as if he beheld an unspeakable mystery" (*VBA,* 32). The quasi simile allows the narrator to present Bishop as an unspeakable mystery at the same time as the narrator reflects both the doubt and the realization that Bishop is a mystery, variously to a number of characters in the story, since he is the object of both baptism and loathing to Francis and the object of both love and loathing to Rayber, his father. Just as there are, to readers relatively familiar with O'Connor's fiction, recognizable and significant hapax legomena, there are also recognizably significant single two-word phrases. There are the unforgettable "cricket choruses" that greet Ruby Turpin as she turns towards home from her revelation at the pig parlor, memorable in part for the metaphorical leveling of the spiritual and animal world (a theme of consistent significance not only in this story but throughout O'Connor) (*ERMC,* 218). There is the "walleyed Guernsey" that greets Asbury on his return to the family farm from the north, where he began to suffer the consequences of drinking unpasteurized milk in a fit of juvenile rebellion against his mother during an earlier visit home (*ERMC*, 88). There is the fence post to which Lucynell Crater the senior is compared in "The Life You Save May Be Your Own": "She was about the size of a cedar fence post" (*GM*, 54). The reduction of the human to the inanimate, particularly, the unattractive inanimate, is a consistent stylistic trait of O'Connor's, as is the interpenetration of the spiritual and the purely physical.[17] That interpenetration is evident in the memorable phrase "silver-white sunlight" in the following equally memorable sentence from "A Good Man Is Hard to Find," narrated as the grandmother points out the interesting, and poetic, bits of the scenery that the family passes on the highway: "The trees were full of silver-white sunlight and the meanest of them sparkled" (*GM*, 11). Of course, just as there are many forgettable hapax legomena in O'Connor, there are many forgettable two-word phrases that occur only once: "courthose porch," "narrow collar," "profane hands." Just as with individual lexical items, the value of frequency counts involving collocations is the discovery of patterns that are not the more obvious either because O'Connor herself makes much of them in her letters and essays or because critics and readers have latched onto them in their symbolic or characterological or thematic development. Thus, as I will detail below and in chapter 5, although the word *eyes* is stylistically important in O'Connor's fiction, some of the collocations into which the word *eyes* enters are also important for specific yet widely recognized themes in her fiction: for example, "closed eyes" and "rolled eyes." Although those and other collocational patterns are not so obvious or overwhelmingly symbolic as perhaps Hazel's blinding himself at the end of *Wise Blood*, they are nevertheless of a piece with O'Connor's thoroughgoing incarnational art.

Frequency Formula

In the last section, I treated frequency counts almost as if they were nonproblematic, as if they were simply a matter of totaling up the individual tokens of a word or a phrase in the O'Connor texts and the Brown texts and comparing those frequencies. However, there are many different ways of treating frequency counts in further attempts to make the counts even more interpretable. In considering various ways of tabulating frequency counts for words in different corpora, we will come ever closer to a measure that better serves the purposes of corpus stylistics. And in consideration of even measures that turn out on closer inspection to be inadequate, we will determine the factors of importance in frequency distributions. Occasionally in both stylistic and corpus linguistics work, some readers' perceptions, at least, are that the statistics and measures are used with insufficient indication of how to think meaningfully about the resulting figures. In a 2002 review of Geoffrey Leech, Paul Rayson, and Andrew Wilson's *Word Frequencies in Written and Spoken English*, which is an extended investigation of word frequency patterns in the British National Corpus, Susan Hunston praises the book for clarity, even with regard to "statistical methods" sufficiently detailed for "duplication," but then writes: "As a non-statistician, though, I would have liked to have . . . further indication of how to interpret the statistical information in the lists as well as how to arrive at the figures." Hunston indicates that the book is strong in illustration of range and dispersion, but then he also indicates some frustration with interpretation of log-likelihood (abbreviated as *LL*): "For example, what does a LL difference of 305 'mean' in looking at the difference between speech and writing?" Elena Semino and Mick Short's 2004 *Corpus Stylistics* is a model of explicitness in its description of the construction and qualitative and quantitative analysis of Semino and Short's speech, writing, and thought presentation corpus; however, there are no specific examples of the calculation for the log-likelihood test that they use for significance testing of frequency differences. Such detail is not integral or important to their arguments.[18] *The Body in Flannery O'Connor's Fiction* is not as statistically sophisticated as some studies are; however, for those who are interested, the remainder of this chapter details the calculations of the statistics behind the stylistics for the entire book. In this section we will see that use of frequency is interestingly not as simple as merely counting words in a text.

One simple problem with raw frequencies is that one often finds oneself working with corpora of different lengths.[19] Although the Brown texts and the O'Connor texts are close to one another in length, the first is 235,431 words long while the second has 293,360 words. This difference of 57,929 words makes direct comparison of raw frequencies difficult and potentially misleading. Thus to say that the word *damn* occurs 31 times each in the Brown and O'Connor texts is slightly misleading in the absence of the total word count and at best difficult to interpret in the context of the total word count. One can, however, conclude that the word *damn* is slightly unrepresented in the O'Connor texts since with the extra 57,929 words in the O'Connor collection there is opportunity for the word to occur at higher frequency but it does not. Of the 22,515 word types in Brown and O'Connor, there are 1,481 words with exactly the same frequency counts in both texts: for example, *damn, mischief, complaining, engage, squeal, interested, limitations, pearl, perfect, funny.* Interpretation of raw frequency counts is even more difficult with words (the vast majority) that have differing frequency counts in the two collections.

There is one other problem with raw frequency counts: they do not allow direct comparison of several word distributions across different corpora. Paul Rayson and Rayson and Roger Garside point out that Knut Hofland and Stig Johannson use G. Udny Yule's difference coefficient in a groundbreaking frequency comparison of the equal-sized Brown Corpus and LOB Corpus. The difference coefficient provides one comparable figure for each word type. As Rayson details, the difference coefficient is calculated as follows with $Freq_1$ being the word frequency in the foreground corpus, for our purposes the O'Connor texts, and with $Freq_2$ being the word frequency in the background corpus, for us, the Brown texts:

$$\textit{diff. co.} = \frac{Freq_1 - Freq_2}{Freq_1 + Freq_2}$$

The difference coefficient ranges from +1 to -1. A positive score indicates greater use in the foreground corpus. A negative score indicates greater use in the background corpus.[20] Thus the word *saved* occurs 43 times in the O'Connor texts and 5 times in the Brown texts; the word *weakness* occurs 3 times in O'Connor and 11 times in Brown. The calculations for the difference coefficients for each of these words is as follows:

$$\textit{saved diff. co.} = \frac{43 - 5}{43 + 5} = \frac{38}{48} = +.79$$

$$\textit{weakness diff. co.} = \frac{3 - 11}{3 + 11} = \frac{-8}{14} = -.57$$

As is clear from the calculations here, the difference coefficient is the ratio of the total number of target words to the difference in frequencies of the target words in each corpus. The only way to get a perfect +1 or -1 for a particular word is for that word not to occur at all in one of the corpora. For example, the word *redemption* occurs 10 times in O'Connor and 0 times in Brown. The ratio of the total number of target words (10) to the difference between the corpora (10) is a perfect 1. The improvement in the difference over simple frequency counts is, again, that there is a possible direct comparison between figures for individual words. Thus a figure of +.79 for *saved* indicates a larger positive ratio between total number of words to the difference in frequencies than a figure of +.60 for the word *serpent.* There are two problems with the difference coefficient for our uses in this book. First, like raw frequency counts, it does not reflect the total number of words in each corpus. Thus it can overestimate or underestimate the representation of a word if the corpora are different in size, a situation that almost always holds in corpus stylistics. The word *arm,* for example, occurs 122 times in O'Connor and 65 times in Brown, with a difference coefficient of .30. This figure already overestimates the coefficient since there are 57,929 more words in the O'Connor texts than in the Brown texts. If we hypothetically double the number of words in the O'Connor texts, also hypothetically doubling the number of tokens of the word *arm,* the difference coefficient is even more misleading at .57. Yule, Hofland and Johannson, Rayson and Garside, and Rayson all assume or use corpora of the same size in their applications or references to the difference coefficient; thus the application of the difference coefficient to corpora of unequal sizes as in this book was never intended. In fact Yule assumes that the word frequencies "are representative samples of one and the same work."[21]

The inapplicability of the difference coefficient is revealing of what a successful measure for our purposes would do: account for corpora of differing size. The second problem is more subtle: the difference coefficient is not scaled for the total number of target tokens that occur in the two corpora. This problem leads to the same difference coefficient (.53) for the body parts *face* and *knees.* The word *knees* occurs 69 times in O'Connor and 21 times in Brown. Because the word *face* occurs 728 times in O'Connor and 220 times in Brown, we have much more evidence for the difference between the words; yet the difference coefficient does not reflect that evidence. The words *prophet, irked,* and *nipple* each receive a +1 difference coefficient because they each occur in O'Connor's texts at least once but do not occur at all in the Brown texts. The specific frequencies in O'Connor are, respectively, 56, 11, and 1. Whatever one might decide about the relative importance of the words *prophet* and *irked,* any frequency measure of use in stylistics should suggest the possibility that *nipple* is less stylistically important than either *prophet* or *irked* in O'Connor's fiction. I am certain that any reader of O'Connor's two novels, in which the word bunches, knows that the word *prophet* is important. A close reader of the fiction also knows that the word *irked* is sometimes used in reflecting the frequent impotent irritation of O'Connor's characters. In "The Life You Save May Be Your Own," Tom T. Shiftlet annoyingly asks Lucynell Crater the senior how she knows his name is not really Aaron Sparks, or George Speeds, or Thompson Bright: "'I don't know nothing about you,' the old woman muttered, irked" (*GM,* 56). The word *irked* occurs in all collections and novels except *The Geranium.* However, even most close readers of O'Connor's texts would be hard pressed to remember even the general vicinity of the word *nipple.* The difference coefficient does not reflect those differing degrees of evidence for the words *prophet, irked,* and *nipple.*

In sum, the difference coefficient represents neither the sizes of the corpora in the calculation nor the amount of information that we have for each word. Two scores that improve on these issues are log-likelihood (G^2) and chi-square (χ^2). To see that there is indeed an improvement in both these issues, consider table 2.

Again, the difference coefficient scores for *face* and *knees* are the same (0.53), as they are for *Jesuits, chloride, asleep,* and *bad* (0.00), and as they are for *nipple, irked,* and *prophet* (1.00). Note, however, that G^2 and χ^2 both distinguish between the use of the words *face* and *knees,* for example, with similar yet significantly scaled differences: (187.03 vs. 17.50 and 174.70 vs. 16.36). I will explain the calculation of these scores below; table 2 demonstrates the motivation for bothering

TABLE 2: **Comparative frequency calculations**

Word	O'Connor	Brown	G^2	χ^2	Diff. Co.
face	728	220	187.03	174.70	0.53
knees	69	21	17.50	16.36	0.53
Jesuits	1	1	0.02	0.02	0.00
chloride	1	1	0.02	0.02	0.00
asleep	26	26	0.62	0.63	0.00
bad	55	55	1.32	1.33	0.00
nipple	1	0	1.17	0.80	1.00
irked	11	0	12.96	8.82	1.00
prophet	56	0	65.99	44.94	1.00

with G^2 and χ^2 at all. Note, second, that where the difference coefficient makes no distinction between the O'Connor and Brown uses of the words *prophet, irked,* and *nipple* (for the superficial reason that the Brown texts contain no instances of any of these words), both χ^2 and G^2 make distinctions; furthermore the scores are distinguished in the way in which we would expect, reflecting the amount of information that we have about the use of each word.[22] As the frequency increases for each word, both the G^2 and the χ^2 scores go up. Finally, note from table 2 that the same pattern occurs with the words *Jesuits, chloride, asleep,* and *bad.* The difference coefficient does not distinguish among these words for the reason that the ratios of the frequencies of the words in each corpus are the same. However, both G^2 and χ^2 distinguish among the words in the direction in which we would expect, except for the words *Jesuits* and *chloride,* with identical frequencies in the two corpora.

In order to determine how the G^2 and χ^2 figures are produced, we first consider the model table 3, which is generally called a contingency table:[23]

TABLE 3: **Model contingency for frequencies**

	Corpus 1		*Corpus 2*		*Total*
	Observed	Expected	Observed	Expected	
word	freq cell 1	freq cell 4	freq cell 6	freq cell 9	freq cell 11
other	freq cell 2	freq cell 5	freq cell 7	freq cell 10	freq cell 12
TOTAL	freq cell 3		freq cell 8		freq cell 13

In this typical 2X2 comparison of the occurrence of a word frequency in two corpora, the first row of numbers is the frequency of the word in each corpus in the first and third columns of numbers and then the total of the word frequencies in both corpora in the fifth column of numbers. The second row of numbers is the frequency of words in each corpus that are not the target word (other) in the first and third columns, for each corpus, and then the total of the "other" word frequencies in the fifth column of numbers. The third row of numbers contains the totals for each column, in the first and third columns the totals for each corpus and in the final the total for all words in both corpora. The frequencies for the target words and other words in both corpora are referred to as the "observed" values; those observed values are entered into both the χ^2 and G^2 calculations. The "expected" frequencies for each of the observed frequency cells are also entered. The "expected" frequencies for each cell are arrived at by first assuming that both individual corpora are together one larger corpus. Then the expected frequencies are specifically calculated by determining the proportion of each individual total on the basis of the proportion in the hypothetical larger undifferentiated corpus. The usual calculation for expected scores is the following:[24]

$$\text{expected value} = \frac{\text{row total} * \text{column total}}{\text{total of all words}}$$

Thus to determine the expected value for cell 4 in table 3, we multiply the row total for that cell (cell 11) by the column total for that cell (cell 3) and then divide that product by the total of all words (cell 13). The formula above is efficient, yet it does not make obvious exactly what the expected value is. If we transform the formula above into the formula below we see much more clearly what is being done:[25]

$$\text{expected value} = \frac{\text{row total}}{\text{total of all words}} * \text{column total}$$

What is happening in this formula is that first the ratio of the total of all words to the row total is determined. This is the ratio, in the case of determining the expected value for cell 4, of the frequency of target words to the total words in the hypothetical larger corpus composed of both corpora. The calculation determines the ratio of target words under the hypothesis that there is no difference between the individual corpora. In the second part of the formula, that ratio is multiplied by the total number of words in the first corpus (that is, the number in our particular case here of cell 3). This, then, provides the specific expected frequency of target words under the hypothesis that the ratio distribution will be the same in the individual corpus as it is in the hypothetical large undifferentiated corpus. Each expected frequency is determined in the same way. Thus the specific calculation of the expected frequency of cell 5 in table 3 is the following:

$$\text{expected value of cell 5} = \frac{\text{row total (cell 12)}}{\text{total of all words (cell 13)}} * \text{column total (cell 3)}$$

In order to clarify these calculations fully, table 4 provides the observed and expected values for the word *arm* in the O'Connor and Brown texts:

TABLE 4: **Contingency for *arm***

	O'Connor		*Brown*		*Total*
	Observed	Expected	Observed	Expected	
arm	122 (c 1)	104 (c 4)	65 (c 6)	83 (c 9)	187 (c 11)
other	293,238 (c 2)	293,256 (c 5)	235,366 (c 7)	235,348 (c 10)	528,604 (c 12)
TOTAL	293,360 (c 3)		235,431 (c 8)		528,791 (c 13)

The calculation of the expected frequency for cell 4, that is, the frequency of *arm* in O'Connor if there were no difference between the corpora, is the following:

$$\frac{187}{528{,}791} * 293360 = .000353636881 * 293360 = 104$$

Thus the observed frequency (122) of the word *arm* in O'Connor is higher than the expected frequency (104), that expectation being based on the assumption that the O'Connor texts and the Brown texts are from some hypothetical larger corpus. The converse of the frequency of *arm* in O'Connor is that the observed frequency (65) of the word *arm* in the Brown texts is lower than the expected frequency (83).

With the observed and expected frequencies for the target words and other words in both corpora, we have all the figures that are necessary to calculate the χ^2 measure for frequency differences. As is indicated in table 2, both χ^2 and G^2 distinguish among frequency distributions for words that have individually the same frequencies in the numerically unequal Brown and O'Connor texts. To determine why either the χ^2 or the G^2 is preferable to the difference coefficient, we must examine the calculation of χ^2 and G^2. Consider, then, the formula for χ^2:

$$\chi^2 = \sum_{i,j} \frac{(Oij - Eij)^2}{Eij}$$

This formula reads that χ^2 is calculated by summing (Σ) the results of dividing the square of the difference between observed and expected values for each of the four central frequency cells (for a 2X2 table) by the expected frequency for each cell.[26] Thus the calculation for the basic chi-square of table 4 is as follows:

$$\chi^2 = \frac{(122 - 104)^2}{104} + \frac{(293{,}238 - 293{,}256)^2}{293{,}256} + \frac{(65 - 83)^2}{83} + \frac{(235{,}366 - 235{,}348)^2}{235{,}348} = 7.21$$

There is an adjustment that is frequently made for 2X2 chi-square calculations when probability is an issue, but because we will not be considering statistical probability, we will ignore those complications.[27] Each of the results of the subtractions in the numerators, some of which are negative after subtraction, is squared before division in order to make all numbers positive. The essential reason that both χ^2 and the G^2 are better indications of frequency distributions than the difference coefficient is that both figures are based on observed and expected frequencies, the latter of which is based both on the total frequency of words in the corpora and the total number of words in each individual corpus. To see how these factors help both χ^2 and G^2 to reflect the amount of information that is available, consider the hypothetical contingency tables 5 and 6.

TABLE 5: **Hypothetical contingency a, $G^2 = 1.24$, $\chi^2 = 1.21$**

	O'Connor		*Brown*		*Total*
	Observed	Expected	Observed	Expected	
Word	16	13.31	8	10.69	24
Other	293,344	293,346.69	235,423	235,420.31	528,767
TOTAL	293,360		235,431		528,791

TABLE 6: **Hypothetical contingency b, $G^2 = 2.49$, $\chi^2 = 2.43$**

	O'Connor		*Brown*		*Total*
	Observed	Expected	Observed	Expected	
Word	32	26.63	16	21.37	48
Other	293,328	293,333.37	235,415	235,409.63	528,743
TOTAL	293,360		235,431		528,791

The difference coefficients for the data in both tables are the same (.33), for the same reasons that the difference coefficients are identical for the words *Jesuits, chloride, asleep,* and *bad* in table 2: the ratios between the words in question are identical, in tables 5 and 6, 2 to 1 (specifically 16 to 8 and 32 to 16). However, in tables 5 and 6 because the expected frequencies are determined by calculating proportion of words in the merged corpus and because both the χ^2 and G^2 calculations include relationships between the observed and expected figures, both χ^2 and G^2 figures increase as the absolute frequencies of the target words increase, that is, as the formula has more and more information to work with.[28] Thus, although the ratio between 16 and 8 on the one hand and 32 and 16 on the other is the same, the absolute difference between the numbers is greater and thus, the difference between the observed and expected frequencies is larger as well.

The log-likelihood G^2 (alternately noted LL and -2lnλ) calculation uses the same observed and expected figures as the χ^2 calculation. A widely cited version of the Dunning calculation for G^2 is as follows (with minor variations in some publications):[29]

$$\begin{aligned} LL = 2 \text{ x } (&a \log a + b \log b + c \log c + d \log d \\ &- (a + b) \log (a + b) - (a + c) \log (a + c) \\ &- (b + d) \log (b + d) - (c + d) \log (c + d) \\ &+ (a + \mathrm{b} + c + d) \log (a + b + c + d)) \end{aligned}$$

Although this version of Dunning's formula is relatively easy to calculate and although this is the specific formula that I use in Textant to calculate G^2, it is not as transparent as it could be, largely because it does not look anything like the χ^2 formula. A G^2 formula used by Leech, Rayson, and Wilson; Rayson; and Garside and Rayson that is more transparent is as follows:

$$-2\ln\lambda = 2\sum_{i} O_i \ln\left(\frac{O_i}{E_i}\right)$$

The formula above is equal to the following, as Leech, Rayson, and Wilson; Rayson; and Garside and Rayson detail:

$$LL = 2\mathrm{x}((a\mathrm{xln}\ (a/\mathrm{E1})) + (b\mathrm{xln}(b/\mathrm{E2})))$$

The symbols a and b refer to the observed frequencies of the target words in, respectively, the first corpus and second corpus, and E1 and E2 refer to the expected frequencies of the target words in, respectively, the first and second corpus.[30] An even more transparent formula that provides the same G^2 score as the version of Dunning above is my alteration of the formula above to the following:

$$-2\ln\lambda = 2\sum_{ij} O_{ij} \ln\left(\frac{O_{ij}}{E_{ij}}\right)$$

The difference between my formula and the one used by Leech, Rayson, and Wilson; Rayson; and Garside and Rayson is that mine calculates over all four cells of a 2X2 table rather than two. The formula above is, thus, equivalent to the following even more transparent formula below:

$$G^2 = 2*((\mathrm{Freq1}*\ln(\mathrm{Freq1}/\mathrm{E1})) + (\mathrm{Freq2}*\ln(\mathrm{Freq2}/\mathrm{E2})) + (\mathrm{Freq3}*\ln(\mathrm{Freq3}/\mathrm{E3})) + (\mathrm{Freq}_4*\ln(\mathrm{Freq}_4/\mathrm{E}_4)))$$

Freq1 and Freq2 refer to the observed frequencies of the target words in, respectively, the first corpus and second corpus and E1 and E2 refer to the expected frequencies of the target words in, respectively, the first and second corpus; and Freq3 and Freq4 refer to the observed frequencies of the "other" words in the first corpus and second corpus, and E3 and E4 refer to the expected frequencies of the other words in the first and second corpus. Thus the log-likelihood figure is scaled for both the natural log of the ratio between the observed and expected figures of the target words and other words for both corpora. Like the χ^2 figure, the G^2 figure reflects the size of the corpus, the absolute frequency of the target word, and the absolute difference between the observed and the expected frequencies. Table 2 indicates that the G^2 figure and χ^2 figure for *face* are close to one another. For almost all the practical purposes of this book, the G^2 and χ^2 are equivalent. Under conditions that are more common in the analysis of collocations than in the analysis of word frequencies, the χ^2 test can overestimate the significance of rare events, as Dunning points out.[31] We will consider that problem specifically in the next section. However, to keep the statistical analysis as consistent as possible and to stay in conformance with the widespread practice of using log-likelihood for word frequencies as well, we will use G^2 for both frequency and collocation ranking.

Collocation Measures

When we measure collocations rather than simple word frequencies, we measure the frequencies of particular combinations of words, anywhere from two to perhaps eight words, although collocations, or combinations that occur more than once in a particular text, decrease in frequency as the number of words in the collocation is increased. A quick post hoc analysis of the *as-if* quasi simile as a collocation in O'Connor's fiction and the Brown texts will serve as an introduction to the procedure of collocation analysis before we apply it to the more subtle collocations involving body parts. Edward Kessler has called the *as-if* quasi simile "O'Connor's poetic signature." This construction is of vast interpretive importance in O'Connor's poetics in part because, as David R. Mayer argues, it "enjoys the advantages of a biblical parable. . . . Like the parable, the 'as if' allows readers to stay merely on the obvious story level if they wish, but signifies deeper truths for those who are willing to accept them." Generally, in O'Connor's fiction the interpenetration of the animate with the inanimate helps to signal O'Connor's sacramental viewpoint.[32] In particular, the *as-if* quasi simile frequently occasions the interpenetration of such seemingly incompatible layers of being. In *Wise Blood,* for example, Enoch goes on a cleaning spree in preparation for his theft of the shrunken man as a "new jesus" for Hazel's "Church Without Christ," but his chair is not up to the challenge: "The gold began to appear with the first touch of water but it disappeared with the second and with a little more, the chair sat down as if this were the end of long years of inner struggle. Enoch didn't know if it was for him or against him" (*WB,* 141, 131). The grotesque and the sacred interpenetrate in "The Lame Shall Enter First," in which, for example, Johnson's incarnational attitude towards his club foot is communicated through a quasi simile: "Johnson was as touchy about the foot **as if** it were a sacred object" (*ERMC*, 162).

There are three primary methods that have been used to rank collocation scores: mutual information, χ^2, and G^2. The mutual information score and χ^2 demostrate exactly the same problem: they tend sometimes to overestimate the importance of rare events, in this case, rare collocations.[33] As indicated above, we will use the G^2 ranking for both word frequencies and collocations, but to explain both collocation ranking with G^2 and why χ^2 can severely overestimate the importance of rare collocations, we will briefly consider the calculations of both G^2 and χ^2 for collocations. In order to do so, we need to consider just one more model contingency table, table 7, which is a modification of one in Dunning:[34]

TABLE 7: **Model contingency for collocations**

	A		*~A*		*Total*
	Observed	Expected	Observed	Expected	
B	Freq (A B)		Freq (~A B)		Freq (X B)
~B	Freq (A ~B)		Freq (~A ~B)		Freq (X ~B)
TOTAL					

In calculating collocation measures in this book, we compare not frequencies of individual words but instead frequencies of combinations of words. We are also not directly calculating collocations across different corpora but instead are calculating collocations within individual corpora. If we happen to be investigating *as if* as a collocation, in table 7, Freq (A B) is the frequency of the bigram (two-word combination) *as if* in the text collection under investigation; Freq (~A B) is the frequency of the bigram "other word" *if,* where "other word" is any word except *as;* Freq (A ~B) is the frequency of the bigram *as* "other word"; and Freq (~A ~B) is the frequency of the bigrams without *as* in first position and without *if* in second position. Thus, analogously to testing a 2X2 contingency table of word frequencies with column 1 being one corpus and column 2 being the other corpus, with the 2X2 contingency table for collocations (for example, *as if*) we are testing the difference in frequency distribution of the "B" term (for example, *if*) between the first column, when we know that the "A" term (for example, *as*) occurs, and the second column, when we know that the "A" term does not occur.

As Dunning points out in detail, although the χ^2 and G^2 tests usually give approximately equivalent results, the χ^2 can overestimate the significance of frequencies, especially of very low-frequency collocations. Consider, then, the bigram "duplex bungalow," which occurs in O'Connor's fiction exactly twice, once in "A Stroke of Good Fortune," in (1, below), to signal Ruby's lower-middle-class dreams of getting out of her high-rise apartment building, and once in "Greenleaf," in (2), to signal the government-sponsored upward mobility of Mr. Greenleaf's sons:

1. "She had her eye on a place in Meadowcrest Heights, a **duplex bungalow** with yellow awnings." (*GM*, 71)
2. "The two of them were living now about two miles down the highway on a piece of land that the government had helped them to buy and in a brick **duplex bungalow** that the government had helped to build and pay for." (*ERMC*, 33)

Now, one might justifiably make much out of the contextual use of the phrase "duplex bungalow" as a post–World War II signifier for the increasing size of the middle class and in particular in (2) the resentment of some towards that rise. The narrator tells us Mrs. May's thoughts and words on the issue: "If the war had made anyone, Mrs. May said, it had made the Greenleaf boys." She concludes "blackly" that the Greenleaf children will be "society" in twenty years because of their father's rising fortunes and the civilizing influence of their French mothers, women that the Greenleaf boys met during the war (*ERMC*, 33). Whatever the contextual importance of "duplex bungalow" in these two O'Connor stories, one would not want a collocation calculation that overestimated its stylistic significance.

Because the absolute difference between the observed and expected frequencies is explicitly represented in the χ^2 formula, in the case of collocations of very low frequency, the difference between the observed and the expected frequencies scaled by the expected frequency, as in the χ^2 calculation, will result in disproportionately large χ^2 figures, as in the case of "duplex bungalow," with a χ^2 of 293,309. The G^2 figure for the same collocation is 51.58. To put these figures into context, consider table 8, which contains three high-frequency collocations and three low-frequency collocations, including "duplex bungalow:"

TABLE 8: **Collocations with log-likelihood and chi-square figures**

Collocation	Frequency	G^2	χ^2
as if	739	5,778.92	57,580.09
he said	984	2,836.61	6,949.41
and then	383	1,357.12	3,908.06
Ignatius Vogle	2	51.58	293,309.00
duplex bungalow	2	51.58	293,309.00
rabble rouser	2	51.58	293,309.00

What these figures show is remarkably close agreement for the three high-frequency collocations at least in the sense that they are ranked in the same order for both G^2 and χ^2 calculations. However, with the low-frequency collocations, the G^2 figure is quite low and the χ^2 calculation is extraordinarily and unrealistically high.[35] One would not want to conclude that "Ignatius Vogle," "duplex bungalow," and "rabble rouser" are characteristic of the whole of O'Connor's fiction. The first two are particular to two short stories. The last occurs in the speech of one unnamed character in *Wise Blood,* in response to Hazel's sermon on the Church Without Christ: "'Rabble rouser,' the little man said. 'One thing I can't stand it's a rabble rouser'" (*WB,* 104). However, the collocation *as if,* with a much lower χ^2 figure than any of the three low-frequency collocations is certainly more broadly characteristic of O'Connor's fiction, as will be detailed below. Note that the G^2 figure for the low-frequency collocations is much smaller than that for *as if.*

Table 9 presents the frequencies of the top five collocations with initial *as* ranked by G^2 score in O'Connor's fiction and the Brown texts. For contrastive purposes it also contains one relatively low-ranked collocation.

TABLE 9: **Collocations with initial *as* in O'Connor and Brown texts**

O'Connor			*Brown*		
Collocation	Freq	G^2	Collocation	Freq	G^2
as if	**739**	**5,778.92**	***as if***	**96**	**465.20**
as soon	60	513.84	*as he*	160	307.85
as well	32	122.95	*as though*	38	238.13
as he	158	114.92	*as a*	121	153.59
as they	53	107.65	*as well*	32	132.40
. . .			. . .		
as this	6	0.002	*as my*	4	0.030

The G^2 scores for O'Connor's *as if* in table 9 confirm what one would already strongly suspect from reading O'Connor's fiction—that *as* and *if* strongly collocate. However, the table demonstrates that the highest scoring collocation for initial *as* in the Brown texts is also *as if.* The G^2 score for *as if* is far higher in O'Connor than in Brown, and the proportions are much higher in O'Connor (2.51 per 1,000 words) than in the Brown texts (.40 per 1,000 words). These two figures confirm the stylistic value of *as if* for O'Connor's fiction even though *as if* remains an interesting collocation in the Brown texts as well. Although *as if* in the O'Connor and Brown texts is certainly worthy of further investigation in future research, the collocation analysis of most other words in O'Connor's fiction demands, at least initially, a much subtler approach than that which is necessary for *as if.*

One way to determine words that might be interesting in a collocation analysis is a frequency analysis. There are seven body parts that appear in table 10 (below), four of which have G^2 scores that are relatively high, three of which have scores that are relatively low. The four that have the highest—*face, head, eyes,* and *mouth*—are the highest scoring body parts in O'Connor's fiction.

TABLE 10: **Body parts and log-likelihood**

Word	*O'Connor* Freq	*O'Connor* Ratio-1000	*Brown* Freq	*Brown* Ratio-1000	G^2
face	748	2.48	220	0.93	187.03
head	519	1.76	210	.89	76.13
eyes	592	2.01	286	1.21	52.28
mouth	214	0.72	67	0.28	51.94
ear	40	0.13	13	0.05	9.12
toe	7	0.02	4	0.01	0.3
collarbone	1	0.003	1	0.004	0.02

Tony Berber-Sardinha argues that for keyword analysis the recommended size of the standard corpus (in our case the Brown texts) is five times the size of the target corpus (in our case the O'Connor texts) for the reason that smaller standard corpora produce fewer keywords and larger standard corpora do not produce significantly more keywords than a standard corpus of five times the size of the target corpus. Rayson uses a target corpus that "is less than or equal in size" to the standard corpus.[36] As I have pointed out, the O'Connor texts have more words than the Brown texts. As a result I do not claim that I am performing keyword analysis in the methodological sense of Scott or Berber-Sardinha or Rayson. However, in the interests of methodological comparison, I created a standard corpus of 1,510,911 words, which is 5.15 times the size of the O'Connor texts. This larger standard corpus was created by combining the literary texts from Brown, Frown (a 1990s version of Brown), LOB (a British version of Brown), FLOB (a 1990s version of LOB), ACE (an Australian corpus), WC (a New Zealand corpus), and Kolhapur (an Indian English corpus). While the number of keywords does increase in the comparison of O'Connor with this larger corpus—what I call the fiction corpus—the ranking of the body parts in table 10 is exactly the same, except that *mouth* and *eyes* flip places. More important, the top ranking four body parts remain exactly the same. Thus because I am interested only in very highly ranked words in this study, the smaller size of the Brown texts is not a methodological problem.

The sheer high frequency of the word *eyes* in O'Connor's fiction, evident in table 10, reinforces the intuitional observation that O'Connor's aesthetics are both theoretically and practically visual. However, the frequency statistics in themselves tell us nothing about the fine-grained contextual use of the word *eyes.*

Considering three collocations with relatively high log-likelihood scores from the O'Connor and Brown texts, as in table 11 (below), we see that examining simple fixed collocations with the word *eyes* will not automatically uncover interesting patterns in the texts:

TABLE 11: ***Eyes* collocations without stoplist**

O'Connor			*Brown*		
Collocation	Freq	G^2	Collocation	Freq	G^2
his eyes	229	1,097.73	*his eyes*	72	316.63
her eyes	105	436.05	*her eyes*	45	187.38
eyes were	58	253.80	*eyes were*	28	127.64

Table 11 illustrates the well-known collocational phenomenon in which grammatical morphemes such as the pronouns *his* and *her;* the linking verb/auxiliary verb *were;* and words from categories such as prepositions, articles, conjunctions, and modal verbs are likely, in part due to frequency, to surface in collocations. It is not that these grammatical collocations are never interesting stylistically; indeed, the most interesting collocation in table 9 is a grammatical collocation—*as if.* However, if one is concerned with content words, such as *eyes,* it is usually preferable to exclude the grammatical words that collocate in order to discover the content words that collocate.

A text analysis program with the feature of a stoplist allows one easily to exclude grammatical morphemes from the collocation analysis.[37] Table 12 contains the top log-likelihood scored two-word fixed-phrase collocations with a minimum frequency of five, minus grammatical words in the Textant stoplist, for *eyes* in O'Connor and Brown:

TABLE 12: ***Eyes* collocations with stoplist**

O'Connor			*Brown*		
Collocation	Freq	G^2	Collocation	Freq	G^2
closed eyes	14	78.99	*closed eyes*	10	72.61
opened eyes	15	67.54	*blue eyes*	10	66.00
shut eyes	11	53.82	*opened eyes*	6	32.02
eyes glittered	5	42.50	*dark eyes*	6	25.83
rolled eyes	8	42.24			

I explain the minimum frequency cutoff of five in the next chapter.

The stoplist for the figures in table 12 includes the following word classes: personal pronouns, reflexive pronouns, determiners, modal verbs, auxiliary verbs, prepositions, coordinating conjunctions, and subordinating conjunctions. Thus in (3), below, we find one token of the collocation *rolled eyes* from O'Connor's "A Good Man Is Hard to Find," even though there is a possessive determiner between the constituents of the collocation:

3. "She **rolled her eyes** and screwed up her mouth and stuck her leathery thin face into his smooth bland one." (*GM,* 12)

More interesting than the number of different collocations in O'Connor versus Brown are the formal and semantic classes of the words involved in the collocations in table 12. Thus of the four top collocations in the Brown texts, two are modifier-noun combinations, and two are noun-verb combinations (the "noun-verb" label is not necessarily representational in constituent order). In the O'Connor texts all five are noun-verb combinations. Both of the modifier-noun combinations in the Brown texts are a combination of a color term or shade term and *eyes.* Chapters 4 and 5 will return to the interpretive significance of these and other collocational patterns.

Dispersion Measures

One last family of statistical measures of importance in this study includes range and Juilland's *D,* both measurements of dispersion of words. As Leech, Rayson, and Wilson and Rayson explain, these measures allow us to specify how widely, or narrowly, a lexical item is spread through a text split into equal-sized units.[38] Only those words that are relatively widely dispersed can be logically said to be generally characteristic of an author's style. For example, the word *haze* (or *Haze)* has a very high G^2 figure: 416.56. The word occurs 392 times in O'Connor's fiction but only 5 times in the Brown texts. However, all but two of those 392 occurrences in O'Connor's fiction name a major character of *Wise Blood.* Although *Haze* is characteristic of *Wise Blood,* it is not characteristic of the remainder of O'Connor's fiction. In fact, it occurs more frequently (5 times, as *haze*) in the Brown texts in its more normal sense than it occurs in the O'Connor texts (only twice).

For both range and Juilland's *D,* Textant splits the text under analysis into segments of 20,000 words each and then determines how many of those segments contain the word or construction in question. The entire O'Connor fiction corpus is 293,360 words. Thus there are 14 segments checked in any range calculation. The remaining words, the entirety of "Judgement Day" and about the last 2,641 words of "Parker's Back" do not figure in the range or Juilland's *D* calculation. This truncation is necessary in order to make range and Juilland's *D* calculations comparable within and across both the Brown and O'Connor texts. The Brown texts number 235,431 words and divide into 11 full segments of 20,000 words each. In any direct range or Juilland's *D* comparison of the O'Connor and Brown texts, we would then count only the first 11 segments of the O'Connor texts. All range and Juilland's *D* comparisons in chapters 4 and 5 will be made solely within the O'Connor texts, so this truncation is mostly not of concern to us. As Leech, Rayson, and Wilson, and Rayson explain, the range is a count of the number of sections of text that a word or construction appears in. The range for *haze* in the first 11 segments in the O'Connor texts is 5; the range in the Brown texts is 2. Because the category of the word *haze* is almost always a proper noun in O'Connor and a common noun in Brown and because *Wise Blood* is spread over three segments, one must be cautious about overinterpreting the range figure, especially with highly bunched lexemes.

Juilland's *D*, whose calculation is detailed by Anthony A. Lyne; Oakes; Leech, Rayson, and Wilson; and Rayson, is a more representative measure of dispersion because it measures how evenly or unevenly distributed a word or construction is in segments of equal size. As Lyne points out, range is a "rather crude measure of dispersion" because it tabulates only "the number of sections of the corpus in which an item had at least one occurrence."[39] A simple range measure would be 11 if the target appeared once in each of 10 segments and 100 times in the remaining segment. The range score of 11 would, therefore, not represent the target's very uneven frequency distribution across the segments.

As Rayson and Oakes detail, in calculating Juilland's *D*, one first calculates the standard deviation(s) of the frequencies of the target in equally sized word segments, 20,000 in Textant. The standard deviation is the square root of the average of the sum of absolute differences between the average frequency ($\bar{x}$) and the individual frequencies (x_i), as follows:

$$s = \sqrt{\frac{\Sigma\,(x_i - \bar{x})^2}{n}}$$

Then, one calculates the variation coefficient (*V*) in order to norm the potentially widely variant standard deviations by the average frequency of the target across the segments:

$$V = \frac{s}{\bar{x}}$$

Finally, the coefficient of dispersion (Juilland's *D*) is calculated as follows:

$$D = 1 \frac{V}{\sqrt{n - 1}}$$

This formula results in scores ranging from 0 to 1. A score of 1 indicates perfectly even distribution across the segments (for example, exactly 10 in each segment) to a hypothetical 0, indicating maximally uneven distribution.[40] In the

O'Connor texts distribution of the word *teeth* has a Juilland's *D* of .83 and a range of 14 while the word *face* has a Juilland's *D* of .95 and the same range of 14. The lower Juilland's *D* score for the word *teeth* results from two relatively high bursts of occurrence in the stories of O'Connor's M.F.A. thesis stories and the story "Everything That Rises Must Converge."

This chapter has presented detailed explanation and justifications for the particular calculations used in the remainder of the book: log-likelihood, range, and Juilland's *D.* Chapter 4 continues the discussions of the middle from chapter 2 and our discussions of quantitative method from this chapter in an exploration of O'Connor's literary body, body parts, and the ergative middle verbs with which they pattern.

The Body

Actions and Parts

There's one of these doctors in Atlanta that's taken a knife and cut the human heart . . . out of a man's chest and held it in his hand, . . . and studied it like it was a day-old chicken, and lady, . . . he don't know no more about it than you or me.

Tom T. Shiftlet (*GM*, 55)

As I indicated in chapter 1, the body and its importance in O'Connor's understanding of the incarnational and sacramental is generally well recognized. As Srigley points out, "The Incarnation . . . represents [for O'Connor] the mystery of embodied spiritual life, both by mirroring the human condition of an interwoven physical and spiritual existence and by revealing the connection of human beings to God that is known through love and lived in both body and soul." The body, even the occasional individual body part, is well analyzed as metaphor in O'Connor's fiction. For example, Avis Hewitt finds metaphorical significance in Mary Fortune Pitts's "very fine, sand-colored hair": "Hair that could have been yellow is instead sand-like, a mineral-world opposition to clay, perhaps that clay of [her grandfather's] which she is 'thoroughly of'—a salutary mixing that constitutes loaming soil far superior to either sand or clay alone." Similarly and equally metaphorically, Natalie Wilson argues that some O'Connor stories imply that "the head is a suspect part of the body, for it seems to house patriarchal law." For example, in "The Comforts of Home," "the mother's incongruously small head can be read as symbolizing her unwillingness to abide by societal codes of conduct and respectability." Although *The Body in Flannery O'Connor's Fiction* is more relentlessly about the specificity of individual body parts than Lake's *Incarnational Art of Flannery O'Connor,* Lake's generalization about grotesques in O'Connor's fiction might serve just as well for my approach to the individual body part: "Whatever else the grotesques may represent in O'Connor's fiction, they never cease to be physical bodies and to make us vividly aware of that fact. They are never merely symbols."[1]

This chapter of *The Body in Flannery O'Connor's Fiction* explores the details of the fundamental embodiment of O'Connor's fiction as that embodiment is realized in her unrelenting concentration on body parts as well as in her use of ergative middle verbs and body-part subjects to those ergative middle verbs. The chapter demonstrates both quantitatively and qualitatively that the most centrally important body-part terms in O'Connor's fiction are *head, mouth, face,* and *eyes,* and that among the centrally important ergative middle verbs in O'Connor's fiction are *turned, thrust, leaned, rested,* and *jerked.* The chapter also provides quantitative analysis of body-part collocations as preparation for and supplement to the qualitative discussion of middle-voice constructions involving body parts as both subjects and objects. Middles and body-part subjects to ergative middle verbs are treated in this chapter, while body-part objects in middle-related constructions are treated in chapter 5.

Frequency and Use of Body Parts

As explained earlier, the minimum cutoff log-likelihood (G^2) score for an "interesting" word in O'Connor and Brown in this study is 6.635. In this chapter and the next I will use the terms *significant* and *significantly* in the statistically nonprobabilistic sense of "interesting." Most body-part terms do not reach this cutoff point, including *lap, shoulder, nerves, hand, tears, hair, cheek, arms, toes, back, hip, ankles, neck, hips, lungs, bone, teeth, skull, shoulders, waist, lip, fingers, wings, ribs, thumb, eyebrows, brain, tongue, bones, nerve, ears, nose, muscles, fist, muscle, throat, cheeks, heels, legs, guts, skin, chest, chin, wing, sweat,* and *corpse.* There are sixteen body-part terms that are far more frequent in the O'Connor texts than in the Brown texts and only eight body-part terms that are significantly more frequent in the Brown texts than in the O'Connor texts: *flesh, lips, belly, beard, hoofs, forefinger, breasts,* and *body* itself. *Body,* for example, is three times as concentrated in the Brown texts as in the O'Connor texts. When the word *body* does occur in O'Connor's texts, it refers to the whole body, undifferentiated for parts. Sometimes that simple wholeness is emphasized, as in *The Violent Bear It Away* when Francis is drugged by the man who picks him up in his car and the drug effects radiate throughout his body: "The liquor lay like a hot rock in the pit of his stomach, heating his whole body . . ." (*VBA,* 230). Sometimes that wholeness of the body is contrasted with individual body parts, as when Mr. Fortune is attacked by his granddaughter, Mary Fortune Pitts, in "A View of the Woods": "She was on him so quickly that he could not have recalled which blow he felt first, whether the weight of her whole solid body or the jabs of her feet or the pummeling of her fist on his chest" (*ERMC,* 79). Here the girl's body has a wholeness and a particularity that are threatening and dangerous in both. It makes good stylistic sense that *body*—undifferentiated—would occur in relatively low proportions in O'Connor's body-part-rich fiction. The body parts that do occur in greater proportions in O'Connor's fiction are stylistically marked in the sense that they are not only frequent but also relatively transparent as manifestations of O'Connor's concerns with the incarnational and the grotesque. The words in table 13 are arranged in two groups of descending strength of the G^2 score (one each for words significant in O'Connor and for words significant in Brown).

For comparative purposes consider the words *Jesus* and *Bible* in table 13. They, too, are significant in the O'Connor texts, scoring far above the 6.635 G^2 level. It is difficult but not impossible to overestimate the importance of the words *Jesus* and *Bible* in O'Connor's fiction of Christian redemption and grace. The words are used in both incarnational and sacrilegious ways. *Wise Blood* is rich in examples of each usage. Hazel Motes's "grandfather had been a circuit preacher, a waspish old man who had ridden over three counties with Jesus hidden in his head like a stinger" (*WB*, 20). The embedding of Jesus metaphorically

TABLE 13: **Body parts in O'Connor and Brown texts**

Word	O'Connor Freq	O'Connor per 1000	Brown Freq	Brown per 1000	G^2	O'Connor D	O'Connor Range
face	728	2.48	2.20	0.93	187.03	.95	14
Jesus	226	0.77	13	0.05	186.44	.77	12
head	519	1.76	210	0.89	76.13	.96	14
eyes	592	2.01	286	1.21	52.28	.92	14
mouth	214	0.72	67	0.28	51.94	.93	14
foot	103	0.35	24	0.10	37.09	.89	14
Bible	44	0.15	8	0.03	20.14	.65	7
eye	124	0.42	48	0.20	20.13	.90	14
knees	69	0.23	21	0.08	17.50	.89	14
elbow	31	0.10	5	0.02	15.61	.73	8
forehead	43	0.14	11	0.04	13.88	.88	14
blood	92	0.31	37	0.15	13.67	.82	14
feet	148	0.50	77	0.32	9.89	.88	14
ear	40	0.13	13	0.05	9.12	.82	13
tail	23	0.07	5	0.02	8.91	.83	13
heart	101	0.34	49	0.20	8.78	.90	14
arm	122	0.41	65	0.27	7.37	.89	14
leg	59	0.20	26	0.11	6.92	.76	11
body	45	0.15	107	0.45	41.52	.87	13
belly	0	0.00	10	0.04	16.18	0.00	0
flesh	11	0.03	30	0.12	13.82	.68	6
hoofs	0	0.00	7	0.03	11.32	0.00	0
lips	36	0.12	55	0.23	9.27	.83	13
beard	5	0.01	16	0.06	8.73	.52	2
forefinger	0	0.00	5	0.02	8.09	0.00	0
breasts	0	0.00	5	0.02	8.09	0.00	0

in this passage as a body part (*stinger*) inside another body part (*head*) reflects an incarnational strategy, the merger of the spiritual with the physical. Jesus is just as deeply embedded in Hazel as in his grandfather. In one of Hazel's first denials of his redemption, he says that there is no Jesus: "Nothing matters but that Jesus don't exist" (*WB*, 54); then later when he is preaching his "Church Without Christ" he contradicts himself with "Nothing matters but that Jesus was a liar" (*WB*, 105), indicating his failure to rid himself of the very assumption of the existence of Jesus in spite of his denial of his existence.[2] Hoover Shoats, Hazel's competition in the "new jesus" business, reflects the centrality of the Bible to fundamentalist Protestantism when he attempts to explain what Shoats calls "The Holy Church of Christ Without Christ": "It's based on your own personal interpitation of the Bible, friends. You can sit at home and interpit your own Bible however you feel in your heart it ought to be interpited" (*WB*, 153). Whether charlatans like Shoats and the itinerant Bible salesman Manley Pointer or deeply flawed but sincere Christians like Mrs. Shortley or Rufus Johnson, O'Connor's Protestants hold the Bible dear to their hearts. On the day that Mrs. Shortley guesses that the priest is plotting to bring another Polish refugee family to Mrs. McIntyre's farm, Mrs. Shortley began "to read her Bible with a new attention. She pored over the Apocalypse and began to quote from the Prophets and before long she had come to a deeper understanding of her existence" (*GM*, 217). And Rufus Johnson of "The Lame Shall Enter First" literally eats pages of his Bible in an attempt to show the atheist Sheppard that he really believes what the Bible says. Although Rufus is certainly a force for evil in the story, he believes, or acts as if he believes, that he is made of the same stuff as Ezekiel, who ate the scroll from heaven on the command of God: "His eyes widened as if a vision of splendor were opening up before him. 'I've eaten it!' he breathed. 'I've eaten it like Ezekiel and it was honey to my mouth!'" (*ERMC*, 185).

It is true that *Jesus* is almost the most highly marked word in table 13, more so than both *Bible* and all body part words but *face*. However, *face, head, eyes, mouth*, and *foot* all occur with higher G^2 scores than *Bible*. Furthermore, both Juilland's *D* and Range scores for O'Connor's fiction are relatively low for the words *Jesus* and *Bible* when compared to the same figures for the top scoring body parts. Note from table 13 that Juilland's *D* is above .90 and that the Range is 14 for *face, head, eyes*, and *mouth* while Juilland's *D* is .77 and .65 and Range is 12 and 7, respectively, for *Jesus* and *Bible*. The word *Jesus* in O'Connor's fiction is concentrated in *Wise Blood*, with more than half of its 226 occurrences in that novel. The word *Bible* is even more concentrated, with almost half of its 44 occurrences appearing in one short story, "Good Country People," with Manley Pointer, the Bible salesman, as one of the central characters. Simply because the body parts *face, head, eyes*, and *mouth* have higher Juilland's *D* and Range is not in itself meaningful. After all, the word *the* has a very high Juilland's *D* of .97 and a Range of 14; however, *the* has a G^2 score of only .76. Thus, a combination of high G^2, Julliand's *D*, and Range signals not only words that are significantly relatively more common in a text collection but also words that have relatively equal distribution throughout that text collection.

The body parts *face, head, eyes,* and *mouth* and their detailed occurrences are the subjects of most of the discussion of body parts in this chapter. As I will explain later, there are qualitative judgment calls as well as statistical tests involved in deciding to concentrate on these four body parts in the bulk of my body-part analysis in this chapter and the next. However, I will also briefly consider the use of some of the other body parts of interest in O'Connor's fiction. As I pointed out in chapter 1, *leg* functions as local metaphor in "Good Man Is Hard to Find" and *foot* as local metaphor in "The Lame Shall Enter First." In O'Connor's fiction *blood, heart,* and *tail* are the most consistently and widely symbolic of the body-part terms listed in table 13. In *Wise Blood* blood is an animate force, speaking to Enoch and motivating him. When he and Hazel visit the city museum for Enoch to show Hazel the mummy, Enoch's blood moves him past the sleeping guard: "Enoch's blood began to beat again, urging him forward" (*WB,* 97). Although blood, particularly mysteriously communicative wise blood, is especially prevalent in O'Connor's first novel, it surfaces in many of the same ways in *The Violent Bear It Away* and in her short stories. The hunger for Christian salvation runs through the very bodies of many of O'Connor's characters. In *The Violent Bear It Away* Francis fears becoming a prophet like his great-uncle, and he fears particularly that the call will come through his blood: "what he was secretly afraid of was that [his great-uncle's hunger for Jesus] might be passed down, might be hidden in the blood and might strike some day in him and then he would be torn by hunger like the old man, the bottom split out of his stomach so that nothing would heal or fill it but the bread of life" (*VBA,* 21). And, very prominently, blood also serves as the literally incarnational in many stories, especially in descriptions of nature. In a rare moment of near insight in "A View of the Woods," Mr. Fortune almost sees the truth of the incarnational world, the world that he reduces to "progress" and commercial greed in his plans to sell his family's front lot to Tilman. He stares at the woods across the lot that he sells to Tilman as if he is "in the midst of an uncomfortable mystery that he had not apprehended before. He saw it, in his hallucination, as if someone were wounded behind the woods and the trees were bathed in blood" (*ERMC,* 71). Perhaps the most obviously sacramental of O'Connor's stories is "A Temple of the Holy Ghost." The child's revelation at the very end of the story presents an incarnational vision of the world that is startling in its dense weaving of the spiritual and the physical. On the way back from services at the convent the child looks out the window of the car: "The sun was a huge red ball like an elevated Host drenched in blood and when it sank out of sight, it left a line in the sky like a red clay road hanging over the trees" (*GM*, 101). There are characters in O'Connor that have a nonincarnational viewpoint, and their view on the significance of blood is telling. Tom T. Shiftlet in "The Life You Save May Be Your Own" is indignantly dissatisfied with the blood test that he must get to obtain the license for marrying Lucynell Crater the junior. He complains: "What do they know about my blood? If they was to take my heart and cut it out . . . they wouldn't know a thing about me" (*GM*, 64). Shiftlet believes that his real self is separate from his body. The self is in all ways unknowable through the body for him. Blood, as part of the dismembered body, is also a signal of the grotesque in O'Connor, one of the most grotesque images in her fiction being the description of the doctor's waiting room in "Revelation": "The table was cluttered with limp-looking magazines and at one end of it there was a big green glass ash tray full of cigaret butts and cotton wads with little blood spots on them" (*ERMC*, 192–93).

The heart has some of the more obvious metaphorical connections to "essence" or "soul" in O'Connor's fiction, as in the priest's admonition to Asbury in "The Enduring Chill": "you must pray to the Holy Ghost for [purity]. Mind, heart and body. Nothing is overcome without prayer" (*ERMC*, 106). There is the occasional character in O'Connor's fiction who, perhaps unconsciously, recognizes the literal incarnational connection between the soul and the body. Mrs. Greenleaf, for example, is in every way, sexually and spiritually, of the earth, as is revealed in her healings: "'Oh Jesus, stab me in the heart!' Mrs. Greenleaf shrieked. 'Jesus, stab me in the heart!' and she fell back flat in the dirt, a huge human mound, her legs and arms spread out as if she were trying to wrap them around the earth" (*ERMC*, 31). Gentry refers to Mrs. Greenleaf as "probably O'Connor's most grotesquely religious character."[3] Sabbath Lily, in her attempt to seduce Hazel while he mistakenly believes that he is attempting to seduce her, indicates her fundamentally incarnational, although unconscious, understanding, of spirituality: "'I can save you,' she said. 'I got a church in my heart where Jesus is King'" (*WB*, 121). One of the more common patterns for the body part *heart* occurs in a comic grotesque simile or metaphor in which the heart is compared to an inanimate mechanical object or an animate nonhuman. In *Wise Blood*, when Enoch recognizes Hazel in the city park, Enoch's heart was "moving so fast it was like one of those motorcycles at fairs that the fellow drives around the walls of a pit" (*WB*, 83). When Hazel goes to visit Mrs. Watts for the second time, he is nervous because his "performance" the first night was less than impressive: "His throat got dryer and his heart began to grip him like a little ape clutching the bars of its cage" (*WB*, 60). The grotesque heart is a common trope throughout O'Connor's fiction. In fact it occurs even in the last story that she worked on before her death, "Parker's Back." When Parker is flipping through the book of tattoos in his search for what will be the Byzantine Christ, his "heart began to beat faster and faster until it appeared to be roaring inside him like a great generator" (*ERMC*, 234).

There is at least one body-part term—*tail*—the more common occurrence of which in O'Connor than in the Brown texts is explainable by O'Connor's interest in peacocks and other barnyard animals, as in the following description from "The Displaced Person": the peacock "had jumped into the tree and his tail hung in front of her [Mrs. Shortley], full of fierce planets with eyes that were each ringed in green and set against a sun that was gold in one second's light and salmon-colored in the next. She might have been looking at a map of the universe but she didn't notice it any more than she did the spots of sky that cracked the dull green of the tree. She was having an inner vision instead" (*GM,* 204–5). Here, Mrs. Shortley characteristically ignores the embodiment of the mystery of the universe in the physical by turning inward to contemplate her own prejudices and fears, especially with regard to the Guizacs and all they represent. More than one third of the twenty-three total occurrences of *tail* occur in "The Displaced Person," accounting for its relatively low Juilland's *D* of .83. The peacock tail commonly represents for O'Connor the spirit in the physical world. In "Good Country People" Hulga Hopewell is "as sensitive about [her] artificial leg as a peacock about his tail." And of course, as noted in chapter 1, her leg is a well-worked symbol for her soul, as the story makes clear: "She took care of it as someone else would his soul, in private and almost with her own eyes turned away" (*GM,* 192). The peacock's tail is the central emblem of "The Displaced Person." It provides a focus for the priest's childlike wonder when the McIntyre peacock spreads his tail: "'Christ will come like that!' [the priest] said in a loud gay voice and wiped his hand over his mouth and stood there, gaping" (*GM,* 239). It also occasions the display of Mrs. McIntyre's crass materialism: "'What a beautiful birdrrrd!' the priest murmured. 'Another mouth to feed,' Mrs. McIntyre said, glancing in the peafowl's direction" (*GM,* 202).

The remaining body-part terms that occur with at least a 6.635 G^2 figure (*knees, feet, forehead, elbow, leg, arm, ear*) are all used in ways that increase the specificity of the body in O'Connor's descriptive language. The knees occur in variable collocational patterns with hands: for example, "hands and knees," "hands on his knees," "hands hung between his knees." When these collocations occur in O'Connor, there is frequently a contextual focused attention on the body, as when Hazel and Sabbath Lily are off for their afternoon in the woods, with Hazel attempting to get to the theological bottom of Sabbath's father's self-blinding and Sabbath's "bastardhood" and Sabbath herself attempting a seduction of Hazel: "He put his hat over his face and folded his arms across his chest. She lifted herself up on her hands and knees and crawled over to him and gazed at the top of his hat. Then she lifted it off like a lid and peered into his eyes" (*WB,* 123). The collocation "hands and knees" is naturally specifically used most frequently for occasions in which a character crawls or otherwise humbles himself or herself on the ground. Sabbath is on her hands and knees in an unsuccessful seduction in the passage quoted above. Equally scandalous to many of O'Connor's self-satisfied and deeply proper and insincere religious characters is a Protestant sacramental connection to the body. In "Greenleaf" Mrs. May, whose own body will be merged with the bull god in her goring at the end of the story, is horrified by Mrs. Greenleaf's prayer-healing that she performs in the woods over a buried collection of newspaper clippings of "morbid stories." One day Mrs. May happens across one of these prayer-healings: Mrs. Greenleaf "swayed back and forth on her hands and knees and groaned, 'Jesus, Jesus.'" Then the narrator makes explicit the implicit connections among Jesus, the body, and sex: "Mrs. May winced. She thought the word, Jesus, should be kept inside the church building like other words inside the bedroom" (*ERMC*, 31).[4]

One of the narratological reasons that parts of the face are prominent statistically in O'Connor's fiction is that the characters themselves in addition to the narrator spend a good bit of time paying attention to the parts of the face. In "The Lame Shall Enter First" Johnson's forehead is described by the narrator in one of the many instances in which he fools Sheppard: "A faint light shone on his forehead but the rest of his face was invisible" (*ERMC*, 173). In many other cases, as when the women notice Hazel's jaw in the dining car of the train, the narrator explicitly notes that it is the characters themselves who notice the parts of the face. In "A Circle in the Fire," Mrs. Cope tries hard to keep her temper with the three juveniles who have invaded her peace and her farm, but when they let the bull out and drain the oil from three tractors her emotion shows: "Two blue veins had come out on either side of Mrs. Cope's forehead and Mrs. Pritchard observed them with satisfaction" (*GM*, 147).

The forehead and the ear are prominent in descriptions of the appearance of characters, probably because they are, like the eyes and mouth, part of the face. Some constituents of O'Connor's faces are grotesquely disproportionate. Thus Tom T. Shiftlet's "face descended in forehead for more than half its length and ended suddenly with his features just balanced over a jutting steel-trap jaw" (*GM*, 54). A facial body-part term that does not occur in table 13 but comes very close to being statistically significant (with a G^2 of 6.48 and a frequency of 26) is *jaw*. The term is particularly commonly used in the exploration of the grotesque. Mr. Head's focalized self-congratulatory assessment of his character at the beginning of "The Artificial Nigger" contrasts sharply with the narrator's grotesque and bathetic description of his appearance: "Sixty years had not dulled his responses; his physical reactions, like his moral ones, were guided by his will and strong character, and these could be seen plainly in his features. He had a long tube-like face with a long rounded open jaw and a long depressed nose" (*GM*, 103). The open jaw foreshadows the gap-mouthed wonder and stupor that both Nelson and Mr. Head experience in their hellish journey through the city. In *Wise Blood* Hazel's jaw serves as the focal point of attention for both the women with whom he sits in the train's dining car and Enoch as Enoch futilely pursues Hazel's friendship. The focalization in the first scene shifts from the women to Hazel, but the women observe him first: "He began eating slowly at first, then faster as the women concentrated on watching the muscles that stood out on his jaw when he chewed. He was eating something spotted with eggs and livers" (*WB,* 17). What they notice about his jaw is consistent with another common use of the jaw in O'Connor's fiction, to signify psychological tension and repression. When Enoch follows Hazel down the streets of Taulkinham, he observes to Hazel, "Your jaw just crawls" (*WB,* 48). In *The Violent Bear It Away* Rayber realizes upon hearing a bellow from the lake that Francis has drowned his son Bishop: "He clenched his teeth. The muscles in his face contracted and revealed lines of pain beneath harder than bone. He set his jaw. No cry must escape him" (*VBA,* 202). There is a good bit of truth denial in characters who set their jaws in this way in O'Connor. Rayber is denying not only the pain that he feels in his own betrayal of Bishop but also the love that he feels for his son, a love that he has sought to deny through his entire life. In "A View of the Woods" Mary Fortune denies the physical abuse that she suffers at the hands of her father: "She had jumped up and started backing away from him with her jaw stuck out. 'Nobody beat me,' she said" (*ERMC,* 61).

The Head and Its Parts: Cognition, Vision, Expression

In this chapter we narrow our focus to concentrate on four extremely frequent and significant body parts in O'Connor's fiction: the face, the head, the eyes, and the mouth. These are four of the most commonly occurring body parts in O'Connor's fiction. Furthermore they are the body parts that exhibit the greatest proportional difference between O'Connor's texts and the Brown texts as reflected in G^2 figures. Table 13 illustrates that the G^2 score for each of these four body parts is far above the minimum cutoff point of 6.635 for an "interesting" lexeme. This study concentrates on these four body parts and not *foot* or any other body part below *Bible* on the log-likelihood scale that table 13 represents. There are several reasons for my concentration on *face, head, eyes,* and *mouth:* 1) unlike *foot,* they are all in the same semantic field of "head body parts"; 2) once *foot* is excluded from concentrated examination, it is consistent to exclude body parts with even lower G^2 scores; and 3) detailed examination of even the four body parts on which I have chosen to concentrate, including their use in middle voice and middle-voice related constructions, will take a surprising amount of space.

Regardless of voice, O'Connor's heavy use of the words *face, head, eyes,* and *mouth,* demonstrable in table 13, makes them simply a potentially important locus for incarnational and grotesque meaning. Statistically, if not thematically, *face* is the most important body-part term in O'Connor's fiction. Table 13 reveals that *face* has more than three times the G^2 figure as *eyes,* the most commonly recognized body parts in the critical literature on O'Connor; *face* also has a higher Juilland's *D* figure. The face is a locus of psychological revelation in O'Connor's fiction. In *The Violent Bear It Away* Rayber wants to see Francis as a younger version of himself, capable of being reasoned out of his religious impulses and convinced of a godless intellectual self-sufficiency. In one argument between Rayber and Francis, the narrator writes of Rayber's vision of Francis that he saw "himself so clearly in the face before him that he might have been beseeching his own image" (*VBA*, 105). It is Rayber's face that engages Francis's imagination as well when Mason tries to describe Rayber to him: "The boy kept trying to find eyes that fit mouth, nose that fit chin, but every time he thought he had a face put together, it fell apart and he had to begin on a new one" (*VBA*, 55). But when Francis goes to the city and meets his uncle in person, he is disappointed, partially because he was hoping for too much and partially because his uncle is spiritually and emotionally impoverished: "Then he gave the schoolteacher a long appraising look, tracing the line of his jaw, the two creases on either side of his mouth, the forehead extending into skull until it reached the pie-shaped hairline. He gazed briefly at the pained eyes behind his uncle's glasses, appearing to abandon a search for something that could not possibly be there" (*VBA*, 105).

As I pointed out in chapter 1, Gary M. Ciuba notes that the failure to find significance in the human face is a common and revelatory shortcoming of O'Connor's reluctant prophets when they are in denial of their spiritual selves.[5] Thus, proselytizing for his Church Without Christ, Hazel has a message that stresses the meaninglessness of both the so-called human conscience and the reflection of matter: "'Your conscience is a trick,' he said, 'it don't exist though you may think it does, and if you think it does, you had best get it out in the open and hunt it down and kill it, because it's no more than your face in the mirror is or your shadow behind you'" (*WB*, 166). It is normally O'Connor's narrator who draws the reader's attention to the divine in the human face. Towards the end of *Wise Blood* the policeman who stops Hazel just because he doesn't like his face pushes his car over an embankment; Hazel then has a revelation, which is reflected in his face: "His face seemed to reflect the entire distance across the clearing and on beyond, the entire distance that extended from his eyes to the blank gray sky that went on, depth after depth, into space" (*WB*, 209). That the human face can reflect the divine is strongly hinted at in *The Violent Bear It Away* in a description of the retarded boy Bishop's face: "Then the light, falling more gently, rested like a hand on the child's white head. His face might have been a mirror where the sun had stopped to watch its reflection" (*VBA*, 164). The face occasionally reflects revelation in the short stories as well. In "A Good Man Is Hard to Find" the grandmother makes her move to comfort The Misfit immediately after she sees "the man's face twisted close to her own as if he were going to cry." The Misfit shoots her for her trouble, and she dies "in a puddle of blood with her legs crossed under her like a child's and her face smiling up at the cloudless sky" (*GM*, 29).

Given that there is almost three times the density of *face* tokens in O'Connor's fiction as there is in the Brown texts, one might expect a variety of literary roles for *face* besides the reflection of grace, the divine, the grotesque, and the incarnational. As we will see later in this chapter, *face* has no collocations at the 6.635 G^2 level or above as subject with ergative middle verbs. However, I will engage here in a brief qualitative analysis of some grammatical and accompanying literary patterns of *face* as subject to ergative middle verbs. Tokens of the word *face* are considered in this chapter mostly as subjects to both clauses (dependent and independent) and phrases. Most of the tokens of *face* in O'Connor's fiction occur in nonmiddle and nonreflexive active constructions such as those in (1)–(3), below, all from "The Lame Shall Enter First":

1. "Sheppard's face was haggard." (*ERMC*, 171)
2. "Sheppard scrutinized his face." (*ERMC*, 151)
3. "The light from the window fell on his face." (*ERMC*, 149)

In (1) there is no conceptual separation or merger of the initiator and endpoint because there is neither an agent/actor nor a medium/goal; (1) is a stative construction with an experiencer subject. In the transitive (2) Sheppard examines another character's face; thus, there is maximum conceptual and formal separation of the initiator and endpoint. And in (3) the noun phrase referring to a character's face serves as a locative, completely separate from the initiator.

The function of the lexeme *face* in O'Connor's prototypical ergative middle constructions is to reveal emotion, usually unconsciously on the part of the agent:

4. "Her face squared up instantly." (*ERMC*, 260)
5. "Norton's face began to twist." (*ERMC*, 165)
6. "He saw his mother's face change as the woman settled herself next to him and he realized with satisfaction that this was more objectionable to her than it was to him." (*ERMC*, 16)
7. "His eyes glinted through his tears and his face stretched in an evil crooked grin." (*WB*, 59)

Each of the tokens of *face* in (4)–(7) minimally serves as the subject of an ergative middle body-action verb. In (4), from "Judgement Day," Tanner's daughter reacts to her father's announcement that he has discovered a black man and woman living next door to them. She fears, rightly, that Tanner's racism and ignorance of race relations in the North will land him in trouble. In (5), from "The Lame Shall Enter First," Norton's face begins to register his despair after his father tells him that his dead mother isn't in heaven, that she isn't in hell, that she "isn't anywhere," that she "just isn't." Examples (4) and (5) are relatively unremarkable.

There are many interpretively more interesting passages in which *face* as a middle subject reveals emotion, or even sometimes helps reveal misperception of emotion on the part of another character, as in (6), from "Everything that Rises Must Converge." There, Julian mistakes the change in his mother's face as racist consternation that a black woman sat down next to him on the bus on which they are riding. In fact, she has just recognized that she and the woman happen to be wearing the same hat. In (7) O'Connor writes of Enoch Emery's reaction in a one-sided argument with Hazel Motes over who has the wiser blood. Enoch's face might be one of those body parts that Yaeger refers to as having a will of its own. If part of O'Connor's sacramentalism, as Brinkmeyer suggests, plays itself out as struggles internal to a character's own body, we might expect the middle and middle-related constructions to play an important grammatical role in signaling those struggles.[6] One of the major thematic points made by body-action middles, then, is that it is the body itself that frequently reveals the emotion of the spirit.

As indicated earlier, *face* as a grammatical subject has no statistically significant collocations with middle verbs. However, it does have three very specific and interesting uses as subject, usually to nonmiddle verbs. In one striking use the face synecdochically announces the arrival of the owner of the face, as in (8) and (9):

8. "After a moment one leg emerged, then her small white crooked face appeared and stared up at him." (*ERMC,* 126)
9. "He felt five claws in the flesh of his upper arm where she was hanging from while her feet mechanically battered his knees and her free fist pounded him again and again in the chest. Then with horror he saw her face rise up in front of his, teeth exposed, and he roared like a bull as she bit the side of his jaw. He seemed to see his own face coming to bite him from several sides at once but he could not attend to it for he was being kicked indiscriminately, in the stomach and then in the crotch. . . . She began a fresh assault on his jaw. 'Stop stop!' he wheezed. 'I'm your grandfather!' She paused, her face exactly on top of his. Pale identical eye looked into pale identical eye." (*ERMC,* 79)

In (8) and (9) the focus on body parts supports the interpretation that, in both cases, the male characters experience the horror of the physicality of the body. In (8), from "The Comforts of Home," first Star Drake's leg and then her face appear as she slides out of Thomas's car. In (9), from "A View of the Woods," Mary Fortune Pitts attacks her grandfather, Mr. Fortune, after he dares to attempt, unsuccessfully, to whip her. This passage, like that in (8), demonstrates the stylistic reliance in O'Connor's fiction on a variety of body parts, in the case of (9), claws, flesh, arm, feet, knees, fist, jaw, stomach, crotch, eyes, and face.

In another use of *face* as a subject, it occurs as the subject of a body-action verb, whether ergative middle, as in (10), or not, as in (11)–(13):

10. "A long way off he saw the blue figure spring and pick up a rock, and he saw the wild face turn, and the rock hurtle toward him; he shut his eyes tight and the rock hit him on the forehead." (*WB*, 99)
11. "When they reached the house he went in and straight to his bed without turning to look at the boy's white face which, drained but expectant, lingered a moment at the threshold of his door as if waiting for an invitation to enter." (*VBA*, 137)
12. "'What's that, Brother?' Scofield asked, his broad face grinning into the thin constricted one across from him." (*ERMC*, 44)
13. "How'd you like a couple of black faces looking at you from the back of your classroom?" (*CS*, 19)

In each of these examples, a noun phrase containing a modifier and the lexeme *face* occurs as the specific subject of a body-action verb. Thus in (10) Enoch Emery sees Hazel's face turn. In this and the remaining examples here, I specifically classify the constructions as heavy body-part actions because the body-part subject *face* can be replaced with a simple pronoun or name referring to the owner of the body part. For instance, example (10) could read "he saw him (or 'Hazel') turn." These examples are characteristic of the pattern in O'Connor's fiction for the heavy body-part actions and heavy body-part reflexives to have modifiers for the lexeme *face.* I am using the term *heavy* here by analogy with Kemmer's "heavy-marked reflexive," a phonologically heavy reflexive morpheme with some middle verbs indicates specific reflexivity rather than simple middle identity of initiator and endpoint which is indicated by a phonologically "light" form, an analogous point to which I return in chapter 5.[7] The body-part term *face* is then made even more specific by the modification. In (11) Tarwater's "white face," which is also "drained but expectant," reveals that he is uncharacteristically vulnerable and probably open to suggestion from his uncle Rayber after having just attended a fundamentalist revival meeting. The next chapter begins with the statement that Rayber "had the sense of opportunity missed" because "Tarwater's face had hardened again" (*VBA,* 139). In (12), from "Greenleaf," Scofield's face need not be mentioned at all, but instead the name *Scofield* in the preceding clause could serve as the underlying subject of the participial "grinning into the thin constricted face across from him." However, the modification as it is helps to differentiate the personalities of the two May brothers, Scofield being the jolly, foolish businessman and Wesley the sour, dissatisfied professor with the "thin constricted" face. And in (13) a racist customer in the barbershop in "The Barber" attempts to scare Rayber, yet another dour professor, with the image of "black faces" looking at him from "the back" of his classroom.

Face in O'Connor sometimes also has a much more purely human rather than incarnational function in reflecting "social" meaning. In Penelope Brown and

Stephen Levinson's social sense, *face* represents interpersonal power,[8] as is illustrated in the following passage from "Greenleaf":

> "Do you see that if I hadn't kept my foot on his neck all these years, you boys might be milking cows every morning at four o'clock?" Wesley pulled the paper back toward his plate and staring at her full in the face, he murmured, "I wouldn't milk a cow to save your soul from hell."
>
> "I know you wouldn't," she said in a brittle voice." (*ERMC*, 36)

In this passage Wesley, one of the many spoiled intellectual offspring in O'Connor's fiction, demonstrates his dominance of his mother by "staring at her full in the face" as he also demonstrates a complete absence of both love and respect for her. In the same story Mr. Greenleaf, the hired help that Mrs. May speaks of in the passage above as needing to be controlled, is described in the following way: "He walked with a high-shouldered creep and he never appeared to come directly forward. He walked on the perimeter of some invisible circle and if you wanted to look him in the face, you had to move and get in front of him" (*ERMC*, 26). To assert social dominance in O'Connor, at least in part, one stares at the face of the person whom one wants to dominate.

There are numerous literary effects of O'Connor's use of the word *head* to refer to the body part. Probably most obviously in many places, the head functions symbolically as the seat of the hyperextended intellect, one of the well-recognized themes running throughout O'Connor's fiction.[9] Horton, for example, refers to the girl in "A Temple of the Holy Ghost" as a "cephalocentric subject" for many reasons, one being that she is intellectually proud, believing herself to be "about a million times smarter" than practically everyone around her (*GM*, 96).[10] In *The Violent Bear It Away* one of the many things that Francis Tarwater fears about his uncle Rayber, the school teacher, is his acquisitive rationality: "If the schoolteacher had got hold of him, right now he would have been in school, one among many, indistinguishable from the herd, and in the schoolteacher's head, he would be laid out in parts and numbers" (*VBA*, 18). The elder Tarwater, Francis's great-uncle, also has reason to distrust Rayber's "head," since while Tarwater was staying with him Rayber secretly observed his uncle and wrote a study of his observations: "The old man had not known when he went there to live that every living thing that passed through the nephew's eyes into his head was turned by his brain into a book or a paper or a chart" (*VBA*, 19). Julian, another cephalocentric character, in "Everything That Rises Must Converge," dramatizes his hyperintellectualism in an argument with his mother about "culture": "He thrust his face toward her and hissed, 'True culture is in the mind, the *mind*,' he said, and tapped his head, 'the mind.' 'It's in the heart,' she said, 'and in how you do things and how you do things is because of who you *are*'" (*ERMC*, 9). Both Rayber and Julian are freaks of the intellect in O'Connor, and part, perhaps a small part but still a part, of that characterization is due to references to their heads, especially in the case of Rayber. Their intellectual freakishness is one manifestation of their spiritual impoverishment, as O'Connor makes generally clear in an essay about the grotesque, the South, and the theological: "Whenever I'm asked why Southern writers particularly have a penchant for writing about freaks, I say it is because we are still able to recognize one. To be able to recognize a freak, you have to have some conception of the whole man, and in the South the general conception of man is still, in the main, theological" (*MM,* 44).

It is certainly not the case that every time O'Connor wishes to lampoon the hyperinflated intellect that the "head" as body part wells up into prominence. For example, there are eight tokens of *head* in "Good Country People," with O'Connor's most widely known hyperintellectual—Hulga Hopewell, the Ph.D. in philosophy, who as the narrator puts it "all day . . . sat on her neck in a deep chair, reading" (*GM,* 176). Yet none of those eight tokens is obviously metaphorical for the intellect, although one could perhaps force the reading since the story is saturated with O'Connor's ironic treatment of human rationality. Neither is it the case that *head* simplistically equates to "intellect." Of its many literary uses, one important to my discussion of the grotesque is one that Yaeger notices in the changeability of the bodies of O'Connor's characters: "This constant mutability of forms moves the human body toward dismemberment."[11] The mutability of the head as a body part is one of the most clearly recognizable patterns throughout O'Connor's fiction. In "A Stroke of Good Fortune" Ruby Hill's body, specifically her head, takes on the characteristics of the (vegetable) life that she so consistently tries to deny: "She was too tired to take her arms from around it [her grocery sack] or to straighten up and she hung there collapsed from the hips, her head balanced like a big florid vegetable at the top of the sack" (*GM,* 69). Mr. Head of "The Artificial Nigger" takes on the characteristics and behavior of a turtle in his fear of the women who are accusing his grandson Nelson of causing one of them injury: "The old man's head had lowered itself into his collar like a turtle's; his eyes were glazed with fear and caution" (*GM,* 123). The reptilian Tilman of "A View of the Woods" appears so in part because of his snakelike head: "He sat habitually with his arms folded on the counter and his insignificant head weaving snake-fashion above them" (*ERMC,* 76). In "Greenleaf" the nonhuman morphs to the human when the bull gores Mrs. May: "She stared at the violent black streak bounding toward her as if she had no sense of distance, . . . and the bull had buried his head in her lap, like a wild tormented lover, before her expression changed" (*ERMC,* 52). And Mrs. Shortley of "The Displaced Person," in reference to the ultimate morphing dismemberment of death in the Holocaust, "recall[s] a newsreel she had seen once of a small room piled high with bodies of dead naked people all in a heap, their arms and legs tangled together, a head thrust in here, a head there, a foot, a knee, a part that should have been covered up sticking out, a hand raised clutching nothing" (*GM,* 200). Thus in addition to symbolizing the hyperextended intellect, there are at least two more ways to make sense of the abundance of the word *head* in O'Connor's fiction: 1) O'Connor was an incarnational writer, so an abundance of body imagery is to be expected; and 2) she was a writer of the grotesque, so one might expect a number of references to body parts in her fiction, particularly of the "dismembered," or isolated, sort.

The mouth in O'Connor's fiction is a primary indicator of both the physical and the spiritual, the incarnational and the grotesque, from the early to the late fiction. In *Wise Blood* "Mrs. Watts's mouth split in a wide full grin that showed her teeth. They were small and pointed and speckled with green and there was a wide space between each one" (*WB*, 33–34). The woman whom Hazel and Enoch see swimming at the city park is also characterized as grotesque partly through descriptions involving her mouth: "First her face appeared, long and cadaverous, with a bandage-like bathing cap coming down almost to her eyes, and sharp teeth protruding from her mouth" (*WB*, 84). Later we will explore in some depth the collocational patterns that are common in the creation of the incarnational and the grotesque. One of those interesting patterns is for the mouth to serve in both revelation and concealment. It is particularly susceptible to both, as is hinted at in the following description of Asa Hawks in *Wise Blood:* "The mouth had a look that might have been either holy or calculating, but there was a wildness in the eyes that suggested terror" (*WB*, 112). The late story "The Lame Shall Enter First" figures the mouth as a central body part in its exploration of the body versus the spirit and skepticism versus belief. The first and last mentions of the body part mouth demonstrate the spiritual progress of the shallow intellectual Sheppard. At the beginning of the story, when Sheppard promises to find the homeless juvenile delinquent Johnson and bring him home to live with them, his son expresses his displeasure and "Sheppard's mouth stretched in disgust" (*ERMC*, 145). The use of a body part as the subject of an ergative middle verb, as explained in chapter 2, indicates a lack of full control, primarily indicating here that Sheppard is on automatic, as he is throughout most of the story. He spends his time with his son berating him for what he sees as his son's unreasonable grief over the death of his mother. After the revelation at the end of the story that Rufus Johnson has indeed betrayed him and lied to him, Sheppard's messianic thoughts return to his own son. Defending himself by recalling all that he has done for Rufus, he says, "'I did more for him than I did for my own child.' He heard his voice as if it were the voice of his accuser. He repeated the sentence silently. Slowly his face drained of color. It became almost grey beneath the white halo of his hair. The sentence echoed in his mind, each syllable like a dull blow. His mouth twisted and he closed his eyes against the revelation" (*ERMC*, 189–90). There is, of course, no one-to-one correspondence between meaning and form, but the presence of *mouth* as subject to another ergative middle verb—*twisted*—

just as Sheppard is overwhelmed by his guilt supports the argument that the body part mouth is expressive of the unity of the spirit and the body.

As we have seen, there are other body parts that figure prominently in O'Connor's fiction (for example, the face, the head, the mouth); however, the eyes are certainly the most thematically important. Eyes are prominent—spiritually, socially, and physically—throughout O'Connor's two novels and irregularly but frequently through the twenty-five short stories in three collections. In *Wise Blood* it is Hazel Motes's spiritually tortured eyes that most frequently attract the attention of the other characters. The narrator comments towards the beginning of the novel that Hazel's "eyes were what held [Mrs. Hitchcock's] attention longest" (*WB*, 10). Later in the novel Sabbath Hawks, in love with Hazel by this point, says, "I like his eyes. . . . They don't look like they see what he's looking at but they keep on looking" (*WB*, 109). At the end of the novel, after Hazel has blinded himself and while he lies dead in her bed, Mrs. Flood, his landlady, "sat staring with her eyes shut, into his eyes, and felt as if she had finally got to the beginning of something she couldn't begin, and she saw him moving farther and farther away, farther and farther into the darkness until he was the pin point of light" (*WB*, 232). In *The Violent Bear It Away* the eyes of the elder Tarwater command his great-nephew in life and in death. As he sits across from his great-nephew after having just died at the breakfast table, Mason Tarwater is described as "a bull-like old man with . . . silver protruding eyes that looked like two fish straining to get out of a net of red threads." Even in death those "eyes, dead silver, were focused on the boy across from him" (*VBA*, 10–11). Compared to the elder Tarwater's prophetic eyes, those of Francis Tarwater, the reluctant prophet, are spiritually impoverished: "He tried . . . to keep his vision located on an even level, to see no more than what was in front of his face and to let his eyes stop at the surface of that." For O'Connor moral depth and the physical act of vision are literally intertwined. As noted in chapter 1, the narrator comments that Francis "did all he could to avoid [the] threatened intimacy of creation" (*VBA*, 21–22). In a 1956 letter to Shirley Abbott, O'Connor wrote, "I believe that the writer's moral sense must coincide with his dramatic sense and this means that moral judgment has to be implicit in the act of vision" (*HB*, 147). It is in his eyes that Francis seems both to accept and to realize at the end of the novel his destiny to become a real prophet: "His singed eyes, black in their deep sockets, seemed already to envision the fate that awaited him but he moved steadily on, his face set toward the dark city, where the children of God lay sleeping" (*VBA*, 243). In the 1946 "Geranium," O'Connor's first published short story, Old Dudley—the displaced racist Southerner living in New York City with his daughter and son-in-law—has a physical reaction to a black man's treating him in what he considers to be a too familiar fashion, a reaction that is concentrated in his eyes: "His eyes felt strange in their sockets. They were swelling in them and in a minute there wouldn't be any room left for them there" (*CS,* 13). And in one of O'Connor's most remarkable stories demonstrating the incarnation of spirituality—"A Temple of the Holy Ghost"—there are numerous delicate but important reminders of human embodiment, including details of the anatomy and behavior of the eyes: while primping in preparation for the visit of the two boys Wendell and Cory, the adolescent Susan "push[es] her face up close to the mirror to watch the pupils in her eyes dilate" (*GM,* 90).

For good reasons—for example, the sheer predominance of eye imagery—scholars have made much of the eye, whether literal or figural, in O'Connor's fiction.[12] O'Connor herself says in *Mystery and Manners,* her posthumously published collection of occasional essays, "For the writer of fiction, everything has its testing point in the eye, an organ which eventually involves the whole personality and as much of the world as can be got into it" (*MM,* 144). One dominant critical tradition has been the demonstration that the eye and vision in general are central to O'Connor's exploration of the mismatch between perception and reality. Patricia D. Maida, for example, argues that a "focus on the eyes . . . increases the reader's awareness of the conflict between individual perception and truth." In the same spirit Sloan explores eye imagery, perception, and perspective as unifying metaphors and themes in the late story "Revelation." In *Narrating Knowledge in Flannery O'Connor's Fiction,* I devote the bulk of two chapters to the exploration of how the verb *see* and clausal and phrasal complements to the verb *see* reflect O'Connor's concern with both physical and spiritual sight. Malin argues generally that much of the distortion seen through the eyes of O'Connor's characters is caused by narcissism. Gentry and Mellard bend the psychological note towards the psychoanalytic in analyses of *Wise Blood,* Gentry arguing that the focus on a connection between sight and sin leads to a connection between the penis and the eye and Mellard that the eye functions to frame the Lacanian gaze.[13]

The Ergative Middle Verb

Thus far in this chapter we have concentrated on body parts and their statistical distribution as well as their literary significance. Another approach to the body is through ergative middle verbs themselves without statistical concern for the participants of such verbs. Later we will put the two halves together and examine collocations of our four body parts of interest and ergative middle verbs. Ergative middle verbs that are significant in the O'Connor texts are those included in table 14, below.

Ergative middle verbs that occur more frequently in Brown than in O'Connor, to the 6.635 G^2 level, are *clicked, nodded, popping, arched,* and *dripped.* Rather than discriminate in table 14 among those verbs that are more or less evenly

TABLE 14: **Some ergative middle verbs in O'Connor and Brown texts**

Word	O'Connor Freq	O'Connor per 1000	Brown Freq	Brown per 1000	G^2	O'Connor D	O'Connor Range
turned	464	1.58	206	0.87	53.36	.93	14
stopped	225	0.76	85	0.36	38.53	.91	14
thrust	63	0.21	10	0.04	32.10	.89	14
leaned	107	0.36	31	0.13	29.23	.87	14
pushed	95	0.32	27	0.11	26.67	.87	14
stuck	61	0.20	16	0.06	19.08	.84	13
shut	93	0.31	34	0.14	17.05	.84	14
opened	154	0.52	71	0.30	15.81	.88	14
eased	22	0.07	2	0.00	15.39	.80	11
move	114	0.38	49	0.20	14.32	.89	14
moving	92	0.31	40	0.17	11.20	.87	14
bent	50	0.17	17	0.07	10.53	.84	13
folded	40	0.13	12	0.05	10.37	.79	11
moved	166	0.56	89	0.37	9.76	.93	14
rested	21	0.07	4	0.01	9.23	.84	12
leaning	38	0.13	12	0.05	9.09	.80	12
jerked	34	0.11	10	0.04	9.08	.82	11
clenched	19	0.06	4	0.01	7.60	.72	8

distributed in O'Connor's fiction, in this section I will illustrate some of the typical ways in which some of these verbs (all of which occur above the 6.635 G^2 level) pattern in O'Connor's fiction. Some of those ways are illustrated by means of the verb *turned* in (14)–(18), below:

14. "Night after night she turned and tossed and very definite lines began to appear in her face, so she had him dug up and shipped the body to Corinth." (*ERMC*, 269)
15. "He tightened his grip on Tarwater's arm and his eyes turned, glowering, toward the front door, which was still open." (*VBA*, 89)
16. "She turned herself in the direction of the barn, musing on this, her expression lofty and satisfied." (*GM*, 205)
17. "Bailey turned his head sharply and said something to his mother that shocked even the children." (*GM*, 22)
18. "He squatted down and put his mouth to the nozzle and turned a cold stream of water into his throat." (*GM*, 125)

In (14) the ergative middle verb *turned* occurs with an undifferentiated whole agentive subject. That is, the initiator and endpoint are the same. Tanner's daughter in "Judgement Day" is described as tortured by her betrayal of her father in burying him in New York rather than sending his body back south, where he wanted to be buried. The initiator and endpoint are undifferentiated in (14) in a way that does not hold for the remaining sentences. Example (15) isolates the verb's ergative one-participant body part. Here Rayber's eyes turn in distrust looking for his uncle lurking in the yard because he suspects the appearance of Francis at his doorstep to be part of a plot of his uncle's to baptize his son, Bishop. Example (16) partially bifurcates the initiator and endpoint with the reflexive *herself.* Here Mrs. Shortley of "The Displaced Person" is intensely and reflexively self-absorbed as she contemplates her exalted and privileged place in creation. She has just told Astor, the old black man who works on the McIntyre farm, that his place is in danger because of all the displaced people in the world, like the Guizacs: "She was seeing the ten million billion of them pushing their way into new places over here and herself, a giant angel with wings as wide as a house, telling the Negroes that they would have to find another place" (*GM,* 205). Example (17), with a specific body part as the object of the ergative middle verb *turned,* is a construction that will be dealt with extensively in chapter 5 along with the reflexive. In this passage the grandmother has just announced her recognition of The Misfit, whose gang will murder the grandmother's entire family, including her son Bailey. The initiator and endpoint are partially bifurcated here into a subject that acts on a specific body part. Example (18) demonstrates that even when the body is not the subject or direct object of one of the ergative middle verbs there is sometimes an element of body effect in the proposition. Here, in "The Artificial Nigger," Mr. Head who has just betrayed Nelson, his grandson, quenches what must be a considerable thirst since the text tells us that he had not had a drink of water since the morning although he and Nelson have walked the city all day long. Mr. Head turns the cold stream of water into his throat, the narrator thus indicating the effect on his body.

As demonstrated in chapter 3, collocational analysis allows us to discover the grammatical patterns into which individual words tend to enter. That is, collocational analysis allows us to rise to at least one level above the individual word to consider phrasal patterns. In analysis of collocations I will consider a collocation significant if it reaches the 6.635 G^2 level and occurs with a frequency of five or more, the arbitrary frequency requirement of five assuring that there are enough examples in the text to support a pattern of literary interpretation. The fixed phrase collocations (and their frequencies) of *turned* with body parts in O'Connor's texts are "turned head" (49), "head turned" (9), "turned face" (11), and "turned eyes" (7). I will have a good bit to say about these collocations later in this chapter as well as in chapter 5. In O'Connor's fiction no significant body-part subjects or objects occur with the verb *leaned.* By far the most common use of *leaned* in O'Connor's fiction is without an object. In fact, the most common statistically significant collocation with *leaned* in O'Connor is "leaned forward" (39), in which the grammatical subject is an undifferentiated subject/self, as in the following:

19. "'That hat looks like a preacher's hat.' 'It ain't,' Haze said, and leaned forward and gripped the back of the front seat. 'It's just a hat.'" (*WB*, 31)
20. "'He's president of the local Historical Society this year.' The girl leaned forward and gave Thomas an even more pointed attention. 'Fabulous!' she said in a throaty voice." (*ERMC*, 123)

In most examples of "leaned forward" the character subject of the collocation is acting in an aggressive fashion of some sort. In (19) Hazel Motes is arguing with his taxi driver over whether Hazel himself is a preacher and whether his black hat makes him look very much like a preacher, as the taxi driver claims when he says, "That hat looks like a preacher's hat." And in (20) Star Drake makes one of several sexual advances towards Thomas, the reluctant object of her affections. When the adverbial *forward* does not occur with *leaned*, the verb usually does not indicate aggression of any sort, as is the case in the following, in which the copper flue salesman Meeks is described as he gives Francis a ride into the city after his great-uncle Mason dies: "Meeks leaned casually against the door of the car, driving with half his attention and giving the other half to Tarwater" (*VBA*, 78).

The aggression of leaning forward is repeated in the collocations for another significantly common ergative middle verb in O'Connor's fiction: *thrust*. The significant collocations (with *forward* or body parts) and their frequencies are "thrust forward" (16), "neck thrust" (8), "head thrust" (11), "thrust head" (9), and "thrust face" (5). These collocations with *thrust* in O'Connor's texts give us some of the most memorable descriptive sentences in all of her fiction:

21. "His neck was thrust forward as if he were trying to smell something that was always being drawn away." (*WB*, 37)
22. "His uncle thrust his head forward and his eyes began to bulge." (*VBA*, 27)
23. "Mrs. Shortley recalled a newsreel she had seen once of a small room piled high with bodies of dead naked people all in a heap, their arms and legs tangled together, a head thrust in here, a head there, a foot, a knee, a part that should have been covered up sticking out, a hand raised clutching nothing." (*GM*, 200)

All of these examples support the stylistics of the grotesque in O'Connor's fiction in two ways. First, there is the concentration on isolated body parts, Hazel's neck as he is walking the streets of Taulkinham, Mason Tarwater's head and eyes as he reacts in outrage to Francis's arrogant and impudent challenge that he prophesize in the city when he has come only to speak with a lawyer, and Mrs. Shortley's remembered Holocaust vision of victims' bodies and body parts. Second, there is the insistence of the body parts themselves, thrusting, tangling, bulging, sticking out, clutching.

Although the verb *rested* is much more common in O'Connor's fiction than in the Brown texts, there are only two collocations in the O'Connor texts with *rested* and neither occurs with a minimum frequency of five: "rested chin" (3) and "rested head" (2), both of which are consistent with O'Connor's use of ergative middle verbs to concentrate on body parts. There are only four tokens of *rested* in the Brown texts while the O'Connor texts have twenty-one. Even though there are only two "nonsignificant" collocations with *rested* in the O'Connor texts and none in the Brown texts, there is what Sinclair calls "semantic preference," one of a body part occurring as subject or object of the verb. As Sinclair explains, "Semantic preference is the restriction of regular co-occurrence to items which share a semantic feature."[14] In the Brown texts two of the four examples of the verb *rested* occur with the body parts *hand* and *back.* In O'Connor's texts eleven of twenty-one examples occur with a subject or object body part: *chin, hand, eyes, head, cheek, arms.* O'Connor's use of *rested* with body part subjects and objects helps to highlight the body, as in her description of Ruller in "The Turkey" after he collides with the tree while chasing the wounded turkey. This collision is in many ways a reminder, at least to the reader, of Ruller's corporeality: "He sat up and looked at his white ankles sticking out of his pants legs into his shoes. They looked like they didn't belong to him. He gripped a hand around each ankle and bent his knees up and rested his chin on a knee" (*CS,* 46).

Like the verb *rested,* the verb *jerked* has no collocations in the Brown texts and only a few low-frequency ones in the O'Connor texts: for example, "jerked arm" (3) and "head jerked" (3). However, all but one of the nouns that follow *jerked his* in O'Connor's texts are body parts: *hand, hands, head, arm, thumb, feet.* And seventeen of the thirty-four total occurrences of *jerked* have a body part either as subject or object of the verb. This variety of body parts once again illustrates the importance of considering semantic preference. Only two of the ten occurrences of *jerked* in the Brown texts have body part objects (*thumb, head*).

Many of the ergative middle verbs that I consider in this section, and others in table 14, are attractants for body parts in O'Connor's fiction, as I have indicated in analyses of collocations and semantic preference. The combinations of these ergative middle verbs and body parts frequently help signal O'Connor's exploration of the body, the mind, and the grotesque. In *Wise Blood,* for example, part of Hazel Motes's awkwardness is simply his being uncomfortable in his skin and with his body. On the train going to Taulkinham, his experiences in the dining car and his encounter with the three women there epitomize his sexual and physical discomfort: "Finally a woman at the far end of the car got up and the steward jerked his hand. Haze hesitated and saw the hand jerk again. He lurched up the aisle, falling against two tables on the way and getting his hand wet in somebody's coffee. The steward placed him with three youngish women dressed like parrots. Their hands were resting on the table, red-speared at the tips. He sat down and wiped his hand on the tablecloth" (*WB*, 15–16). Hazel clearly has no control over his body here. It is the contrast of the steward's control of his hand in ordering Hazel to his table and then the steward's hand by itself ordering Hazel to his table along with the women's red-speared resting and controlled hands that sets Hazel's hands in relief. He accidentally sticks his hand in someone's coffee cup and then wipes his hand on a tablecloth. His hands always serve as objects rather than ergative subjects. However, there is no one-to-one semantic mapping between ergative subjecthood and control, as we saw in detail in chapter 2. Just as frequently, lack of control on the part of the ergative subject will be made clear through context. In "A Good Man Is Hard to Find" the grandmother lives long enough to know that her entire family is murdered by The Misfit and his gang. When the shots ring out that have killed her son Bailey and her grandson John Wesley, "The old lady's head jerked around. She could hear the wind move through the tree tops like a long satisfied insuck of breath" (*GM*, 25). The grandmother's head is clearly acting without control here. Surprise is one of the contextual elements that occasion the use of the verb *jerked.* In *Wise Blood* the grotesque woman with the "sharp teeth protruding from her mouth" comes into the museum and stands over the display case, which reflects her face: "When Haze saw her face on the glass, his neck jerked back and he made a noise. It might have come from the man inside the case" (*WB*, 99). The isolation of body parts that is prevalent in a grotesque style is evident here, as not Hazel's head but his neck jerks back and as his own voice, or unspecified noise, appears not to come from him but from the shrunken mummy inside the museum case. In "The Displaced Person" Mrs. Shortley is horrified by both the manners and the bodies of the members of the displaced family, the Guizacs. When the Guizacs arrive on the McIntyre farm, Mr. Guizac kisses Mrs. McIntyre's hand on being first introduced to her. Mrs. Shortley has a surprised instantaneous involuntary reaction: "Mrs. Shortley jerked her own hand up toward her mouth and then after a second brought it down and rubbed it vigorously on her seat" (*GM*, 199).

Collocational Analysis of the Head and Its Parts

The collocations that appear in table 15 occur with a G^2 of at least 6.635 and occur at least five times.

As explained in chapter 3, there is a 57,929 word difference between the Brown texts at 235,431 words and the O'Connor texts at 293,360 words. Numbers of words can make a difference in numbers of significant collocations in a corpus, especially given the requirement in my analysis that a "significant" collocation demands both a G^2 score of 6.635 or above and a frequency of five or more. Thus in an effort to make certain that it is not simply the size of the Brown texts that

TABLE 15: ***Eyes*-ergative-middle-verb collocations in O'Connor and Brown texts**

O'Connor			*Brown*		
Collocation	Freq	G^2	Collocation	Freq	G^2
closed eyes	14	78.99	*closed eyes*	10	72.61
opened eyes	15	67.54	*opened eyes*	6	32.02
shut eyes	11	53.82			
rolled eyes	8	42.24			
eyes fixed	7	39.97			
eyes closed	8	35.76			
eyes moved	8	24.95			
turned eyes	7	7.96			

caused the differences in collocation behavior outlined in tables 15–18, I added to the Brown texts the Frown general-fiction K subcorpus, which brought the Brown-Frown fiction texts to 293,758 words, slightly over the number of words in the O'Connor texts. This addition of words made no difference at all in the types of significant collocations for analysis in this chapter; thus the figures for Brown in tables 15–18 reflect only the Brown texts. Earlier in this chapter we examined the frequencies and literary significance of middle ergative middle verbs with and without a variety of body parts as subjects or objects. In this section we examine four central body parts only in collocation with ergative middle verbs. The Brown texts have the not surprising noun-ergative-middle-verb collocations of "opened eyes" and "closed eyes." The O'Connor texts have not only these two specific noun-ergative-middle-verb collocations but also six more. One of the consistent patterns in tables 15–18 is evident in table 15: most collocations with these body-part terms and ergative middle verbs occur with the body-part terms as objects rather than subjects of the ergative middle verbs. As I indicated earlier, this chapter will consider those collocations with body-part subjects; chapter 5 will concentrate on ergative middle verbs in collocation with body-part objects and on reflexives as middle-related constructions. The collocations that involve *head* and an ergative middle verb in Brown and O'Connor appear in table 16. The most common collocation in O'Connor is "Mr. Head," from "The Artificial Nigger," which we will ignore because *head* there does not refer to a body part. There are fully ten collocations with the minimum numerical requirements in O'Connor with *head* as a body part, but only one such collocation in Brown. There are no collocations with the minimal numerical requirements that involve *mouth* or *face* and an ergative middle verb in the Brown texts; thus tables 17 and 18 contain the collocations that meet the requirements in O'Connor.

TABLE 16: ***Head*-ergative-middle-verb collocations in O'Connor and Brown texts**

O'Connor			*Brown*		
Collocation	Freq	G^2	Collocation	Freq	G^2
turned head	49	244.47	*shook head*	32	343.09
shook head	15	101.05			
stuck head	12	74.80			
head thrust	11	65.70			
thrust head	9	49.87			
turn head	9	45.39			
lifted head	8	38.61			
head lowered	5	28.29			
raised head	6	23.04			
head turned	9	15.64			

TABLE 17: ***Mouth*-ergative-middle-verb collocations in O'Connor**

Collocation	Freq	G^2
shut mouth	9	58.43
mouth stretched	7	52.40
mouth twisted	6	51.78
opened mouth	8	41.78
closed mouth	5	27.53
mouth opened	5	21.41

TABLE 18: ***Face*-ergative-middle-verb collocations in O'Connor**

Collocation	Freq	G^2
thrust face	5	18.42
turned face	11	16.70

The function of the appearance of the word *eyes* as the subject in body-action middles seems to be at least in part to draw attention to the grotesquery of the body itself, as in (24)–(26), below:

24. "and then [Madam Zoleeda] had sat back grinning, a stout woman with green eyes that moved in their sockets as if they had been oiled." (*GM*, 71)
25. "her eyes moved directly to Rayber's face in the window and he knew they sought it." (*VBA*, 132)
26. "All at once the ugly girl turned her lips inside out again. Her eyes fixed like two drills on Mrs. Turpin." (*ERMC*, 203)

In each of these examples the eyes evoke for the reader the astonishing merger of the spirit and the flesh, a merger that is at once incarnational and grotesque. In each the eyes act as affected agents. Van O'Connor characterizes the aesthetic of the grotesque as one in which the human is seen as "caught in his [or her] own biological nature" in a "tangle of rationality, irrationality, love and hatred, self-improvement and self-destruction."[15] In (24) the seer Madam Zoleeda's oily eyes move like those of a charlatan; in (25) Lucette Carmody's eyes seek out Rayber's face in the window of the church in which she preaches; in (26) Mary Grace, the agent of Ruby Turpin's revelation, has eyes that fix on their target like a machine.

Examples (24) and (25) are broadly representative of the body-action middle semantics of the collocation "eyes moved" in O'Connor's fiction. All occur in finite clauses, either main or subordinate, each reporting an event rather than a state. However, that in (26)—"eyes fixed"—is rare in O'Connor's fiction in reporting events; the more usual pattern is for the verb *fixed* to be stative, as in the following:

27. "the grey eyes were fixed on him as if they were waiting serenely for a struggle already determined." (*VBA*, 215)

In (27) Bishop is reduced to a set of grey eyes that are fixed on Tarwater before Tarwater drowns Bishop. Regardless of the state or event status of the verb, all of these constructions in which eyes function as the subject of middle verbs draw attention to the body acting on its own to affect itself.

In table 16 there are three body-action-middle-verb collocations with *head* as the subject—"head thrust," "head lowered," and "head turned." Consider, then, the following example from *Wise Blood:*

28. "Mr. Hazel Motes's head turned very slowly, following her down the pool." (WB, 84)

The head both initiates and undergoes the activity of turning. In (28) Hazel Motes's head follows the woman who is sunning herself at the swimming pool, the same woman who is described in exquisitely grotesque detail. In this case and those discussed below in this section, the middle-voice constructions signal the total or partial collapse of the distinction between the initiator and the endpoint. Two of the specific literary effects of this frequent collapse are the suggestions, made within the context of the incarnational and the grotesque, 1) that the human body—and its parts—has a will (or spirit) of its own of which the human mind may be entirely unaware and 2) that the decisions and actions of the human mind have a reflexive effect on the body that the mind inhabits.

The other significant body-action middle collocations with *head* as the subject in O'Connor's fiction are examples of specifically what Givón calls the "adjectival-lexical passive." This construction is middle in the sense that it is not truly passive but instead a one-participant body-action event with a subject as initiator and endpoint, as in the following:

29. Hazel's "head was thrust forward as if he had to use his whole face to see with." (*WB,* 187)
30. Sally Virginia "went off to the woods as if she were stalking out an enemy, her head thrust forward and each hand gripped on a gun." (*WB,* 150)
31. "The shoat climbed the two steps onto the back porch and stood outside the screen door, looking in with his head lowered sullenly." (*GM,* 37)

As Ward, Birner, and Huddleston and Givón argue, adjectival passives of the sort that we see in (29)–(31) and in (27) above, whether clausal or phrasal, are more adjectival (participial) than verbal. Operational tests for the adjectival status of these constructions include that one can substitute, or insert, for *be* other verbs that take predicative complements such as *remain,* as in "his head remained thrust forward." That substitution is not possible with a verbal passive. Thus one cannot substitute *remained* for *was* in "He was killed."[16]

Table 17 indicates three subject-ergative-middle-verb collocations for *mouth:* "mouth stretched," "mouth twisted," and "mouth opened." All three indicate an ambiguous lack of control on the part of the agent:

32. "Here she was, wearing her best clothes and a string of beads, and now bounding forward with her mouth stretched." (*GM,* 198)
33. "His mouth twisted and he closed his eyes against the revelation." (*ERMC,* 190)
34. "Sitting upright and rigid in the cab of the truck, his muscles began to jerk, his arms flailed, his mouth opened to make way for cries that would not come. His pale face twitched and grimaced." (*VBA,* 216)

The focalizer of (32), Mrs. Shortley, observes Mrs. McIntyre bounding forward with a grotesque smile on her face to meet and greet the Guizacs, the newly arrived displaced family of "The Displaced Person." In (33) Sheppard of "The Lame Shall Enter First" reacts in self-revulsion to the revelation that he has neglected his own son in an effort to support his own ego as a salvation figure to the juvenile delinquent Johnson. And in (34) Francis Tarwater reacts in horror to the memory of drowning his own cousin, Bishop.

Table 18 demonstrates an initially curious pattern for *face.* Even though *face* is the most statistically prominent of the body parts in table 13, it has only two collocations with ergative middle verbs and in neither of those collocations is *face* the subject. As I demonstrated earlier in this chapter, there are constructions in O'Connor's fiction with *face* as the subject of an ergative middle verb. Yet the relative lack of statistically "interesting" such collocations highlights an obvious intuition: the face is less animate as a whole and thus much less likely to serve as a collocationally interesting middle agent, or middle medium as we will see in chapter 6, than *head, eyes,* or *mouth.* The head can turn or nod; the eyes can move; the mouth can twist or stretch or open. The face can grimace, but neither *grimace* nor *frown* is an ergative middle verb. An important point to notice here is that even though there are no statistically "interesting" collocations for *face* and ergative middle verbs, the qualitative analysis of *face* with ergative middle verbs earlier in this chapter led to the discovery of "heavy body-part actions," a category that will have an important corollary in chapter 5 when we examine objects to ergative middle verbs.

The overall greater concentration of body parts and ergative middle verbs in O'Connor's fiction supports a stylistics of the embodiment of spirit or at least of embodiment itself. In chapter 5 we will examine ways in which middle-related constructions may become more elaborated than the prototypical middles but yet remain less elaborated than prototypically transitive constructions.

The Bifurcated Self

Body Parts and Reflexives

Lady, a man is divided into two parts, body and spirit.
Tom T. Shiftlet (*GM,* 62)

As one would notice in even a casual reading, conceptualizations of the mind and body are central to O'Connor's fiction. In "A Temple of the Holy Ghost" the twelve-year-old focalizing girl is hyperaware of bodies and the spiritual and emotional questions that they pose. The entire story can be read as an exploration of the relationships between the body as temple and the conscious mind. When her mother sternly reminds her cousins, the fourteen-year-olds Joanne and Susan who have been joking about boys and the backs of automobiles, that they are "Temples of the Holy Ghost," the girl has the revelation that she herself is a "Temple of the Holy Ghost": "It made her feel as if somebody had given her a present" (*GM,* 88). In addition to the general thematic attention to the body as an incarnational temple in the story, there is of course O'Connor's characteristic attention to concrete detail, in particular to individual body parts. The mind is always capable of recognition of the body and its parts. Joanne and Susan are fascinated with their own legs as objects: "They put on lipstick and their Sunday shoes and walked around in the high heels all over the house, always passing the long mirror in the hall slowly to get a look at their legs" (*GM,* 85). In another story of coming of age, "A Circle in the Fire," the twelve-year-old focalizing Sally Virginia is also alive to the presence of the body. At the end of the story, as Powell and his juvenile delinquent gang bathe in the cow trough, Sally Virginia watches from the edge of the woods. When the boys jump out of the trough and run around it, Sally Virginia, as focalizer, notes "the sun glinting on their long wet bodies" (*GM,* 152). As we saw in detail in chapters 2 and 4, it is possible for body parts to act as if they are the controlling agents. In a brilliant manipulation of point of view O'Connor has Sally Virginia observe, from the vantage point of leaning over the stair banisters, her mother and Mrs. Pritchard, the hired help, having a conversation about the juvenile boys: "She got up and went out into the hall and leaned over the banisters. Mrs. Cope's and Mrs. Pritchard's legs were facing each other in the back hall" (*GM,* 138).[1]

In this chapter we will be less concerned with body parts such as legs acting on their own or even with the extent to which characters notice the bodies of other characters. Instead the focus will be on how characters act upon themselves and their own body parts, as in the following passage from *Wise Blood:*

> The woman was climbing out of the pool, chinning herself up on the side. First her face appeared, long and cadaverous, with a bandage-like bathing cap coming down almost to her eyes, and sharp teeth protruding from her mouth. Then she rose on her hands until a large foot and leg came up from behind her and another on the other side and she was out, squatting there, panting. She stood up loosely and shook herself, and stamped in the water dripping off her. . . . The woman sat down in the spot of sun and took off her bathing cap. Her hair was short and matted and all colors, from deep rust to a greenish yellow. She shook her head and then she looked up at Hazel Motes again, grinning through her pointed teeth. She stretched herself out in the spot of sun, raising her knees and settling her backbone down against the concrete. (*WB,* 84–85)

In this passage describing a grotesque at the swimming pool in the city park, there are three verb-reflexive-pronoun constructions: "chinning herself," "shook herself," and "stretched herself." Each sentence could occur with approximately the same meaning without the pronoun *herself:* for example, "chinning up on the side," "shook," and "stretched out in the spot of sun." However, the reflexives are consistent with the concentration on the body in this passage. That is, the reflexives introduce a split between the initiator and the endpoint, or the mind and the body. Consider the list of body parts that explicitly occur in the passage above: *face, eyes, teeth, mouth, hands, foot, leg, hair, head, knees, backbone.* Many of these body parts occur not only as grammatical subjects ("face appeared," "teeth protruding," "foot and leg came up") but more important for this chapter as grammatical objects ("shook her head," "raising her knees," and "settling her backbone"). Thus the use of the reflexives as well as the body-part objects contributes to the partial separation of the body (the endpoint) from the mind (the initiator). That partial separation allows for a variety of specific literary effects, among them O'Connor's focus on the grotesque and the spiritually damaging preoccupation with isolation.

There are any number of reasons for calling attention to the split between the mind and the body. Besides the attention to grotesque detail that we see in the passage above from *Wise Blood,* another common motivation seems to be the signaling of a disjunction between the actions of the body and the will of the mind, as we see clearly in the following passage from "Greenleaf":

> He detached himself from the car slowly. . . . Presently he emerged again with the gun, circled behind the car, opened the door violently and threw

> himself onto the seat beside her. . . . "Spring is here!" she said gaily. Mr. Greenleaf lifted one muscle somewhere near his mouth as if he found this the most asinine remark ever made. When she stopped at the second pasture gate, he flung himself out of the car door and slammed it behind him. Then he opened the gate and she drove through. He closed it and flung himself back in, silently, and she drove around the rim of the pasture until she spotted the bull, almost in the center of it, grazing peacefully among the cows. . . . He flung himself out again, this time deliberately leaving the car door open so that she had to lean across the seat and close it. . . . He seemed to throw himself forward at each step and then pull back as if he were calling on some power to witness that he was being forced. (*ERMC,* 48–49)

Here Mr. Greenleaf and Mrs. May are going to shoot the scrub bull of Mr. Greenleaf's sons because it has escaped from the sons' farm and has been in among Mrs. May's cattle. Mr. Greenleaf is described six times as acting on himself reflexively to "throw himself" or "fling himself" in or out of Mrs. May's car or across Mrs. May's field to go shoot the bull. As the last sentence makes clear, Mr. Greenleaf is "being forced" to go shoot his sons' bull. Unlike the verbs *chin* and *stretch* in the passage above from *Wise Blood,* neither *throw* nor *fling* is an inherently middle verb. Thus the reflexive pronoun is obligatory if the subject and the object have the same referent. In this passage as well there is a reminder of the split between the mind and the body, although that reminder is less insistent than in the passage from *Wise Blood.* In describing a smirk on Mr. Greenleaf's face the narrator says that he "lifted one muscle somewhere near his mouth."

Just as there are a multitude of reasons for calling attention to the mind/body divide, there are a multitude of reasons for conflict between the mind and the body besides reluctance of the subject to perform the event in the first place, as in Mr. Greenleaf's case. There might simply be inertia to overcome, as in the following from "A Circle in the Fire": "Mrs. Pritchard heaved herself from the chimney and waved her arm in a fierce circle but he pretended not to hear" (*GM,* 132). Mrs. Pritchard is a less than enthusiastic worker on Mrs. Cope's farm. At the beginning of the story, just before Mrs. Pritchard heaves herself away from the chimney, Mrs. Cope is described as "squatting down pulling grass out of the border beds around the house." However, "Mrs. Pritchard was leaning against the chimney, her arms folded on a shelf of stomach, one foot crossed and the toe pointed into the ground" (*GM,* 130). She is, then, the picture of indolence and inertia.

In the subjects of the one-participant ergative verbs that we analyzed in chapter 4, we have the relatively nonproblematic unity of mind and body; however, as we will see in this chapter, in the use of body-part objects as well as reflexive and intensive pronouns, the bifurcation of the mind and the body is made explicit. This chapter explores the split of the individual into a subject and a self with subject understood as mind and self referred to by means of body parts first and then by means of reflexive pronouns. The chapter will demonstrate and analyze both the linguistic and the literary complexities of standard reflexive constructions in O'Connor and how body-part reflexives are used as well.

Subject and Self

Kemmer's view of the middle as being characterized most clearly through relative elaboration of the initiator and endpoint provides three specific benefits in this study of the body in O'Connor's fiction, the second and third benefits being particularly relevant in this chapter. First, it gives us a unified view of the relationships among active constructions, passive constructions, and core middle constructions. Second, it suggests a motivated place for the middle-related reflexive construction. Third, it provides hypothetical parallels between ontological subject/initiator and bodily self / endpoint. As John Haiman argues, reflexives in English are frequently "indicative of a divided self."[2] In a related vein George Lakoff points out that some grammatical patterns of English indicate that the human person can be conceptualized as a combination of a "Subject" and a "Self." He defines *subject* as "the locus of subjective experience: consciousness, perception, judgment, will, and capacity to feel." *Self* is, for Lakoff, at least in part "the body" but it can also be understood as the conceptualized remainder of a person after the abstraction of the most immediate and foregrounded "subjective experience." Lakoff contends that the following sentences, among others, prove the potential linguistic bifurcation of the person into subject and self:

1. If I were you, I'd hate me.
2. If I were you, I'd hate myself.

As Lakoff argues, traditional logical semantics would have to argue that (1) and (2) mean the same thing since *I, me,* and *myself* are supposed to be all co-referential. Both (1) and (2) would then have the logical form of, as Lakoff writes, "If X were Y, X would hate X." However, he continues, the sentences do not mean the same thing. If we understand *subject* and *self* in Lakoff's terms, the difference in meaning can be made clear. In (1) the speaker is hypothesizing that if her subject were the same as the subject of her addressee, then that subject would hate the speaker's self. As Lakoff explains, a context for (1) might be that the speaker is not a nice person at all and that the addressee is. Thus if the speaker's subject were the addressee's subject, that subject would hate the speaker's self. Example (2) again hypothesizes that the speaker's subject is the same as the addressee's subject. But this time, as Lakoff says, the context might be that the addressee is an unpleasant person. Thus if the pleasant speaker's subject replaced the unpleasant addressee's subject, that subject would hate the addressee's unpleasant self.

Lakoff explores various expressions in English that demonstrate some of the details of the complex split of subject and self. That split, Lakoff argues, is frequently at odds with our normal, everyday understanding of the relationship between subject and self, or mind and body. For example, subject is normally seen to be in control of self; however, there are conflicting expressions that indicate that true control is gained by being true to self (for example, the body). Consider the following instantiations of these conflicts, all from Lakoff:

3a. I made myself get up early.
b. I restrained myself from hitting him.

4a. Don't betray yourself.
b. Be true to yourself.

The sentences in (3) indicate a nonproblematic relationship of subject control and self subservience. The mind seems quite rightly to control the body. The sentences in (4) from Lakoff, however, demonstrate a more problematic relationship where self, as the central entity of the person, is seen as being truer than subject; subject is, thus, urged to cede control to self. As Lakoff details, there are many more complexities in our understandings of the relationship between subject and self, but those above are central to our concerns in this chapter: that is, whether the subject or the self, the mind or the body, is the locus of control, whether the true person is aligned more with the subject/mind or the self/body.

There are explicit realizations of the complicated relationship of Lakoff's subject to self throughout O'Connor's fiction. One of the more obvious threads is the distinction between "internal" and "external" causation.[3] For example, in *The Violent Bear It Away* Mason Tarwater is angered by the "schoolteacher" article that his nephew Rayber writes claiming that Tarwater called himself to be a prophet because of his own insecurity: "'Called myself!' the old man would hiss, 'called myself!' This so enraged him that half the time he could do nothing but repeat it" (*VBA,* 19–20). Tarwater's understanding of the true person is "self" that responds solely to its ultimate instigator subject, the Old Testament God. It is perhaps obvious that O'Connor would explore internal versus external causation in the arena of human versus divine will. However, just as frequently O'Connor explores the internal dynamics of subject versus self. Consider, then, one of O'Connor's most frequent character types, one who doesn't understand himself/herself or his/her own motivations. For example, O. E. Parker of the late story "Parker's Back" is certainly moved by the mysterious external force of grace, as is evident in his pursuing the tattoo of the Byzantine Christ on his back. However, O'Connor makes it clear through explicit narrative commentary that Parker is clueless about his own motivations. O'Connor's narrator says of Parker's understanding of himself and his understanding of his fundamentalist wife, Sarah Ruth, "He could account for her one way or another; it was himself he could not understand" (*ERMC*, 220). It is both Sarah Ruth and his inexplicable (for him) attraction to tattoos in general, set in motion by his seeing a tattooed man at a fair, and to the Byzantine Christ in particular that wake his self up: "Parker had never before felt the least motion of wonder in himself. Until he saw the man at the fair, it did not enter his head that there was anything out of the ordinary about the fact that he existed" (*ERMC*, 223). Perhaps the most comic version of the O'Connor bifurcation of subject and self is Enoch Emery's relationship to his wise blood: "His blood was more sensitive than any other part of him; it wrote doom all through him, except possibly in his brain, and the result was that his tongue, which edged out every few minutes to test his fever blister, knew more than he did" (*WB*, 129–30). Both Enoch and Francis Tarwater engage in long dialogues with their other selves, Enoch's dialogue being between his conscious mind and his controlling wise blood, Francis's dialogue being between himself and the devil as alter ego. The narrator says of Francis and his conversation with the "stranger," "He began to feel that he was only just now meeting himself, as if as long as his uncle had lived, he had been deprived of his own acquaintance" (*VBA*, 35).

Reflexivity as a Continuum

The reflexive pronoun is both a measure of elaboration in Kemmer's sense and a morpheme that helps one to express the division of "Subject" and "Self" in Lakoff's sense. Consider the following examples:

5a. "Mrs. Turpin **herself** was fat but she had always had good skin." (*ERMC*, 194)
 b. Mrs. Turpin was fat but she had always had good skin.
6a. "She had **herself** a stroke on the day she left out of here." (*GM*, 240)
 b. She had a stroke on the day she left out of here.
7a. "She had given thirty dollars for it and hadn't bought **herself** anything else big again." (*WB*, 26)
 b. She had given thirty dollars for it and hadn't bought anything else big again.
8a. "This morning she was threatening to kill **herself** again." (*ERMC*, 118)
 b. This morning she was threatening to kill again.

These examples illustrate both the reflexive and emphatic uses of the X-*self* pronouns in English. As Faltz, Givón, and P. K. Saha argue, the emphatic use of the X-*self* pronouns is the origin of the reflexive use. The examples in (5)–(8) are arranged in increasing approximation to the purely reflexive use of these pronouns in (8). The (a) examples are from O'Connor; the (b) examples are altered for the purpose of comparison. Example (5a) is prototypically of the emphatic use of the X-*self* morpheme. The word *herself* occurs after the subject, and, as Givón argues of the emphatic reflexive in general, "the contrasted item is unexpected or goes against the hearer's likely belief."[4] Defining the unexpected or likely belief is naturally very hard to do. However, since these items are pragmatic, we look to the context to determine whether the concepts have any heuristic value. The context in which (5a) occurs is the doctor's waiting room where Mrs. Ruby Turpin sizes up the waiting patients and makes friends with the "pleasant" lady, the mother of Mary Grace, a severely acned "fat girl of eighteen or nineteen, scowling into a thick blue book" (*ERMC,* 193). Thus any unexpectedness or comparison here probably resides solely in Ruby Turpin's mind since all of the other people in the waiting room, as well as O'Connor's readers, have already seen that she is fat. What might be unexpected to Ruby is that both she and Mary Grace are fat and thus share something although Ruby believes that they are radically different in temperament as well as skin quality. Kaoru Fukuda points out that one way to tell the difference between an emphatic reflexive and a normal reflexive is that an emphatic reflexive, unlike a normal reflexive, may be removed from the sentence without affecting its grammaticality or core meaning, as one can do quite easily in (5b).[5] If we skip to example (8a), we can see at the other end of the continuum that the pronoun *herself* here is grammatically reflexive rather than emphatic. First, as Givón says, the reflexive use of the X-*self* pronouns requires not only that the "referent is *mentioned twice* in the same clause," which is true of the emphatic as well, but also that the "referent participates in the clause *in two different roles.*"[6] The canonical reflexive may not be removed from the clause in which it appears if one wants a roughly synonymous sentence for the reason that what results is a sentence with different participants, as in (8b). There Star Drake is reported simply to have threatened to kill, presumably someone else, not herself, as in (8a). Example (6a) is as close to the emphatic use as it is to the reflexive use of the pronoun *herself* in the operational sense that one can leave the pronoun out and the omission does not significantly affect the meaning of the sentence, as one can see in (6b). Yet the pronoun occurs in postverbal object position. This use in (6a), then, is similar to what Kemmer refers to as the "heavy-marked reflexive." Kemmer notes this similarity as well.[7] I will refer to it as the "heavy reflexive." Example (7a) is even closer to a prototypical reflexive in that *she* and *herself* clearly have different roles in the sentence and because it is possible to interpret (7b) as referring to a situation in which she does not buy anything for anyone ever again. Thus we can think of the emphatic and reflexive uses of the X-*self* pronouns as lying on a continuum from prototypical emphasis to prototypical reflexivity with at least one clearly recognizable position in the middle—the "heavy reflexive."

Heavy Reflexives, Heavy Body-Part Reflexives, and Body-Part Reflexives

In chapter 4 we analyzed a construction that I referred to as "the heavy body-part action," on analogy with Kemmer's "heavy-marked reflexive." In the heavy body-part action, a body-part term, such as *face,* functions synecdochically for the whole human. Thus the clause "the boy's white face . . . lingered a moment at the threshold of his door" (*VBA,* 137), is a heavy body-part action because O'Connor could have simply written, nearly synonymously, "the boy lingered a moment at the threshold of his door." This chapter extends the analysis to "heavy reflexives," "heavy body-part reflexives," and "body-part reflexives" in O'Connor's fiction.

The prototypical body-action construction in O'Connor can be represented by (9), below, from "A View of the Woods":

9. "He got up and dressed and went outside." (*ERMC,* 72)

In (9) Mr. Fortune gets himself up and dresses himself. There is no explicit specification in the body-action middle that he acts on himself. When there is specification of the reflexive self in a body-action construction, there is frequently an additional contextual meaning that the body action was either unexpected or achieved with some difficulty. Kemmer notes, "The reflexive form implies a physical barrier between the person intending to carry out the action, and the body on which it is carried out. Along the same lines, it may be noted that the English phrase *dress herself* is quite appropriate to use of a small child who does not yet have full control of her limbs, or of a recuperating hospital patient."[8] The following passage from *The Violent Bear It Away,* in which the retarded boy Bishop is described, makes strategic use of the "heavy reflexive":

10. "The afflicted child looked as if he must have dressed himself. He had on a black cowboy hat and a pair of short khaki pants that were too tight even for his narrow hips and a yellow t-shirt that had not been washed any time lately. Both his brown hightop shoes were untied." (*VBA,* 154–55)

In the first sentence of (10) it is implied that Bishop has done a bad job of dressing himself; that extra contextual meaning is signaled in part by the "heavy reflexive," in English a reflexive construction that contains a reflexive morpheme even though the verb is inherently middle.[9] The extra meaning that is encoded by a heavy reflexive varies widely depending on context. In the following passage the displaced person Mr. Guizac is described as he works underneath the tractor that is shortly to roll over him, killing him:

11. "He had on rubber boots that were cracked and splashed with mud. He raised one knee and then lowered it and turned himself slightly." (*GM,* 249)

O'Connor could have written simply that he "turned slightly." The heavy reflexive "turned himself slightly," however, is syntactically parallel with the transitive "raised one knee" and "lowered it."

Analogous to the heavy reflexive and the heavy body-part actions that I discuss in chapter 4 are heavy body-part reflexives, in which body-part terms such as *face* or *head* occur as "heavy objects." These constructions are "heavy" in the sense that they occur with a specific body part when not strictly necessary, just as the heavy reflexive occurs with a reflexive morpheme when it need not. Table 18 in chapter 4 reported that there are only two collocations at or above the 6.635 G^2 with minimum frequencies of five for *face* as object of ergative verbs: "turned face" and "thrust face." The first of these collocations is a heavy body-part reflexive. Other heavy body-part reflexives would be "nod head," "blink eyes," "shrug shoulders," and, for men, "shave face." Although other heavy body-part reflexives, such as "leaned his head back" or "nodded her head," occur in O'Connor's texts, none of them, except "turned head" and "turned face" reach the 6.635 G^2 level with a minimum frequency of five as collocations. The following are typical of "turned face":

12. "Haze turned his fragile placed-looking face toward him." (*WB,* 76)
13. "When she turned her churning face toward the opening, she saw his blue figure struggling successfully over the green speckled lake." (*GM,* 195)
14. "He turned a comical face to the child." (*ERMC,* 156)
15. "The eye shut softly and the owl turned its face to the wall." (*WB,* 95)

As part of her argument that O'Connor uses "intransitive verbs as a means of expressing the stillness of the eternal moment," McMullen recognizes the "reflexive action" of (13), saying that *she* and *face* "are intrinsically one."[10] I label each of the examples in (12)–(15) a "heavy body-part reflexive" since there are approximately synonymous sentences in which one may simply leave out the body-part noun phrase, as in "Haze turned toward him" and "He turned to the child." These approximations are not exactly synonymous, at least in part, because they are missing the emotional specificity that is conveyed by the modifiers to the noun *face.* In (12), then, Hazel's face conveys his "fragile" state of mind when he is confronted by a truck driver who is angry with him for blocking the road. Earlier in the chapter in which (12) occurs, the narrator gives a more detailed evocation of that fragility: "[Hazel's] black hat sat on his head with a careful, placed expression and his face had a fragile look as if it might have been broken and stuck together again, or like a gun no one knows is loaded" (*WB,* 68). In (13) Hulga Hopewell's face expresses the humiliation and awakening that she experiences on being duped by the "innocent" Bible salesman Manley Pointer. In (14) the face of the juvenile delinquent Johnson expresses his amusement at the pink paint job in the bathroom of the Sheppard house. And in (15) the indifferent owl in the city park zoo turns its face from Hazel. There are eleven such heavy body-part reflexives with the verb *turn* and the object *face* in O'Connor. There are other heavy body-part reflexives in O'Connor involving the word *face,* as in (16)–(18), but none occurs more than once:

16. "'Noooo,' she said and leaned her round red face between the two nearest poles." (*GM,* 83)
17. "'How does a child like you know so much about these men?' Susan asked and pushed her face up close to the mirror to watch the pupils in her eyes dilate." (*GM,* 89–90)
18. "The stranger twisted his rutted face sharply." (*VBA,* 52)

Notice that both (16) and (18) characteristically have a modified lexeme *face* as the heavy body-part reflexive object. Susan in (17) is earlier described as having "a pretty pointed face" (*GM,* 86).

The other collocation involving *face* as object is not a heavy body-part reflexive, but it is a body-part reflexive: "thrust face." It is not a heavy body-part reflexive because "He thrust toward them" is not roughly synonymous to "He thrust his face toward them" in the same way that "He turned toward them" is roughly synonymous with "He turned his face toward them."

19. "Bishop climbed out of the car and thrust his face against his father's side." (*VBA,* 151)
20. "Tarwater lifted his head and returned the woman's stare. Then he took a stride forward and thrust his face at her." (*VBA,* 153)

Body-part reflexives are like prototypical reflexives in the reflexivity of the subject acting on its self; they are unlike prototypical reflexives in the specificity of the object. The examples in (19) and (20), occurring within two pages of one another in *The Violent Bear It Away,* illustrate the impossibility of establishing a one-to-one correspondence between a specific literary meaning and the body-part reflexive. In (19) Bishop seeks protection by thrusting his face against his father. In (20) Tarwater aggressively thrusts his face at the woman working at the reception desk of the Cherokee Lodge in an effort to challenge her assumption that he, as well as Bishop, is Rayber's son. There is a great variety of O'Connor characters whose actions are described by means of these body-part reflexives, although the examples below contain verb-object combinations that do not reach the 6.635 G^2 level. Each of the following is from a different one of the three O'Connor short-story collections, *The Geranium, A Good Man Is Hard to Find,* and *Everything That Rises Must Converge,* respectively:

21. "He worked his face to look as if he were thinking something out and hurried down the street until he was out of their view." (*CS,* 51)
22. "Across the street at the Empire Hotel, a colored cleaning woman was looking down from an upper window, resting her face on her folded arms." (*GM,* 48)

23. "Just then the inner door opened and a nurse with the highest stack of yellow hair Mrs. Turpin had ever seen put her face in the crack and called for the next patient." (*ERMC*, 193)

Because of his pride and embarrassment over the admiration he receives for the turkey that he has hunted down, Ruller self-consciously attempts to seem preoccupied in (21). In (22) Harry Ashfield incidentally notices a woman who appears and disappears from the narrative in this one sentence. And in (23) a nurse whose actions in the story "Revelation" consist only of calling patients and coming in and out of the waiting room first appears. In each of these examples, the only thematic work done is the incremental calling of attention to the undeniable body.

Significant body-part reflexives with *eyes* as the object include "closed eyes," "opened eyes," "rolled eyes," "shut eyes," and "turned eyes":

24. "She rolled her eyes and screwed up her mouth and stuck her leathery thin face into his smooth bland one." (*GM*, 12)
25. "The doctor, seeing he was awake, made a face like a Chinaman, rolled his eyes almost out of his head and cried, 'Say AHHHH!'" (*ERMC*, 93)
26. "The ride had made her sleepy and as soon as she got up on the stool, she rested her head on the counter and shut her eyes." (*GM*, 65)
27. "As soon as she got in the house, she lay down on her bed and shut her eyes and pressed her hand over her heart as if she were trying to keep it in place." (*GM*, 231)

Note that in each of the examples (24) through (27), the subjects act on more body parts than just the eyes. In (24) the grandmother attempts to amuse her grandchild by reflexively acting on her mouth, her eyes, and her face; in (25) Doctor Block attempts to amuse Asbury, his reluctant patient, by reflexively acting on his mouth and eyes; in (26) Lucynell Crater the younger reflexively acts on her head and eyes; and in (27) Mrs. McIntyre reflexively acts on her eyes and her hand.

Head occurs as the grammatical object in seven significantly common collocations: "turned head," "shook head," "stuck head," "thrust head," "turn head," "lifted head," and "raised head." Consider the following two examples, the second of which is a heavy body-part reflexive:

28. "The child suddenly stuck her head far out the window and said, 'Ugggghhrhh,' in a loud voice, crossing her eyes and hanging her tongue out as far as possible as if she were going to vomit." (*GM*, 143)
29. "The child turned her head, slowly, as if it worked on a screw, and watched his car pass. His face was so close to the glass that it looked like a paper face pasted there." (*WB*, 103)

I chose the examples in (28)–(29) to illustrate not just the body-part reflexive but also O'Connor's consistent focus on the body, as each example mentions at least one other body part in addition to the body-part reflexive objects.

Finally the following examples are typical of the "opened mouth," "closed mouth," and "shut mouth" collocations in O'Connor, all three of which reach the 6.635 G^2 level with a minimum frequency of five:

30. "She opened and closed her mouth several times before anything came out." (*GM,* 27)
31. "'I takes a little turpentine and sugar when I has a cold,' Morgan said. 'Shut your mouth,' Randall said, turning on him. 'Shut your own mouth,' Morgan said. 'I know what I takes.'" (*ERMC,* 111)

Strikingly, but consistently, when O'Connor's narrator reports that a character opens his or her mouth, that character has difficulty speaking, as in (30), in which the narrator reports on the grandmother's inability to speak when she finds herself alone with The Misfit, whose fellow killers have just dragged off the last of the grandmother's family to murder. Example (31) is representative of the tendency of O'Connor's characters to spend a fair amount of time telling one another to shut up.

The Literary Significances of the Divided Individual

Although less well recognized than many features, the divided individual has received some attention in O'Connor's fiction, two of the more obvious cases being Enoch Emory and Francis Tarwater. Suzanne Morrow Paulson, for example, approaches the issue "through Freud and the psychology of the divided self" while Mellard explores the mirror stages of Lacan as they are manifested in doubled characters such as Mary Fortune and her grandfather in "A View of the Woods." That doubling can take the form of a bifurcation of the individual or of another individual who mirrors a first.[11] More subtle than O'Connor's doppelgangers are her characters who are internally divided, sometimes through intense psychological distress and sometimes through a pathological self-absorption. In the epigraph to this chapter is quoted one of the more paradoxically unselfaware but yet self-absorbed characters in O'Connor's fiction, the flimflam man Tom T. Shiftlet: "Lady, a man is divided into two parts, body and spirit." Just after his philosophical pronouncement of dualism, Shiftlet makes his startling analogy: "The body, lady, is like a house: it don't go anywhere; but the spirit, lady, is like a automobile: always on the move, always" (*GM,* 62–63). This is the hint that Lucynell Crater the senior needs. She in effect offers to paint the automobile that Shiftlet has repaired in return for his marriage to her mute daughter, Lucynell Crater the junior: "In the darkness, Mr. Shiftlet's smile stretched like a weary snake waking up by a fire. After a second he recalled himself and said, 'I'm only saying a man's spirit means more to him than anything else. I would have to take my wife off for the week end without no regards at all for cost. I got to follow where my spirit says to go'" (*GM*, 63). This passage nicely illustrates O'Connor's use of body parts as subjects in middle constructions to communicate the almost independent nature of self (the body), a pattern that we analyzed extensively in chapter 4. Shiftlet's smile stretches metonymically for his mouth, but recognizing that his "self" is giving too much away, he recalls "himself"; that is, his subject mind takes control of his self body. And then his mind attempts to clarify his position but confuses it more. His body must follow where his spiritual subject—the automobile—leads him.

The bifurcation of the individual into subject and self, in Lakoff's sense, provides the opportunity for an exploration of self-involvement, that is, an exploration of the hyperawareness and sense of importance of self that are common among O'Connor's characters. The sense of importance takes many specific realizations, probably most obviously in the pathological isolation and intellectual hubris that many O'Connor characters exhibit. Rayber of *The Violent Bear It Away* might be a self-righteous intellectual, and Hazel Motes might be a prideful "hillbilly nihilist";[12] however, the similarity of Rayber's self-aggrandizement to that of Hazel indicates a kinship in O'Connor's mind between this isolated intellectual and this Christian incapable of communion in a real church. Rayber tells his uncle Mason Tarwater, "You've got to be born again, Uncle, . . . by your own efforts, back to the real world where there's no saviour but yourself" (*VBA*, 76). Hazel, too, evidences a self-reliance that borders on the comically unrealistic: "When he was eighteen and the army called him, he saw the war as a trick to lead him into temptation, and he would have shot his foot except that he trusted himself to get back in a few months, uncorrupted. He had a strong confidence in his power to resist evil; it was something he had inherited, like his face, from his grandfather." Hazel trusts himself to get back home uncorrupted in a matter of months. The text tells us, "He was gone four years; he didn't get back, even for a visit" (*WB*, 22–23). In his denial of Jesus and his own redemption in preaching the Church Without Christ, he has a persistent doctrine of self-reliance. Asa Hawks, the false blind preacher, tells him, "You still have a chance to save yourself if you repent. . . . I can't save you but you can save yourself." Hazel tells him "That's what I've already done" (*WB*, 111–12).

One connection that a good number of O'Connor's characters share, whether they be intellectuals or flimflam men or reluctant backwoods prophets, is what Srigley refers to as the grotesque "desire for absolute human autonomy." Srigley argues, "The moral choice that O'Connor consistently dramatizes in her stories is between a life of responsibility for others that is ordered by the love of God and other human beings and a life ordered solely by love of the self." Monroe sees this sort of pride and isolation manifested, for example, in Mr. Head and Nelson in

"The Artificial Nigger." He argues that they suffer from "a dignity based on an overweening pride in themselves and a condescension towards others not as good as they." Paul W. Nisly points out that O'Connor's characters find themselves isolated in spite of the many doubles that occur, as for example in the case of Mr. Head and Nelson. And Lake argues that O'Connor's grotesques help destroy "the illusion of the autonomous self," that autonomy being from the body and from the world's grotesques.[13]

A preoccupation with the self and the definition of the self through reflexive pronouns is a general trait of a good number of O'Connor's characters. Sometimes that self-reflexivity reaches a level of banality that is stupefying, as it does in the justification Julian's mother has for buying her ridiculous hat: "'Well,' she said, 'you only live once and paying a little more for it, I at least won't meet myself coming and going'" (*ERMC,* 4–5). She does in a sense meet herself coming and going when the black woman gets on her bus wearing exactly the same hat. At the other end of the continuum, we have The Misfit, who has bifurcated himself in a sincere, although ultimately misguided attempt, to find justice: "'That's why I sign myself now. I said long ago, you get you a signature and sign everything you do and keep a copy of it. Then you'll know what you done and you can hold up the crime to the punishment and see do they match and in the end you'll have something to prove you ain't been treated right. I call myself The Misfit,' he said, 'because I can't make what all I done wrong fit what all I gone through in punishment'" (*GM,* 27–28). He has actually renamed his self in an attempt to somehow make it truer. Another megalomaniac that believes in the purity of the "true" self is the self-righteous, self-satisfied racist Mrs. Ruby Turpin of "Revelation." Mrs. Turpin is particularly well pleased with her own social and racial position as a white landowner. However, she is a bit sensitive and insecure, so she spends too much time thinking about the issue: "Sometimes at night when she couldn't go to sleep, Mrs. Turpin would occupy herself with the question of who she would have chosen to be if she couldn't have been herself." Ruby tortures herself with the dilemma of what she would do if Jesus had given her no real choice but to be black. She stalls but finally relents in her imagination and accepts the place that Jesus has created for her as a black woman: "And he would have made her a neat clean respectable Negro woman, herself but black" (*ERMC,* 195).

O'Connor's characters, especially many of the more self-absorbed types, believe mightily in the power of self-control and self-correction. This hubristic sense of self-determination is often reflected in their use of reflexive pronouns, as in the case of Rayber, the "schoolteacher" nephew of Tarwater the elder: "'You're too blind to see what you did to me. A child can't defend himself. Children are cursed with believing. You pushed me out of the real world and I stayed out of it until I didn't know which was which. You infected me with your idiot hopes, your foolish violence. I'm not always myself, I'm not al . . .' but he stopped. He wouldn't admit what the old man knew. 'There's nothing wrong with me,' he said. 'I've straightened the tangle you made. Straightened it by pure will power. I've made myself straight'" (*VBA,* 73). In this passage Rayber confronts his uncle with his anger over the influence that the uncle had over him in kidnapping him when he was a child and teaching him the basics of Christianity, to which Rayber was powerfully attracted. Rayber clearly conceptualizes a split between subject and self, with self understood as the "true" self. He notes, perhaps rightly, that children's selves are at the mercy of those around them. Then he indicates a perceived split between his subject and self when he notes that he is not always himself. And finally he indicates, probably wrongly, that he has, by sheer willpower, controlled his own self. Rayber is a type in O'Connor's fiction, not only a hyperintellectualized, self-deluded religious skeptic but also a hubristic believer in the power of the individual will. He uses the same argument that he uses on himself to his own uncle Tarwater the elder when he tells him that he has "to be born again . . . by [his] own efforts" (*VBA,* 76). He believes that his sister was just "a good healthy American girl, just beginning to find herself when she was struck down" in a car wreck (*VBA,* 107). Of course, Rayber is himself conflicted, even in his own understanding of self-reflexive behavior. He believes in self-reflexive behavior only when it fits his own prejudices. Thus he considers his uncle's call to prophet status as a self-delusion. In his "schoolteacher" magazine article he writes of his uncle, "His fixation of being called by the Lord had its origin in insecurity. He needed the assurance of a call, and so he called himself" (*VBA,* 19). Self-reflexive behavior is acceptable to Rayber only when it fits his selfishly humanistic prejudices. When he claims the younger Tarwater for himself, he tells Mason, "This one is going to be brought up to live in the real world. He's going to be brought up to expect exactly what he can do for himself. He's going to be his own saviour. He's going to be free!" (*VBA,* 70). Of course, what Rayber means by being free is being like Rayber himself.

The cult of self-reliance is mixed frequently in O'Connor with isolationism and tragic naïveté. Like Srigley, John R. Clark sees "indifference, insensitivity, and isolation" as characteristic of O'Connor's grotesque, notably in Mrs. Shortley's blindness to the peacock in "The Displaced Person":

> Then she stood a while longer, reflecting, her unseeing eyes directly in front of the peacock's tail. He had jumped into the tree and his tail hung in front of her, full of fierce planets with eyes that were each ringed in green and set against a sun that was gold in one second's light and salmon-colored in the next. She might have been looking at a map of the universe but she didn't notice it any more than she did the spots of sky that cracked the dull green of the tree. She was having an inner vision instead. She was seeing the ten million billion of them pushing their way into new places over here and

> herself, a giant angel with wings as wide as a house, telling the Negroes that they would have to find another place. She turned herself in the direction of the barn, musing on this, her expression lofty and satisfied. (*GM,* 204–5)

Clark comments on the fact that "Mrs. Shortley sees nothing";[14] however, the reflexive constructions in which she is first described as seeing herself and then turning herself also, more subtly perhaps, are reflective of her self-involvement. Ruby Hill, whose story is an extended comic denial of her pregnancy, is especially proud of her self-reliance regarding medical care: "She had done all right doctoring herself all these years—no bad sick spells, no teeth out, no children, all that by herself" (*GM,* 73). Harry Ashfield, the naïve and abused child of "The River," demonstrates self-reliance in not only baptizing himself but drowning himself in the process, exactly the nonreflexive fate of Bishop in *The Violent Bear It Away* since Francis both baptizes him and drowns him: "He intended not to fool with preachers any more but to Baptize himself and to keep on going this time until he found the Kingdom of Christ in the river" (*GM,* 51). And the many spoiled and emotionally and spiritually crippled adult children in O'Connor's fiction are delusionally self-reliant, their self-reliance normally shown to be false at some point in the story. Hulga Hopewell ends up one-legged and nearly blind in the hayloft; Asbury Fox is stripped of his ignorance and pride as the Holy Ghost descends upon him; Thomas, the historian, shoots his mother accidentally in an attempt to kill Star Drake, a recipient of her love, that "pure idiot mystery" (*ERMC,* 118). And Julian of "Everything That Rises Must Converge" is convinced that he is free of his mother's love: "Most miraculous of all, instead of being blinded by love for her as she was for him, he had cut himself emotionally free of her and could see her with complete objectivity. He was not dominated by his mother" (*ERMC,* 12).

Even when O'Connor's characters think that they are acting with charity towards others, they are more frequently feeding their own self-aggrandizement. Besides Rayber of *The Violent Bear It Away,* the other great self-righteous do-gooder in O'Connor's fiction is Sheppard of "The Lame Shall Enter First." He too is a great believer in self-control. He tells his own young son, who is missing his dead mother terribly, "If you stop thinking about yourself and think what you can do for somebody else . . . then you'll stop missing your mother" (*ERMC,* 147). He says four times during the course of the story, "I have nothing to reproach myself with," all four times in self-defense for his actions with Johnson, the juvenile delinquent whom he is not able to save after all. Finally, he has a brief moment of real insight at the end of the story: "His heart constricted with a repulsion for himself so clear and intense that he gasped for breath. He had stuffed his own emptiness with good works like a glutton. He had ignored his own child to feed his vision of himself" (*ERMC,* 190). It is too late for Sheppard. His son has killed himself.

Distribution of Reflexives

One measure of the stylistic effect of the conceptualizations of the unified and bifurcated self is the proportion of the use of reflexive pronouns, as we have already seen above in many examples. Rayber of *The Violent Bear It Away* is probably the most intellectually and spiritually corrupt character in O'Connor's fiction. He attempts once to drown his own son and knowingly allows his nephew Francis Tarwater to drown the child. Of Rayber's many problems, his most severe is the overintellectualization of practically everything in his life, including his understanding of his own self. After one of his many missed opportunities to connect emotionally with his nephew, including expressing the real and justifiable anger that he feels towards him, Rayber typically rationalizes his behavior through hyperintellectualization: "Rayber felt afflicted with a peculiar chilling clarity of mind in which he saw himself divided in two—a violent and a rational self. The violent self inclined him to see the boy as an enemy and he knew that nothing would hinder his progress with the case so much as giving in to such an inclination" (*VBA*, 139). It is Rayber more than any other character who is literally described as seeing himself. Out of ten such constructions in O'Connor's texts, six of them describe Rayber. And all of them are used ironically in the sense of either Rayber's false intellectualism, as in the case above, or his false guilt, or his false liberality. After he witnesses the performance of the child evangelist Lucette Carmody, he has a characteristically self-involved fantasy that confuses the Edenic with intellectual fantasies: "Rayber saw himself fleeing with the child to some enclosed garden where he would teach her the truth, where he would gather all the exploited children of the world and let the sunshine flood their minds" (*VBA*, 133).

Table 19 indicates that the reflexive/intensive pronouns *herself, himself,* and *yourself* are differently distributed in frequency in the O'Connor and Brown texts, with O'Connor having the greater proportion of them. The other intensive/reflexive pronouns are approximately evenly distributed for proportion. The figures for *myself* and *itself* are included for comparison with the others.

TABLE 19: **Distribution of reflexive and intensive pronouns in O'Connor and Brown texts**

Word	O'Connor Freq	O'Connor per 1000	Brown Freq	Brown per 1000	G^2	O'Connor D	O'Connor Range
herself	177	0.60	84	0.35	16.57	.81	14
himself	423	1.44	266	1.13	9.88	.89	14
yourself	88	0.30	40	0.17	9.43	.82	14
myself	69	0.23	59	0.25	0.12	.88	14
itself	43	0.14	34	0.14	0.00	.83	13

As the Juilland's *D* scores for *herself, himself,* and *yourself* indicate, all three of these words are relatively unevenly distributed in O'Connor's texts when compared to the four body-part terms that we focused on in chapter 4 and earlier in this chapter: *face, head, eyes,* and *mouth.* Juilland's *D* is .92 or above for all four of these body parts. Each of the words *herself, himself,* and *yourself* has bursts in *The Violent Bear It Away* and stories from *The Geranium, A Good Man Is Hard to Find,* and *Everything That Rises Must Converge.*

The Violent Bear It Away, O'Connor's second novel, is the most "reflexive" of the five main O'Connor works, having 3.60 X-*self* words per thousand words. In fact, O'Connor's fiction generally became more "reflexive" with the publication of *The Violent Bear It Away. The Geranium,* her M.F.A. thesis collection, has 2.27 X-*self* words per thousand; *Wise Blood,* her first novel, 2.19 per thousand; *A Good Man is Hard to Find,* her first short-story collection, 2.27 per thousand. The average for all of O'Connor's fiction is 2.5 X-*self* words per thousand. All of the stories of *Everything That Rises Must Converge,* her posthumously published short story collection, are either at the mean or above it. Of the stories in *Geranium,* only "The Barber" and "The Turkey" are at the mean or above. Of the stories in *A Good Man Is Hard to Find,* only "A Stroke of Good Fortune" and "The Displaced Person" are at the mean or above.

In *The Geranium* "The Barber" is the most reflexive at 3.3 X-*self* words per thousand. Rayber is massively self-involved with his own supposed superiority in intellect and morality. On the night after his first argument with the racist barber, Rayber lies in bed, mulling over what he would have done if "he'd had an opportunity to prepare himself"; Rayber often "amused himself analyzing" his friend Jacobs's way of making people think he knew more than he did; the narrator reports that Rayber is "disgusted with himself for saying" that he would provide rationale for voting for his liberal candidate, presumably because he considers himself above argument with the racist barber and his racist customers (*CS,* 18, 20). "A Stroke of Good Fortune," in *A Good Man Is Hard to Find,* is by far the most "reflexive" of all of O'Connor's narratives, with 4.5 X-*self* words per thousand. This high reflexivity is a result of two tendencies. Ruby Hill is concerned not only with her self as body but also with her self as autonomous entity. When her friend Laverne urges her to see a doctor, she counters, "I can take care of myself" (*GM,* 79). When Laverne, who shows interest in someone outside of herself—Ruby's brother Rufus—asks if Rufus is around, Ruby can barely bring herself even to notice the question or its significance: "I don't know. I kept myself away from doctors all my life. I kept—why?" (*GM,* 79). In the middle of her repeating herself in the last sentence, she suddenly connects to Laverne's question. As obsessed as Ruby is with her autonomous self, she is even more concerned with her body, which is showing itself as nonautonomous and demanding attention from her for that very reason. Her body asserts itself in demanding such attention. As the story begins she "brace[s] herself at the bottom of the steps for the climb to the fourth floor." The climb up the stairs to her apartment is not easy: "She gripped the banister rail fiercely and heaved herself up another step, shaking her head" (*GM,* 70, 72). Even the act of ignoring her body demands that she pay attention to her body. When she is leaving Laverne's apartment, where Laverne has made it abundantly clear that she knows that Ruby is pregnant, Ruby "walked carefully to the door, keeping herself erect and not looking down at her stomach the way she wanted to" (*GM,* 82). Ruby's denial of her body and her self-involvement indicate that although it may be true that most of O'Connor's self-involved characters are failed intellectuals of some sort, not all are.

There are plenty of failed and self-involved intellectuals in the collection *Everything That Rises Must Converge.* For example, there is Asbury of "The Enduring Chill," who comes home a sick intellectual and creative failure, still scapegoating his mother for his lack of talent; there is Thomas of "The Comforts of Home," a historian of some sort, who sponges off his mother while he ridicules the expansive grace of her love; there is Sheppard of "The Lame Shall Enter First," who wants to turn the juvenile delinquent Johnson into an intellectual mirror of himself but who neglects and abuses his own son; and there is Julian of "Everything That Rises Must Converge," who will learn after his mother's death that he is far more dependent on her than he would like to think. All of these intellectuals are self-involved, and that self-involvement is responsible for a good proportion of the X-*self* words in these stories. The narrator tells us, for example, that Julian frequently retreats from life to "an inner compartment of his mind": "This was a kind of mental bubble in which he established himself when he could not bear to be a part of what was going on around him. From it he could see out and judge but in it he was safe" (*ERMC,* 11).

The self-involvement in these stories is not necessarily limited to the intellectuals. In "The Comforts of Home" Star Drake, the manipulative juvenile who latches onto Thomas's mother's charity, is either described or self-describes herself ten times as wanting or attempting to kill herself or hurt herself. Of course, Star Drake has no intention of hurting herself. Furthermore, there are stories in the collection *Everything That Rises Must Converge* that have no intellectuals at all; yet those stories are at or above the mean for the use of X-*self* words. For example, "A View of the Woods" has 3.1 X-*self* words per thousand, although there is not an intellectual in the entire cast of characters. However, Mr. Fortune is just as self-involved as any self-important faux intellectual. The fact that he spends so much time justifying his actions and thoughts to himself indicates at least in part that he senses that he is wrong in selling the Pitts's front pasture to Tilman, the gas-station entrepreneur: "He turned and looked away over the lake to the woods across it and told himself that in five years, instead of woods, there would be houses and stores and parking places, and that the credit for it could go largely to him" (*ERMC*, 65). When his granddaughter abandons him in town because she knows what he is up to, he realizes but does not act on her reproach: "He meant to make his voice severe but instead it came out crushed, as if it belonged to a suitor trying to reinstate himself" (*ERMC*, 69). He refuses to recognize the value of the field and the view across the field to himself and to his family, yet he continues to sense his own delusion: "A pine trunk is a pine trunk, he said to himself" (*ERMC*, 70). And in a final hubristic and self-delusional act he attempts to whip his granddaughter to discipline her but he has again to convince himself of the need and wisdom of it: "He saw that the time had come, that he could no longer avoid whipping her, and as he turned off the highway onto the dirt road leading to home, he told himself that when he finished with her, she would never throw another bottle again" (*ERMC*, 77).

From table 20 we see that there are sixteen different collocations with reflexive pronouns in the O'Connor texts but only six in the Brown fiction subcorpora that have G^2 scores at or above 6.635 and a frequency of at least five.

TABLE 20: **Collocations with reflexive and intensive pronouns in O'Connor and Brown texts**

O'Connor			*Brown*		
Collocation	Freq	G^2	Collocation	Freq	G^2
found himself	15	81.68	*told himself*	12	58.03
called myself	9	74.05	*found herself*	7	45.52
flung himself	7	56.68	*told herself*	6	34.36
steadied himself	5	52.87	*found himself*	6	23.40
threw himself	7	46.75	*find himself*	5	20.81
blinded himself	5	43.15	*made himself*	5	12.60
found herself	6	31.73			
pulled himself	7	25.87			
saw himself	9	22.67			
felt himself	8	22.07			
let himself	7	18.77			
told himself	6	18.60			
see yourself	5	17.01			
called himself	5	16.99			
make himself	6	15.15			
heard himself	5	14.74			

The stoplist used to compute the figures in table 20 does not include reflexive pronouns, of course, but it does include personal pronouns, auxiliary verbs, modal verbs, determiners, coordinating conjunctions, subordinating conjunctions, and prepositions. As I did with collocation tests earlier, I ran collocation tests against the Brown texts with the Frown general-fiction K subcorpus. Only one significantly common collocation, "found myself," was added to the Brown list. Distribution statistics such as Juilland's *D* and range usually cannot be applied to collocations, at least in part because the frequencies are typically low. Compare the frequency of fifteen for the most common collocation in table 20 with the frequency of 423 for the most common X-*self* pronoun in table 19. However, the second of the O'Connor collocations ("called myself") illustrates the necessity of keeping one's eye on the distribution of these collocations in the text since all examples of "called myself" come from one character's dialogue in one chapter in one novel: Mason Tarwater's rant on Rayber's betrayal of him by writing him up for a "schoolteacher magazine": "'His fixation of being called by the Lord had its origin in insecurity. He needed the assurance of a call, and so he called himself.' 'Called myself!' the old man would hiss, 'called myself!' This so enraged him that half the time he could do nothing but repeat it. 'Called myself. I called myself. I, Mason Tarwater, called myself! Called myself to be beaten and tied up. Called myself to be spit on and snickered at. Called myself to be struck down in my pride. Called myself to be torn by the Lord's eye'" (*VBA*, 19–20). Thus one might want to discount these nine examples of "called myself" as a stylistically significant collocation in O'Connor since they all occur in this relatively short passage.

One of the most interesting collocational uses of the reflexive in O'Connor's fiction is the "found X-self" construction, with "found himself" being the most significant X-*self* collocation in O'Connor's fiction. Note that "found X-self" is significant in the Brown texts as well, and recall that adding the Frown general fiction K-subcorpus to the Brown texts adds the significant collocation "found myself." Note, however, that the top ranked X-*self* collocation for the Brown texts is "told himself" while that for O'Connor is "found himself." Note as well the relatively high G^2 score for "found himself" in O'Connor. Even though the "found X-self" construction cannot in itself be called a unique stylistic marker for O'Connor since it does occur significantly in the Brown texts as well, its semantics make especially clear the bifurcation of subject and self, which overall is clearly stylistically marked for O'Connor, as is evident in the number of different X-*self* collocations in table 20. We have already qualitatively examined many of these X-*self* collocations (for example, "flung himself" and "threw himself" in "Greenleaf" and "saw himself" in *The Violent Bear It Away*). The collocation "found X-self" typically has a role in O'Connor's exploration of the failures of the human intellect. In particular, the collocation is almost always used to encode a disjunction between subject and self in the sense that subject is surprised by an action that self performs or by the condition of self. Mrs. Wally Bee Hitchcock, like Ruby Turpin, prefers to place people in the proper position in her mind by determining their worth from their appearance, especially what they wear. Just after she and Hazel Motes meet, Mrs. Hitchcock is conflicted, however: "She wanted to get close enough to see what [his] suit had cost him but she found herself squinting instead at his eyes, trying almost to look into them" (*WB,* 10). Hitchcock is, like a number of other characters in *Wise Blood,* fascinated by Hazel's eyes. She wants to do one thing, and discovers her self doing quite another. Again Enoch Emery is perhaps the most divided character in O'Connor's fiction. Recall that his brain is divided into two parts, the part that is in touch with his blood and the part that is stocked with words. And his body, or self, which is of course in constant contact with his blood, is frequently at odds with Enoch the subject. When it becomes clear to Enoch's blood that he is to act by its wishes, in part to steal the mummy to be the new jesus for Hazel's new Church Without Christ, his self responds but his mind lags behind: "The first thing that he found himself doing that was not normal was saving his pay." Enoch's mindlessness is bestial, foreshadowing his ultimate transformation into a gorilla when he steals the gorilla suit at the end of the novel: "Sometimes he didn't think, he only wondered; then before long he would find himself doing this or that, like a bird finds itself building a nest when it hasn't actually been planning to" (*WB,* 130, 129). Parker of "Parker's Back" also has a very difficult time following through on his intentions. After he meets his wife to be, Sarah Ruth, he intends not to come back to visit; however, he does: "Parker had no intention of taking any basket of peaches back there but the next day he found himself doing it" (*ERMC,* 228). In fact, his puzzling relationship with his wife is a constant motivation for examining and acting on his self. The first paragraph of the story ends with his wondering why he stayed with Sarah Ruth: "He was puzzled and ashamed of himself" (*ERMC,* 219). Parker's problem is that he, too, has a divided subject-self, like Enoch. His self is in fact very much attracted to Sarah Ruth, but his subject mind will have nothing to do with what his body tries to tell him. During their first meeting, when she hits him so hard for his blasphemy that he thinks he has really hurt the hand that he has been pretending was hurt, her physical touch affects him deeply: "Her own hand was dry and hot and rough and Parker felt himself jolted back to life by her touch. He looked more closely at her. I don't want nothing to do with this one, he thought" (*ERMC,* 222). They are married shortly thereafter.

In many cases, the "found X-self" construction is used to encode shock and disorientation on the part of the focalized character. In *The Violent Bear It Away* Rayber chases Francis through alleys following him to the Carmodys' revival meeting. However, he leaves the house shoeless and disheveled. In chasing Francis down an alley, he has an accident: "A garbage can materialized in his path. There was a noise like the collapse of a tin house and he found himself sitting up with his hand and one foot in something unidentifiable" (*VBA,* 123). The surprise and shock that a character experiences in order to find the self again does not have to be physical, although the distinction between the physical and mental is sometimes difficult to make. In "A Good Man Is Hard to Find" the grandmother loses control of her body in exactly the way that she might least expect. She is almost speechless, or at least senseless, when left alone with The Misfit after her entire family has been taken off to be murdered in the woods: "She opened and closed her mouth several times before anything came out. Finally she found herself saying, 'Jesus. Jesus,' meaning, Jesus will help you, but the way she was saying it, it sounded as if she might be cursing" (*GM*, 27). O'Connor's characters frequently "find themselves" just as they are losing everything that they hold most dear, whether that be their lives, as in the case of the grandmother, or their jobs, as in the case of Mrs. Shortley in "The Displaced Person." Mrs. Shortley overhears Mrs. McIntyre telling the priest that it is the Shortleys whom she will dismiss from their jobs since she now has the Guizacs, the displaced family from Poland. Thus the Shortleys are to be the newly displaced: "Mrs. Shortley sat down on an open sack of laying mash with a dead thump that sent feed dust clouding up around her. She found herself looking straight ahead at the opposite wall where the gentleman on the calendar was holding up his marvelous discovery but she didn't see him. She looked ahead as if she saw nothing whatsoever" (*GM*, 220). Here Mrs. Shortley loses control of her self, of her body, on the verge of losing everything she thought secure.

The overcoming of inertia seems to be one of the primary motivations for another of the significant collocations—"pulled himself," which is used most frequently when O'Connor describes a character who struggles back from sickness or unconsciousness. In *Wise Blood* it is used to describe Hazel's actions just after he wakes from his nightmares in his Essex: "He pulled himself over into the front of the car and eased his foot on the starter and the Essex rolled off quietly as if nothing were the matter with it" (*WB*, 161). In "A View of the Woods" it is used to describe Mr. Fortune as he wakes up in the morning looking for his granddaughter Mary Fortune Pitts: "He pulled himself up and looked around the room but she was not there" (*ERMC*, 72). And in "The Enduring Chill" the construction is used to describe Asbury as he climbs to his sickroom after having just returned home with a disease that he mistakenly thinks is going to kill him: "Holding onto the banister, he pulled himself up the steep stairs, across the landing and then up the shorter second flight and into his room." (*ERMC*, 90–91).

In this chapter we have seen a connection between the grotesquery of isolation, especially in Srigley's sense, and the split between the mind and the body, or subject and self, as it is manifested in reflexives. In *The Violent Bear It Away*, one of the recurring problems is the self-involvement and isolation of the major characters. Thus both Rayber and Francis Tarwater attempt to run from involvement with the world. And there are subtle hints throughout the novel that their efforts are doomed. When Francis first meets Bishop he feels a revulsion towards his retarded cousin but senses the connection between Rayber and Bishop: "The boy had a vision of the schoolteacher and his child as inseparably joined. The schoolteacher's face was red and pained. The child might have been a deformed part of himself that had been accidentally revealed" (*VBA*, 93). There are two interesting patterns revealed in this example. First, the reflexive pronoun is separated from its antecedent by two sentence boundaries. Second, the reflexive appears in a prepositional phrase modifying "a deformed part," signaling a connection between Rayber and Bishop that certainly Rayber would not admit. Bishop is, as Lake argues extensively, the representation of the idiot world in O'Connor's fiction, the world that must be embraced and loved in spite of its idiocy and in spite of the illogic of that love.[15] Francis has a blinding moment of insight: "The Lord out of dust had created him, had made him blood and nerve and mind, had made him to bleed and weep and think, and set him in a world of loss and fire all to baptize one idiot child that He need not have created in the first place and to cry out a gospel just as foolish." Francis tells his uncle and himself, "I won't get used to him! I won't have anything to do with him!" (*VBA*, 91–93). Francis refuses to see the divine in himself or in the banal world that surrounds him. His devilish companion speaks for his spiritual hubris: "His friend suggested he demand an unmistakable sign, not a pang of hunger or a reflection of himself in a store window, but an unmistakable sign, clear and suitable—water bursting forth from a rock, for instance, fire sweeping down at his command" (*VBA*, 162). This spiritual hubris that expects God to speak as if speaking to an Old Testament prophet is akin to the intellectual hubris of her hyperintellects such as the two Raybers, Hulga, Julian, Thomas, and Asbury.

The literary significance of body-part reflexives, like the literary significance of middles themselves or body parts themselves, is much more difficult to generalize than the literary significances of reflexives, I believe for the reason that the body and its parts are incarnational for O'Connor. The absence of a clearly defined generalization for the meaning of the body and body-part constructions in O'Connor's fiction is, in fact, the significance of the body in O'Connor—its fundamental resistance to dominance by either the subject or literary interpretation. The arguments of this book do not assume a one-to-one correspondence between meaning and form, say between the middle and the incarnational and grotesque. Instead the middle and body parts fundamentally realize the embodiment of meaning and spirit in O'Connor's fiction. The ambiguities of agent and medium, of actor and goal, and of the initiator and the endpoint are experiential rather than ideational. In the concluding chapter to this book we will explore some of the theoretical problems with attempting to find a direct interpretive connection between middle-voice-related constructions and literary significance.

Conclusions

Literary Metaphors of the Body and Grammatical Voice

Beinst she was kin to us, we gone to see the body.
Mrs. Pritchard (*GM*, 131)

The Body in Flannery O'Connor's Fiction has demonstrated the grammatical effects of O'Connor's concerns with the incarnational and grotesque body, those concerns being in turn the effects of her sacramental theology. The grammatical effects investigated in this book occur at a remarkably finely grained level of the grammar and of the lexicon—the level of voice and the level of body parts. Furthermore, the book has demonstrated that it is possible to investigate the stylistics of a grammatical category—voice—in the fiction of a language that does not formally unify that category. The effects of O'Connor's concerns with the incarnational and grotesque body in fact show the semantic, rather than formal, unity of the middle in her fiction. Those effects are visible in the reflexives, the body-part reflexives, the body-action middles, and the "heavy" versions of reflexives, body-part reflexives, and body-part action middles. As we have seen, it is impossible to assign any specific unitary meaning to O'Connor's middle constructions with lexemes such as *face, head, eyes,* and *mouth.* Instead what seems probable is that O'Connor's concern with the incarnational and grotesque body simply led her to focus on the head and parts of the head as important in that they so often reveal emotion and spiritual turmoil. Voice is conceptually and formally a perfect category for the exploration of the incarnational and the grotesque for two reasons: 1) the categories of reflexive and middle blur but yet do not erase the difference between the initiator and the endpoint; and 2) the use of the heavy constructions and the body-part reflexives manipulate the voice feature of elaboration in a way that highlights the physicality of the body and self, a potentially grotesque view, and the consequent dependency of the spirit on the body, an essentially incarnational view. Thus in the various middle constructions or constructions closely related to the middle explored in this book, the initiator and the endpoint—for example, the human and his/her body—are blurred. Sometimes the face, for example, seems to act on its own, as in body-action middles; sometimes initiators act on their own faces, making themselves both initiators and endpoints. The blurring of the distinction between initiator and endpoint by the action of the agent on his/her own body in body-action middles highlights the facts that the spirit is situated in a body and that, in the incarnational view, the spirit is infused and made manifest through the body; the "heavy" constructions and body-part reflexives call attention to the presence of the body in their use of the body-part words as subject or object when that specificity is not required.

Even today, as we have seen in this book, there continues to be stylistic analysis of the sort that uses linguistics to illuminate literary texts. There are even analyses of voice, in particular passive voice, in some literary works, although fewer than one might expect. Daniel Kies, for example, demonstrates that the high percentage of passive verbs and nominalizations in Orwell's *1984* supports the novel's thematics of reduced agentivity. M. Angeles Martínez argues that reduced transitivity—manifested in increased occurrence of passives, metonymic body parts for whole humans, and ergativity—demonstrates a stylistic move towards reduced agentivity in Thomas Pynchon's revision of the story "Under the Rose" as the third chapter of *V.*[1] And McMullen argues that O'Connor's use of the passive contributes to her stylistic tendency to strip her characters of free will. McMullen comes quite close to recognizing the middle voice in O'Connor's fiction without naming it directly. She quotes Zelda Boyd on agency in psychoanalytic discourse and literature: "English offers many ways of avoiding agency besides the passive construction. . . . Consider . . . 'the impulse seized me,' which reverses the conceptual agent through metaphor, or consider sentences like 'the twig snapped,' 'the water boiled,' which are neither passives nor conventional actor/action sentences but happenings, that is, events represented without referent to an agent or cause . . ." (ellipses in McMullen). Halliday and Matthiessen use the term *happening* to refer to a one-participant ergative, such as Boyd's "the twig snapped."[2] McMullen points out a tendency in O'Connor for the use of "adjectives that have passive intent." In spite of McMullen's assertion of a general stylistic trait of passivization, she discusses only three real examples of the passive voice and then analyzes two examples of "passive intent" from the same story—"Greenleaf." These examples of "passive intent" are the sentences "Bars of light slid across him as the venetian blind was slit" and "Clouds crossing the moon blackened him" (*ERMC*, 24; qtd. in McMullen). McMullen's analyses of "passive intent" and "happenings" in these sentences are examples of literary interpretation driving analysis of form itself. She writes of "Clouds crossing the moon blackened him," "While the sentence structure is overtly active voice, O'Connor suggests a passive intent since the bull, the 'him' of the sentence, is the receiver of the action initiated by the clouds." In other words once McMullen has decided that O'Connor makes her characters passive, even active sentences must be interpreted as having "passive intent," even though O'Connor might just as well have actually written the passive "He was blackened by clouds crossing the moon." McMullen claims that these two sentences "fall into the category of Boyd's 'happenings.'" The verb *blackened* in O'Connor's sense is not an ergative verb, and although *slid* is an ergative, the ergative point is missed by implying that its significance is that "the bull . . . is acted upon by celestial elements (. . . the light)" through "passive intent": "Active participation in these events and decisions remains out of the bull's control because of O'Connor's linguistic choices."[3]

There are many interesting problems, some real and some imagined, in the interaction of literary and linguistic theory. It has been seventeen years since Jacqueline M. Henkel astutely declared in the pages of *PMLA,* "We have just witnessed the rise and fall of linguistic models in literary criticism."[4] Those models, intended variously to provide overarching systems to govern and explain literary production and reception, included structuralism, speech act theory, and Chomsky's transformational-generative grammar, and they failed for a number of reasons, among them, as Henkel argues, the inappropriate metaphorization of those linguistic models within literary criticism. One of the more common and troublesome metaphorical applications was the extension of sentence-level linguistics to text-level literary production and understanding. Thus both Jonathan Culler's *Structuralist Poetics* and Ellen Schauber and Ellen Spolsky's *Bounds of Interpretation* posit a "literary competence" on analogy with linguistic competence in spite of the fact, as Henkel points out, that literary competence is "a very general 'knowing how' [to read or interpret] in exactly the sense Chomsky wishes to exclude" from the almost entirely unconscious linguistic competence. Metaphorization of linguistics is not included among three weaknesses of structuralist narratology that Gerald Prince lists: "lack of completeness," "lack of explicitness," and "ambition to account for" aesthetics and interpretation. However, as both Roger Seamon and Henkel argue, it is precisely the drive for interpretation—one of the faults that Prince does list—that frequently motivates the literary metaphorization of linguistic models.[5]

If structuralism in its various metaphorical manifestations in literary studies has been a long-term failure, that is, if the kind of totalizing systematizing that is common in literary borrowings of linguistic concepts has generally been given up as ultimately a false goal, there is still the question of the microrelation between form and meaning, or form and interpretation. And it is here, at this fundamental level, that linguistics still contributes, although usually unwittingly, to the interpretive humanities (for example, history, literature, philosophy, rhetoric). This chapter, in part, examines the interpretive fate of a form-meaning relation—the middle voice—that has been invoked repeatedly, even since Henkel's article in 1990, in literary criticism, historiography, philosophy, and rhetorical studies. The failure of large-scale structuralist, or even poststructuralist, metaphorical extensions of linguistic theory to the humanities provides the opportunity for examination of smaller-scale homologies, or analogies. That smaller scale allows a much clearer view of the essential differences in the metaphorical applications of linguistics to the humanities and the linguistic analysis of the language of the documents of the humanities. First, I consider the use of the middle voice in interpretation within the fields of literature, history, philosophy, and rhetoric. The chapter next returns to discussions of the body in O'Connor criticism and stylistic analysis of O'Connor's fiction. I then argue that the language of the text and the body of the text are both irreducible, thus providing theoretical justification for text-based stylistic analysis. Finally, I offer thoughts about why at least small-scale metaphorizations of linguistic constructions are likely to continue to occur in the interpretive humanities.

The Middle Voice as an Interpretive Trope

As Henkel argues, what is generally understood to be the failure of structuralism in literary studies refers to the failure of the metaphorical application of the theoretical axioms of structuralist linguistics—for example, competence, performance, grammaticality, kernel sentences, phrase structure rules—to fundamental questions of literature theory and criticism—for example, production and understanding. Prince's *Narratology,* for example, references kernel narratives and rewrite rules for narratives on the analogy of kernel sentences and transformational rules in early transformational grammar. Whereas the kernel sentences of transformational grammar are, essentially, the fundamental simple sentences that are generated by phrase structure rules (those that form noun phrases, for example, from placing a determiner before a noun), Prince's kernel narratives are simple narratives that involve "no more than one modification of a situation or state of things." More complex narratives are formed by conjunctions of narrative sections, which are in turn formed of conjunctions of narrative episodes. While Prince's *Narratology* explicitly argues that "narrative grammar" should not concern itself with interpretation, Culler's *Structuralist Poetics* analogizes a literary competence (governing literary readings) on the basis of the linguistic competence that governs the allowable sentences of a language. As Henkel explains, there are several problematic moves involved in such a structuralist poetics, not least of which is, as she puts it, "the initial analogy between sentence and text, a move that must entail a dramatic inflation of the semantic concerns accounted for." Henkel points out in general that the demand that structuralist poetics govern, or judge, interpretation is its ultimate undoing since the sentence-based linguistic model on which it is analogized is simply not designed to produce such textual interpretations. In fact, Seamon argues, if structuralist poetics had been content with creating structuralist models of the literary system, in the sense of Northrop Frye's anatomy or Roman Jakobson's literariness, "we would now be dealing only with many proposed models of the literary system, a parallel to the many theories of language." However, Seamon concludes, poetics undermined its own systematicity in turning hermeneutic, in producing interpretation of individual works.[6]

Simply that linguistic structuralism as a governing metaphor has been widely judged a failure in literary studies does not mean that metaphorization of linguistics does not continue in the humanities. The linguistic middle voice, for example, has considerable metaphoric currency in the humanities, even though, unlike structuralism—or its attendant large ideas such as competence, performance, grammaticality, kernel sentences, phrase structure rules—the middle voice has specific operational tests for the determination of its presence in a construction.

Although he does not borrow the middle voice, Genette's narratological voice, which we discussed briefly in chapter 1 to distinguish it from grammatical voice, is analogously borrowed from linguistic grammatical voice, just as his order, duration, and frequency are borrowed from linguistic tense/aspect and his point of view is borrowed from linguistic mood (imperative, subjunctive, declarative, and so on). Genette is aware of the stretch involved in these borrowings and in fact claims that he "make[s] no pretense of basing them on rigorous homologies" and that he makes no special interpretive claims for voice other than as a structural principle. However, it is instructive to review a use of Genette's homology here because it is essentially the same one that many other literary theorists make. Lorna Hutchison, for example, first recognizes the difference between narratological voice and point of view but then conflates Genette's narratological voice and grammatical voice in claiming that Margaret Atwood's *Alias Grace* evidences the middle voice, or "middle discourse," in that "the question of 'who "speaks"' remains unresolved, and is indeed unresolvable." The homological connection occurs between the subject of the verb and the narrator of the narration. Just as voice determines the relationship between the subject of the verb and the semantic role that occurs as subject (for example, actor for actives, goal for passives), narratological voice determines the relationship between the narrator and the narration. As Genette argues, a narrative statement "can be interpreted only with respect to the person who utters it and the situation in which he utters it." It is a short step from this homology between narrative voice and grammatical voice to broader homological extensions of the middle voice.[7]

Most contemporary metaphorical discussions of the middle trace their intellectual history to one essay—"To Write—An Intransitive Verb?," in which Roland Barthes metaphorizes Emile Benveniste's exposition of the linguistic middle voice: "the middle voice corresponds exactly to the state of the verb *to write:* today to write is to make oneself the center of the action of speech [*parole*]; it is to effect writing in being affected oneself; it is to leave the writer [*scripteur*] inside the writing, not as a psychological subject . . . , but as the agent of the action."

Thus from the linguistic middle voice, in which the grammatical subject is affected by the action of the verb, Barthes metaphorically derives the rhetorical middle voice, in which the modern writer is affected by the act of writing. The justification for this metaphorization is provided early in Barthes's essay with his remarkable "postulate of *homology*": "the structure of the sentence, the object of linguistics, is found again, homologically, in the structure of works. Discourse is not simply an adding together of sentences; it is, itself, one great sentence. In terms of this hypothesis I would like to confront certain categories of language with the situation of the writer in relation to his writing." Here Barthes explicitly claims one great metaphorical leap and makes another implicitly. The explicit leap is the claim that discourse is one great sentence. Because sentences variously have subjects, objects, and grammatical voice, for example, texts have the same. Even if one were to grant discourse the analogy of a long sentence, still formally absent from that sentence is the writer, whom Barthes implicitly adds when he applies the "hypothesis" to "the situation of the writer in relation to his writing." Thus in Barthes's analogy, because the subject of a middle-voice verb is affected by the action of that verb, the writer of a "middle-voice" text is affected by the writing of that text.[8]

In two essays published in 1992 Hayden White further explores Barthes's conception of intransitive writing. In "Writing in the Middle Voice" he notes similar ideas surfacing in the writings of Michel Foucault, Freud, and earlier writings by Barthes himself. However, in "Historical Emplotment and the Problem of Truth" White invokes Berel Lang's argument that Barthes's "intransitive writing" is the only suitable discourse for representing the Holocaust. White furthers the argument by asserting that the most appropriate representation for the Holocaust is a modernist middle-voice style of writing—one that is characterized by the affectedness of the writer and reader in the event of writing by the use of modernist techniques such as free indirect discourse, narrative questioning, ambiguous point of view, and distortions of realist notions of temporality.[9] Both LaCapra and Hans Kellner pick up White's discussion of a middle voice representation of the Holocaust, clarifying the metaphorization and in Kellner's case thereby making unambiguous the problems of that metaphorization. LaCapra argues that in his "own tentative judgment, the use in historiography of some discursive analogue of the middle voice might be most justified . . . when one is moved, even shaken or unsettled, in such a manner that one is unable or unwilling to judge or even to predicate with any degree of confidence." In these cases, argues LaCapra, the historiographer is in a position of being unable to position himself or herself at any specific distance or proximity to victim/perpetrators, for example. The middle voice is, thus, useful because it provides "modulations of proximity and distance, empathy and irony . . . and . . . need not be understood as ruling out all forms of objectivity and objectification." Kellner, whose essay is footnoted by

LaCapra, also calls on discussions of the middle voice to ground his essay on the representation of the Holocaust. Yet, in passages Kellner's essay demonstrates the logical end of a formless metaphorization of a linguistic construction. Consider his reaching for a (nonexistent) example of "middle-voiced phrasing" in the lyrics of a contemporary songwriter: "To use an analogy, Barry Manilow sings 'I write the songs' actively; a passive phrasing (and reversal of perspective) of this would be 'I am written by the songs' or perhaps 'The songs write (me?)'; a middle-voiced phrasing would be 'I am the song and it (I) is (am) writing me (it).' This last example, which is not so absurd as it seems when seen in a Heideggerian context in which 'language speaks,' throws attention on the being of the agents (subject, object) and their mutual involvement in the historical moment of writing." What is clear in Kellner's Heideggerian, convoluted attempt to write in the middle voice is that the term has no meaning other than the metaphorical. That full metaphorical status, of course, has a tendency towards inflation of meaning and application. Kellner reveals that inflation most clearly when he argues that "if one acknowledges the social construction of the self and reality, or at least their effective linguistic construction as we can know them, all utterances may be understood as middle-voiced, even when they are not explicitly so."[10]

The middle voice has also found a place in philosophy. Jacques Derrida finds it useful in his widely influential essay "Difference." In fact Derrida says that "difference" itself "indicates the middle voice" in that "it precedes and sets up the opposition between passivity and activity." The middle voice is, then, some kind of ur-voice, one that precedes the active and the passive. Later in the essay he makes clear that the use of the middle voice is for him the same as the use that most philosophers and literary critics have for it. It is at least in part "a virtual metaphor," as Vincent P. Pecora points out in his discussion of the following passage from Derrida: "And we shall see why what is designated by 'differance' is neither simply active nor simply passive, that it announces or rather recalls something like the middle voice, that it speaks of an operation which is not an operation, which cannot be thought of either as a passion or as an action of a subject upon an object, as starting from an agent or from a patient, or on the basis of, or in view of, any of these *terms*. But philosophy has perhaps commenced by distributing the middle voice, expressing a certain intransitiveness, into the active and the passive voice, and has itself been constituted in this repression."[11] Now this is quite a bit for the middle voice to be responsible for, as a repressed tool in the creation of philosophy itself. However, as Thomas Pepper details, Heidegger also found the middle voice to be an excuse for "a certain porousness of reflexion for the self-interrogating phenomenon of Dasein." That is *Dasein,* Heidegger's "being," shows itself very much as a middle-voice verb. In both Derrida and Heidegger, and most other nonlinguistic uses of the middle voice, the construction is a trope. Especially evident in Heidegger's and Derrida's use of the middle voice, it is a rhetorical move, not a thing at all, least of all a grammatical construction. Rather like being or difference themselves, it is a no thing, a way of being or differing in the world. As Pepper argues, Heidegger's "deployment of the middle voice could be called more of a mention than a use." And as Pepper says of Derrida's use of the middle voice, it is "a name for a kind of structurally hovering indetermination." That indetermination, Pepper contends, is "why [Derrida] has to say 'something like the middle voice,' rather than to presume to name the middle voice itself."[12] The middle voice is so useful as a philosophical indetermination that it finds use even in its absence, or perhaps especially in its absence. Herwig Friedl argues that "it is the middle voice, the medium, as one of the historically earliest *genera verbi* (or in Greek: *diathesis*), whose absence in contemporary language is putting such a strain on pragmatist thinking once pragmatism begins to try and approach the problem of saying or, at least, of hinting at and of conveying the inner workings of Being as it unfolds." Friedl says that the absence of a robust modern middle voice in English created particular problems for the philosophical pragmatism represented by William James and John Dewey, since their vision of being was that of a self creating and created by experience. Friedl argues that the middle voice would have been of supreme use to James and Dewey because it "implies an existential situation in which the clear-cut contrast of subjective agency and of undergoing become questionable." He writes that the middle voice "does remind us that there may have been a time when the experience of experience . . . could be articulated—but that was, as we have seen in our linguistic excursion, before the subject established itself as the indispensable center of speaking and knowing." As Bradford Vivian writes, "To develop a conception of rhetoric in the middle voice is to develop a conception of rhetoric in which the rhetorical agent is not a subject exterior to the order of discourse but a form of subjectivity that is itself discursively engendered, maintained, and transformed." It is no wonder, then, that Pepper writes, "The twentieth century is the century of the middle voice."[13]

The metaphorical middle voice has been enthusiastically embraced in the ever-expanding world of literary studies as well as historiography. Both Teresa Dovey and Brian Macaskill explore J. M. Coetzee's characterization of at least one potential writing style as middle-voiced in a Barthesian sense: "To write (middle) is to carry out the action (or better, to do writing) with reference to the self." Macaskill points out that "the highly specialized details of such linguistic inquiry are of no concern to [his] argument" but then presents a brief explication of the semantics of the middle voice in English "in the interests of establishing metaphoric grounds for subsequent discussion." That subsequent discussion, based on a metaphoric understanding of the middle voice, leads Macaskill to argue that the character Magda's writing in Coetzee's *In the Heart of the Country* "serves as a medial figure for Coetzee's middle-voice writing, that 'taking place' that here takes place between the strictures of self and other, language and history, intransitive and transitive utterance, practice and theory." As a metaphor the middle voice in literary interpretation can take almost any quality of the middle voice and project it as the quality that makes the literature under question "middle-voice-like." Thus for Macaskill a character's writing provides a "middle" operating at the levels of the self, history, language, and theory.[14]

For David C. Kress, Nathaniel Mackey's novel *Djbot Baghostus's Run* itself becomes a middle-voice verb. Kress argues that "the novel's beginning(s) and ending(s) are dispersed into the unfolding of the novel itself." This "unfolding" and an impression "that the style of the novel is to a large extent non-transitive" are among the reasons that Kress concludes that the novel "apparently has (or takes) no object other than process itself" and that "in this sense the novel could be compared to or thought of as a verb, or at least as having verb-like qualities, a verb in the middle voice." Hutchison's analysis of the metaphorical middle voice in Margaret Atwood's *Alias Grace* concentrates the essence of the literary middle voice in the narrator's voice. She argues that the middle voice lies in "signs of questionable agency in what concerns the narrating act" in the sense of who is speaking in the narrative and who controls the narration. In "Racial Wounding and the Aesthetics of the Middle Voice in *Absalom, Absalom!* and *Go Down, Moses*," Minrose Gwin connects several threads, among them trauma, racial wounding, and the middle voice, appealing to, among others, LaCapra's, Barthes's, Benveniste's, Derrida's, and White's discussions of the middle voice: "LaCapra believes that acting out, which enacts a repetitive resistance to working through trauma, also can be tied to the idea of the discursive equivalent of an extinct rhetorical mode called the middle voice, a model suggested by Hayden White as a form of discourse that might be useful or at least less inadequate than either testimony or interpretation in representing catastrophic events." Gwin's interpretive use of the middle in her discussion of *Absalom, Absalom!*, for example, is as "a voice that evokes not so much the past but the repetitious quality of traumatic wounding that endlessly recoils upon itself." Thus the voices and the pain of Rosa, Sutpen, Bond, and Quentin are merged in a middle voice: "The relationship of subject, object, and action becomes hopelessly muddled."[15]

In a fair indication of the continuing relevance of linguistic metaphors in literary study, the middle voice occasionally serves as the theoretical center of Ph.D. theses (for example, Harbour Fraser Hodder's 1991 exploration of the poetics of the middle in Dickinson, Whitman, and Hopkins and Yael Katz's 2000 use of the middle to explicate Nabokov's *Lolita* as "the fictional diary of a 'murderer,' a 'madman' and a writer" and as "a fictional record of the impossible moment which unites all three in a single voice, in the middle (voice)."[16] The middle voice has also been of use in film studies. Thomas M. Kavanaugh, who, although well before Henkel, announced the "fall of linguistic models in literary criticism," argues that the "actor's film" (for example, the Charles Bronson, Clint Eastwood or Jerry Lewis film) may be understood as discourse instances of the middle voice. Kavanaugh contends that the overwhelming centeredness of the actor in these kinds of movies, in which the plot and characterizations are secondary to the presence of the central actor, reveals the middle voice, "the voice of ideology": "It is the only voice ultimately coherent with that ideology of the unified subject so omnipotent as to appropriate to itself the power to create the entire world in which it acts." And as the best sign that the middle voice will continue to serve the metaphorical needs of interpretive humanities studies, Michael Joyce uses it in an analysis of the new "coherence" of computerized hypertext. Joyce argues that because it involves an affecting as well as affected subject, "the middle voice is a voice of coherence, offering us a lasting presence of particularities as a strategy against the fragmentary plenitude and multiplicity that faces and effaces us." The new coherence, Joyce argues, is characterized by "successive attendings to persisting forms," that is, by the shifting attention that is characteristic of users, producers, and productions of hypertext and the Web.[17]

Thus, as we have seen in this section, it is certainly not the case that linguistic metaphors disappeared with the death of structuralism. In particular, at least this one, the middle voice, serves decidedly poststructuralist uses. Whether those uses be historiographical, literary, rhetorical, political, philosophical, or some "middle" mixture of all or some, they all seem to concentrate on the metaphorical extension of the middle-voice conflation of the affected and the affecting subject. What perhaps best explains the attraction of the middle voice in relatively recent work in the interpretive humanities is that it can be used to explore poststructuralist concerns with, for example, the erasure of the distinction between the "subject" and the "object." And what is perfectly ironic about the middle voice as poststructuralist metaphor is that it was originally metaphorized from linguistics, itself the perfect embodiment of structuralism.

The Body in Literary Theory and O'Connor Studies

There is already a connection between the body and voice in linguistics, as we saw in chapter 2. The question now is what connections there might be in literary theory. Judith Wilt points out that feminist and postcolonial theories have demonstrated the metaphorical use of the body in economics, politics, and art and have argued that such metaphorical use has "played its part in the way we overlook, write out, and even outrage the material bodies of real persons in world culture." Narratology itself, as Daniel Punday observes, has almost nothing to say about the body.[18] What work has been done narratologically on the body in O'Connor is metaphorical. Thus Patricia Yaeger relies on the metaphorization of torture and specifically cutting, the first from Elaine Scarry and the second from Roland Barthes. As Yaeger points out, Scarry's analysis of torture casts the torturer as a bodiless voice and the tortured as a voiceless body. The dynamic is one of enormous power in which the tortured body evidences the power of the all-determining voice of the torturer. Yaeger recognizes her own "hyperbole" and the questionable and perhaps "reprehensible" analogy between real torture and reading; however, she finds it a useful analogy because "the description of O'Connor's writing as torture helps me to grasp something about O'Connor that—without the analogy—I would be unable to grasp." That torture reveals itself to Yaeger in the overwhelming presence of O'Connor's determining critical voice in her letters and essays. If we allow ourselves to be overdetermined by O'Connor's voice, Yeager argues, "we are left, then, with a primitive sadism that most critics convert into an old and comfortable theology." That sadism, then, is the lure for both readers and characters in O'Connor's fiction. As Barthes argues in *The Pleasure of the Text,* there are always "two edges" to reading: the comfortable one and the dangerous, unfamiliar one. Those edges are produced by what Barthes refers to as "cutting." The Barthesian safe edge, for Yaeger, is the visionary lyricism that one finds sometimes in O'Connor's fiction, as in the roadside scenery in "A Good Man Is Hard to Find": "The trees were full of silver-white sunlight and the meanest of them sparkled" (*GM,* 11). The Barthesian dangerous edge is, as Yaeger puts it, "the gritty pain of the body."[19] One sees, or feels, that gritty edge throughout O'Connor's fiction, as in the murders of the grandmother's family.

Perreault also writes against a comfortable theology in the interpretation of O'Connor, especially in the interpretation of the relation between body and spirit in "The Artificial Nigger." In particular, Perreault points out, "The central figure [for Nelson's growth] is the extraordinary body of the black woman, who is drawn for us in a more sensual way than is any other O'Connor character." Perreault is absolutely on target here; there is no other character in O'Connor whose body is so fully described as a signifier for the sexual body. In one sentence in particular Nelson's focalization of the woman's sensual embodiment is intensely revealing: "His eyes travelled up from her great knees to her forehead and then made a triangular path from the glistening sweat on her neck down and across her tremendous bosom and over her bare arm back to where her fingers lay hidden in her hair" (*GM,* 119; qtd. in Perreault). And it is in the concentration of redemption and bodily humanness, the significantly other for both Nelson and Mr. Head, where the problem of the story lies for Perreault: the frequently celebrated redemption of Mr. Head at the end of the story is simply a failure, for the reason that neither of the central white characters—Nelson or Mr. Head—truly identifies with the black body, either in the form of the sexualized woman or the tortured and marginalized "artificial nigger." Perreault recognizes the importance of the incarnational both to O'Connor herself and to her fiction; however, as she points out, the contextualized encounter of the spirit and the body, particularly in "The Artificial Nigger," with an unrepentant racist grandfather and a racist grandson in training, complicates that encounter. As Perreault says, O'Connor's "Catholicism demands a reconciliation of spirit with body, but for O'Connor neither body nor spirit can be abstracted from its material, social condition."[20]

The failure of particular characters to recognize in the racial other the unity of the body and spirit that they so desperately need is a common occurrence in O'Connor. In a letter to John Hawkes, O'Connor complained, "I am afraid that one of the great disadvantages of being known as a Catholic writer is that no one thinks you can lift the pen without trying to show somebody redeemed" (*CW,* 1146). In fact, one of the more interesting patterns in O'Connor is grace rejected, as in the case of Mr. Shiftlet at the end of "The Life You Save May Be Your Own" or Rayber in *The Violent Bear It Away* or Sheppard in "The Lame Shall Enter First" or Thomas in "The Comforts of Home." In her letter to Hawkes, O'Connor could have said the same of being known as an incarnational writer. Just as being a Christian writer does not guarantee redemption, being an incarnational writer does not guarantee recognition of the unity of body and spirit, even when they are presented with what might seem to the reader as an obvious unity. Consider Mrs. McIntyre's response to the sacrificial death of the Christ-like Mr. Guizac: "Mr. Guizac's body was covered with the bent bodies of his wife and two children and by a black one which hung over him, murmuring words she didn't understand. . . . She felt she was in some foreign country where the people bent over the body were natives, and she watched like a stranger while the dead man was carried away in the ambulance" (*GM,* 250). As Rachel Carroll argues, the body of the displaced person, more generally the body of the alien other in the Holocaust, serves as the site of repressed trauma—of unresolved "racial anxiety." Carroll's contention that the repressed trauma of "The Displaced Person" is racial in origin resembles, with the addition of the middle voice, the argument that Gwin makes about the "trauma of race and this history of southern slavery" in Faulkner. Gwin argues that "this repetitive wounding may indeed be heard to cry out in a discursive equivalent of the middle voice."[21] O'Connor repeatedly dramatizes the rejection of the spirit-body connection, whether that rejection be racist or not, specifically in her character's fear and consequent rejection of the body. There is the uncomprehending Hazel hearing the last confession of Solace Layfield as the blood seeps from him. There is Francis Tarwater afraid that he will catch the passion for the bread of life from his great uncle. It is the failure of these characters and many others to see the unity of spirit and flesh that in effect foregrounds O'Connor's concerns with the incarnational body. It may in fact have been possible for O'Connor to pick up a pen without effecting either redemption or the acceptance of the incarnational body; however, the failure of acceptance does not mean that the offer is not there.

A Reconciliation of the Body and Voice, Grammar and Meaning

In his *Narrative Bodies: Toward a Corporeal Narratology,* Punday details several ways in which the body enters meaningfully into a narrative. Among those ways that are interesting in a discussion of voice and the body in O'Connor's fiction are the following:

1. The ways in which authors differentiate between what is a body and what is not a body.
2. The ways in which the body and the not-body make contact.

These two questions, among the many that Punday asks, are fundamental because they explore the very definition of what a body is and what a body does. The answers to these questions allow us to indicate not only the particularities of O'Connor's grotesque bodies but also the stylistic communication of those bodies. Bakhtin argues, in fact, that what defines the grotesque body as different from "the classic and naturalist images" of the body is exactly the boundaries "between the body and the world and between separate bodies." O'Connor's grotesque, yet incarnational, vision is that there is very little separation between the human body and other bodies. As Di Renzo says of Mrs. Shortley's revelatory moment of death in "The Displaced Person," it "is expressed in purely corporeal terms. It is directly related to a new understanding of her body and its relationship to other bodies." In that revelation, Di Renzo argues, she "overcomes her xenophobia."[22] Consider some of the details of the revelation: "She thrashed forward and backward, clutching at everything she could get her hands on and hugging it to herself, Mr. Shortley's head, Sarah Mae's leg, the cat, a wad of white bedding, her own big moon-like knee; then all at once her fierce expression faded into a look of astonishment and her grip on what she had loosened" (*GM,* 223). Mrs. Shortley's final attempt to grasp the material extends not only to the bodies of other humans but also to her own body, the cat, and the inanimate wad of white bedding.

Of course drawing the boundary between the body and the not-body is one of the most vexing issues in human thought and behavior. It is in part what the sacramental theme in O'Connor is meant to address. For O'Connor there is an incarnational sense in which the body is the world. In "Writing Short Stories" she argues, "The fiction writer has to realize that he can't create compassion with compassion, or emotion with emotion, or thought with thought. He has to provide all these things with a body; he has to create a world with weight and extension" (*MM,* 92). The body is also something that O'Connor paid attention to in her reading, as Lake points out in her quotations from Arthur F. Kinney's annotated bibliography of O'Connor's library. O'Connor marked the following passage with marginal lining in Anton C. Pegis's preface to his *Introduction to Saint Thomas Aquinas:* "Man as a knower must be such that he can give existence, within his knowledge, not to abstract essences, but to sensible beings. That is why man as a knower needs a body."[23]

As we have seen throughout this book, O'Connor's literary sacramentalism is realized in part through her unrelenting concentration on the existence and action of the body and its parts. It is by now a well-known and understood human tendency to abstract both the body and language, as Derrida made clear in his explorations of phonocentrism and logocentrism in Western philosophy and Western linguistics. Leena Kore Schröder writes in a discussion of the body and metaphor in Virginia Woolf's writings, "Language is . . . a system that functions by virtue of effacing its own materiality: we find it all too easy to deal in meanings, and overlook the actual linguistics and phonetic conditions in which they are embodied." As I have pointed out elsewhere, the resistance to the abstraction of the body and language is most evident in O'Connor's time in the New Criticism, a theory that is famous for its celebration of the obstinacy of the literary object, its resistance to abstraction, and its potential for the protection of the world itself from pragmatic scientism. John Crowe Ransom, in particular, is insistent on the ability of literature to exceed the very objectivity of "scientific discourse." He says that the "worlds" that are described by "our scientific discourses" are "reduced, emasculated, and docile versions." He maintains that "poetry" (that is, literature) "intends to recover the denser and more refractory original world which we know loosely through our perceptions and memories." This is, of course, very close to the use that Friedl finds for the middle voice in articulating "being." Martin Gliserman has already introduced the final connections that I wish to make here—between the body and the sentence: "The author presents us with the shape and energy of sentences, and as we enter that realm, we try on those shapes and forces, as we might try on someone else's gesture to see what it feels like, or as when our face or hand spontaneously gets into a position that calls to mind another person's gesture and then feeling we understand that person for a moment. The sentence is physical; it puts us in various positions."[24] Gliserman's notion that the sentence is physical, that is, is a bodily experience, provides us with a way to think about the effect of O'Connor's body-filled middle constructions on our own body-filled understanding. Those sentences that describe, for example, eyes moving, faces turning, and heads lowering describe body actions that we find familiar and comfortable yet oddly disturbing as we find our familiar body actions worked out in O'Connor's grotesque world.

Some Final Thoughts

This book has demonstrated the potential of lexical analysis and collocational analysis as discovery procedures and, just as important, has also implicitly demonstrated the value of supplementing such a discovery procedure with further qualitative grammatical analysis. The log-likelihood and dispersion scores help us assemble a collection of statistically interesting collocations involving any particular word. What to make of those collocations, arrived at through computational collection and calculation, is then at least a two-step process. One must determine what, if any, grammatical patterns appear to be represented among the collocations and then what, if any, literary significance might be attached to those patterns. Thus more than half (seven) of the top thirteen collocations in O'Connor with the word *eyes* are representative of middle-voice semantics. These middle-voice semantics, in which the body part is either the agent-experiencer of the verb (for example, "eyes fixed," "eyes closed," "eyes moved") or the body-part reflexive of the verb (for example, "closed eyes," "rolled eyes," "shut eyes," "opened eyes"), can be connected to O'Connor's interest in the incarnational, specifically the spiritual significance of the human body. When O'Connor has the eyes perform events or the subject perform events on the eyes or even when the eyes serve as the focused stimulus for an unnamed experiencer, she makes use of constructions that are, probably individually, below the level of conscious attention of most casual readers. However, these patterns, in combination with many others not investigated here, help explain the wide recognition of the importance of the body and of the incarnational in O'Connor's fiction. There are other patterns involving the word *eyes;* the sheer high-frequency presence of the word *eyes* (and that for other body parts not discussed here) supports the incarnational as well. However, collocation analysis does give us the means to winnow the hundreds of tokens of the word *eyes,* and others, for the phrasal patterns that are statistically significant. Collocation analysis, then, provides us a powerful tool for discovery of stylistic patterns beyond the level of the individual word. However, lexical analysis itself is an effective method for deciding which words to look for in collocational patterns.

Stylistics, also, rather than being an abstraction, allows us to consider the body as it is manifested in the words and sentences of O'Connor's stories. There we find the conflict of the body and the nonbody dramatized repeatedly on the microlevel. In many ways contrary to poststructuralist caricatures of stylistics as part of an attempt to find comfort from the indeterminacies of life in formalism, the use of empirical evidence in stylistic work, at least as practiced in this book, finds tendencies rather than absolutes.[25] When one uses calculations that measure the strengths of relative frequencies, of either words alone or of collocations, the analyst explicitly recognizes the nonabsolute tendencies of word and collocation frequencies. Indeed the use of computers and statistical analysis in stylistics does not preclude rationalist methodologies; however, empirical methods allow the confirmation of literary intuition, allow the discovery of patterns that might otherwise not be noticed, and provide the opportunities for the confirmation of further hypotheses that develop from the empirical analyses themselves.

Occasional modern literary nostalgia for a grammatical construction such as the middle voice and the specific frequent modern literary idealization of the middle voice as a mode of language that fights everything from racism, to classism, to the effects of the Holocaust recalls the politicized, yet idealized, approach of the New Critics to the "truth" of literature. In the influential *Well Wrought Urn* (1947) Cleanth Brooks writes, "It is the scientist whose truth requires a language purged of every trace of paradox; apparently the truth which the poet utters can be approached only in terms of paradox."[26] If the embrace of the "politics" and meaning of the middle voice has any force at all, it should signal an openness not only to the self-affectedness of the historicity of poststructuralism but also to the self-affectedness of recent technological innovations that make possible the kind of relatively small-scale computational analysis such as I have performed in this book.

This book has not demonstrated that the stylistic link between the middle voice and interpretation is any more systematic or "scientific" than the metaphorical link between the middle voice and interpretation. Rather, the difference in analysis is that of the stylistic versus the metaphorical: stylistics looks to find linguistic form and/or semantics in the text as objects of discovery and analysis; the literary, historiographical, philosophical, and rhetorical use of the middle voice concentrates, as did much of structuralist poetics, on the level of the metaphorical, with relatively little attention to sentence-level semantics and form. Both stylistics and the interpretive humanities make interpretive moves at the level of the text. However, whereas the literary, historiographical, philosophical, and rhetorical interpretive use of the middle voice makes a direct connection from the meaning of the middle to the metaphorical meaning of the "middle" text, stylistics, as I have practiced it in this book, understands that the meaning of the text is diffused throughout any number of contextual and formal elements and that the meaning of specific middle or middle-related constructions supports that meaning only indirectly. There is, then, no "middle" O'Connor text. There might be incarnational texts or grotesque texts, however, that middle-voice constructions help to create.

It is unlikely that the continuing metaphorization of linguistic constructions in the interpretive humanities offers new hope of an integration of linguistics and literary study. Rather, it appears that the metaphorization of the middle—to name one example—is a scaled down (and poststructuralist) version of the type of sentence-to-text metaphorization that characterized structuralist poetics. It is likely that smaller scale metaphorized linguistic models, rather than the large-scale models that Henkel announced as having come to an end in literary studies seventeen years ago, will continue to surface sporadically as theorists occasionally discover linguistic constructions, such as the middle voice, that can be metaphorized in ways that support whatever theory (structural, poststructural, cultural) has currency at that time. And those small-scale metaphorizations seem much more desirable than further attempts at grand unification, such as the structuralists' attempts, because at that smaller scale the differences between linguistic stylistics and linguistically metaphorized literary interpretation are clearest and, thus, more likely to engender appreciation for the fundamental differences in the objects and modes of investigation in our respective disciplines.

Appendix

Texts Sampled for the Fiction Brown Subcorpora

The following are the sources for the K, L, M, N, and P subcorpora of the Brown Corpus. Each of the samples of the texts within these subcorpora, randomly selected from the fiction texts in the Brown University library, numbers approximately 2,000 words. The random nature of this sampling ensures that one type of general literature is not sampled more frequently than another. O'Connor's texts are represented as the foreground against this assumed background of statistical literary normality. Please note that material published in fiction anthologies listed below was often published (and copyrighted) before it was collected in these books. This bibliographical information is taken from W. N. Francis and H. Kucera's *Brown Corpus Manual,* Providence, Rhode Island, Department of Linguistics, Brown University, 1979. http://khnt.hit.uib.no/icame/manuals/brown/INDEX.HTM (8.9.07)

K01. Davis, Christopher. *First Family.* New York: Coward McCann, 1961, 204–10.
K02. Barbeau, Clayton C. *The Ikon.* New York: Coward McCann, 1961, 80–85.
K03. Coffin, Tristram. *Not to the Swift.* New York: W. W. Norton, 1961, 200–4.
K04. DuBois, W. E. B. *Worlds of Color.* New York: Mainstream, 1961, 134–39.
K05. Stacton, David. *The Judges of the Secret Court.* New York: Pantheon Books, 1961, 50–56.
K06. Zara, Louis. *Dark Rider.* Cleveland, Ohio: World Publishing, 1961, 40–44.
K07. Pollini, Francis. *Night.* Boston: Houghton Mifflin, 1961, 246–52.
K08. Endore, Guy. *Voltaire! Voltaire!* New York: Simon and Schuster, 1961, 96–100.
K09. Fast, Howard. *April Morning.* New York: Crown, 1961, 130–36.
K10. Barr, Glayds H.. *The Master of Geneva.* New York: Holt, Rinehart and Winston, 1961, 152–57.
K11. Warren, Robert Penn. *Wilderness.* New York: Random House, 1961, 162–70.
K12. Green, Gerald. *The Heartless Light.* New York: Charles Scribner's Sons, 1961, 166–70.
K13. Maxwell, William. *The Chateau.* New York: Alfred A. Knopf, 1961, 240–45.
K14. Stone, Irving. *The Agony and the Ecstasy.* Garden City, N.Y.: Doubleday, 1961, 294–98.
K15. Hebson, Ann. *The Lattimer Legend.* New York: Macmillan, 1961, 190–95.
K16. Longstreet, Stephen. *Eagles Where I Walk.* Garden City, N.Y.: Doubleday, 1961, 92–96.

K17. Uris, Leon. *Mila 18.* Garden City, N.Y.: Doubleday, 1961, 324–29.

K18. Dos Passos, John. *Midcentury.* Boston: Houghton Mifflin, 1961, 94–98.

K19. Duncan, Robert L. 1961. *The Voice of Strangers.* Garden City, N.Y.: Doubleday, 242–48.

K20. Bolton, Guy. *The Olympians.* Cleveland and New York: World Publishing, 1961, 128–34.

K21. Palmer, Bruce. *My Brother's Keeper: Many Are the Hearts.* New York: Simon and Schuster, 1961, 132–38.

K22. Cheever, John. "The Brigadier and the Golf Widow." *New Yorker* 39 (1961): 53–54.

K23. Arkin, Frieda. "The Light of the Sea." In *The Best American Short Stories,* ed. Martha Foley and David Burnett. Boston: Houghton Mifflin, 1961, 2–6.

K24. Gass, W. H. "The Pedersen Kid." In *The Best American Short Stories,* ed. Foley and Burnett. Boston: Houghton Mifflin, 1961, 110–15.

K25. Miller, Arthur. "The Prophecy." In *The Best American Short Stories,* ed. Foley and Burnett. Boston: Houghton Mifflin, 1962, 258–62.

K26. Rushing, Jane Gilmore. "Against the Moon." *Virginia Quarterly Review* 37, no. 3 (1961): 378–83.

K27. Myers, E. Lucas. "The Vindication of Dr. Nestor." *Sewanee Review* 69, no. 2 (1961): 290–95.

K28. Bingham, Sallie. "Moving Day." *Atlantic Monthly* 208, no. 5 (1961): 63–65.

K29. Schiller, Marvin. "The Sheep's in the Meadow." *Antioch Review* 21, no. 3 (1961) 336–40.

L01. Van Atta, Winfred. *Shock Treatment.* Garden City, N.Y.: Doubleday, 1961, 24–31.

L02. Fair, A. A. *Bachelors Get Lonely.* New York: William Morrow, 1961, 82–89.

L03. Dean, Amber. *Encounter with Evil.* Garden City, N.Y.: Doubleday, 1961, 48–54.

L04. Alexander, David. *Bloodstain.* Philadelphia: J. B. Lippincott, 1961, 128–34.

L05. Halliday, Brett. *The Careless Corpse.* New York: Dodd, Mead, 1961, 136–43.

L06. Dewey, Thomas B. *Hunter at Large.* New York: Simon and Schuster, 1961, 118–124.

L07. Holden, Genevieve. *Deadlier Than the Male.* Garden City, N.Y.: Doubleday, 1961, 96–104.

L08. Shannon, Dell. *The Ace of Spades.* New York: William Morrow, 1961, 184–91.

L09. Eberhart, Mignon G. *The Cup, the Blade or the Sword.* New York: Random House, 1961, 126–32.

L10. Olesker, Harry. *Impact.* New York: Random House, 1961, 94–101.

L11. Stone, Hampton. *The Man Who Looked Death in the Eye.* New York: Simon and Schuster, 1961, 56–62.

L12. Masterson, Whit. *Evil Come, Evil Go.* New York: Pocket Books, 1961, 49–55.

L13. Hitchens, Dolores. *Footsteps in the Night.* Garden City, N.Y.: Doubleday, 1961, 156–61.

L14. Lockridge, Frances, and Richard Lockridge. *Murder Has Its Points.* Philadelphia: J. B. Lippincott, 1961, 96–101.

L15. Miles Disney, Doris. *Mrs. Meeker's Money.* Garden City, N.Y.: Doubleday, 72–78.

L16. Gordon, Alex. *The Cipher.* New York: Simon and Schuster, 1961, 238–45.

L17. James, Breni. *Nights of the Kill.* New York: Simon and Schuster, 1961, 114–22.
L18. Harmon Coxe, George. *Error of Judgement.* New York: Alfred A. Knopf, 1961, 24–29.
L19. Williams, Brad. *Make a Killing.* New York: M. S. Mill / William Morrow, 1961, 196–203.
L20. Lacy, Ed. "Death by the Numbers." *Manhunt* 9, no. 4 (1961): 8–12.
L21. McCloy, Helen. "The Black Disk." *Ellery Queen's Mystery Magazine* 37, no. 4 (1961): 23–27.
L22. Barlow, S. L. M. "Monologue of Murder." *The Saint Mystery Magazine* 15, no. 2 (1961): 121–25.
L23. Rose, J. W. "Try My Sample Murders." *Trapped Detective Story Magazine* 6, no. 2 (1961): 45–50.
L24. Brown, Fredric. *The Murderers.* New York: E. P. Dutton, 1961, 116–22.
M01. Heinlein, Robert. *Stranger in a Strange Land.* New York: G. P. Putnam's Sons, 1961, 250–55.
M02. Farmer, Philip José. *The Lovers.* New York: Ballantine Books, 1961, 37–42.
M03. Blish, James. *The Star Dwellers.* New York: Avon, 1961, 83–88.
M04. Harmon, Jim. "The Planet with No Nightmare." *If* 11, no. 3 (1961), 7–12.
M05. McCaffrey, Anne. "The Ship Who Sang." In *The Year's Best S-F,* ed. Judith Merril. New York: Dell, 1961, 311–17.
M06. Smith, Cordwainer. "A Planet Named Shayol." In *The Year's Best S-F,* ed. Judith Merril. New York: Dell, 1961, 353–58.
N01. Overholser, Wayne D. *The Killer Marshal.* 1961; rpr. New York: Dell, 1963, 53–58.
N02. Irving, Clifford. *The Valley.* New York: McGraw-Hill, 1961, 262–67.
N03. Farrell, Cliff. *Trail of the Tattered Star.* Garden City, N.Y.: Doubleday, 1961, 168–73.
N04. Horan, James D. *The Shadow Catcher.* New York: Crown, 1961, 248–53.
N05. Ferber, Richard. *Bitter Valley.* New York: Dell, 1961, 9–17.
N06. Anderson, Thomas. *Here Comes Pete Now.* New York: Random House, 1961, 4–12.
N07. Ballard, Todhunter. *The Night Riders.* New York: Pocket Books, 1961, 5–11.
N08. Savage, Mary. *Just for Tonight.* New York: Dodd, Mead, 1961, 114–20.
N09. Thompson, Jim. *The Transgressors.* New York: New American Library of World Literature, 1961, 9–13.
N10. Chadwick, Joseph. *No Land Is Free.* New York: Avon, 1961, 21–26.
N11. Caesar, Gene. *Rifle for Rent.* Derby, Conn.: Monarch, 1963, 46–51.
N12. Booth, Edwin. *Outlaw Town.* New York: Ballantine, 1961, 103–8.
N13. Ferguson McKeown, Martha. *Mountains Ahead.* New York: G. P. Putnam's Sons, 1961, 390–95.
N14. Field, Peter. *Rattlesnake Ridge.* New York: Jefferson, 1961, 164–72.
N15. Plantz, Donald J. Sweeney Squadron. New York: Dell, 1961, 133–38.
N16. Salisbury, Ralph J. "On the Old Santa Fe Trail to Siberia." *Northwest Review* 4, no. 2 (1961): 52–56.
N17. Prather, Richard S. "The Bawdy Beautiful." *Cavalier* 11, no. 94 (1961): 64–65.
N18. Bains, Peter. "With Women . . . Education Pays Off." *Monsieur* 4, no. 2 (1961): 17, 77–78.

N19. Jackson, David. "The English Gardens." *Partisan Review* 28, no. 2 (1961): 216–21.
N20. McClary, T. C. "The Flooded Desert." *Argosy* 352, no. 4 (1961): 27, 104–6.
N21. Sommers, C. T. "The Beautiful Mankillers of Eromonga." *Cavalcade* (1961): 60, 62.
N22. Johnson, Gordon. "A Matter of Curiosity." *Yale Review* 50, no. 4 (1961): 556–60.
N23. Hall, Wheeler. "Always Shoot to Kill." *Bluebook for Men* 100, no. 7 (1961): 34–35, 52–53.
N24. Brown III, T. K. "The Fifteenth Station." *Playboy* 8, no. 7 (1961): 36–38.
N25. Newton, Wesley. "Aid and Comfort to the Enemy." *University of Kansas City Review* 27, no. 3 (1961): 210–13.
N26. Brock, Paul. "Toughest Lawman in the Old West." *Rage Magazine* 1, no. 4 (1961): 41–43, 60.
N27. Hines, James, and James Morris. "Just Any Girl." *Swank* 8, no. 6 (1961): 37, 66–68.
N28. Grimshaw, Ralph. "Mrs. Hacksaw: New Orleans' Society Killer." *Sir!* 18, no. 1 (1961): 56–58.
N29. Ellison, Harlan. "Riding the Dark Train Out," *Rogue* 6, no. 5 (1961): 14, 30.
P01. Waldo, Octavia. *A Cup of the Sun.* New York: Harcourt, Brace, 1961, 8–14.
P02. Ritner, Ann. *Seize a Nettle.* Philadelphia: J. B. Lippincott, 1961, 158–62.
P03. McMeekin, Clark. *The Fairbrothers.* New York: G. P. Putnam's Sons, 1961, 258–64.
P04. Chute, B. J. *The Moon and the Thorn.* New York: E. P. Dutton, 1961, 34–41.
P05. Bosworth, Allen R. *The Crows of Edwina Hill.* New York: Harper and Brothers, 1961, 26–31.
P06. Tiernan, Richard. "Land of the Silver Dollar." In *The Quixote Anthology,* ed. Jean Rikhoff, Kam Tiernan, and Richard Tiernan. New York: Grosset's Universal Library, 1961, 36–40.
P07. Delmar, Vina. *The Big Family.* New York: Harcourt, Brace, 1961, 206–11.
P08. Gourse, R. Leslie. *With Gall and Honey.* Garden City, N.Y.: Doubleday, 1961, 272–76.
P09. Ford, Jesse Hill. *Mountains of Gilead.* Boston: Little, Brown, 1961, 128–33.
P10. Williams, Jay. *The Forger.* New York: Atheneum, 1961, 4–8.
P11. Breuer, Bessie. *Take Care of My Roses.* New York: Atheneum, 1961, 168–76.
P12. Callaghan, Morley. *A Passion in Rome.* New York: Coward-McCann, 1961, 124–29.
P13. Hanes, Frank Borden. *The Fleet Rabble.* New York: L. C. Page, 1961, 40–44.
P14. Biddle, Jr., Livingston. *Sam Bentley's Island.* New York: Doubleday, 1961, 70–75.
P15. Burrough, Loretta. "The Open Door." *Good Housekeeping* 152, no. 5 (1961): 117–18.
P16. Brown, Margery Finn. "A Secret Between Friends." *Redbook* 116, no. 4 (1961): 104–10.
P17. Hine, Al. "The Huntress." *Saturday Evening Post* (February 4, 1961): 29, 84–85.
P18. [Anonymous.] "No Room in My Heart to Forgive." *Modern Romances* 56, no. 11 (1961): 76–78.
P19. [Anonymous.] "This Cancer Victim May Ruin My Life." *Medical Story* 1, no. 1 (1961): 18–21, 36.
P20. Norris, Spencer. "Dirty Dog Inn." *Dude* 6, no. 1 (1961): 9–10, 28–30.
P21. Spencer, Elizabeth. "The White Azalea." *Texas Quarterly* 4, no. 4 (1961): 112–15.

P22. [Anonymous.] "A Husband Stealer from Way Back." *True Love* 76, no. 3 (1961): 6–7, 12.

P23. Robinson, Barbara. "Something Very Much in Common." *McCall's* 88, no. 11 (1961): 172–74.

P24. Elkin, Samuel. "The Ball Player." *Nugget* 6, no. 5 (1961): 25–26, 31.

P25. Butler, William "The Pool at Ryusenji." *Harper's Bazaar* 94, no. 2990 (1961): 146–47.

P26. Krause, Ervin D. "The Snake." *Prize Stories 1963: The O. Henry Awards.* New York: Doubleday, 1963; first published in *Prairie Schoone*r (Summer 1961).

P27. McGiffin, Lee. "Measure of a Man." *Ladies' Home Journal* 78, no. 6 (1961): 103–4.

P28. Hoover, Carol. "The Shorts on the Bedroom Floor." *Story* 34, no.133 (1961): 38–42.

P29. Carson, Robert. *My Hero.* New York: McGraw-Hill, 1961, 170–74.

Notes

Chapter 1: The Body in Flannery O'Connor's Fiction

1. References to studies that explore this insight will occur throughout the book, but the latest important studies are Susan Srigley, *Flannery O'Connor's Sacramental Art* (Notre Dame, Ind.: University of Notre Dame Press, 2004), and Christine Bieber Lake, *The Incarnational Art of Flannery O'Connor* (Macon, Ga.: Mercer University Press, 2005). Less recent studies are John F. Desmond, *Risen Sons: Flannery O'Connor's Vision of History* (Athens: University of Georgia Press, 1987), 32–50; Kathleen Feeley, *Flannery O'Connor: Voice of the Peacock* (New Brunswick, N.J.: Rutgers University Press, 1972), 113–39. Throughout the text words, parts of words, and phrases under consideration are highlighted in bold type.
2. Gilbert H. Muller, *Nightmares and Visions: Flannery O'Connor and the Catholic Grotesque* (Athens: University of Georgia Press, 1972), 34, 67, 111; James W. Horton, "Flannery O'Connor's Hermaphrodite: Notes toward a Theology of Sex," *Flannery O'Connor Bulletin* 23 (1994–95): 31.
3. Lake, *Incarnational Art,* 9–10; Srigley, *Sacramental Art,* 10, 7.
4. Patricia Yaeger, "The Woman without Any Bones: Anti-Angel Aggression in *Wise Blood,*" in *New Essays on* Wise Blood, ed. Michael Kreyling (Cambridge: Cambridge University Press, 1995), 105.
5. Sharon Cameron, *The Corporeal Self: Allegories of the Body in Melville and Hawthorne* (Baltimore: Johns Hopkins University Press, 1981), 3, 6; for discussions of body parts in Steinbeck, see Geoffrey N. Leech and Michael H. Short, *Style in Fiction: A Linguistic Introduction to English Fictional Prose* (London: Longman, 1981), 191; in Faulkner, see Michael Toolan "Syntactical Styles as a Means of Characterization in Narrative," *Style* 19, no. 1 (1985): 84; in Anderson, Hemingway, and West, see Jeffrey Meyers, "Introduction," *Winesburg, Ohio,* by Sherwood Anderson (New York: Bantam, 1995), xvii; in the Southwestern Humorists, see Milton Rickels, "The Grotesque Body of Southwestern Humor," in *Critical Essays on American Humor,* ed. William Bedford Clark and W. Craig Turner (Boston: G. K. Hall, 1984), 155–66; Jonathan Hall, "The Evacuations of Falstaff (*The Merry Wives of Windsor*)," in *Shakespeare and Carnival: After Bakhtin,* ed. Ronald Knowles (New York: Macmillan, 1998), 123–51; Sean Benson, "'Even to the Gates of Rome': Grotesque Bodies and Fragmented Stories in *Coriolanus,*" *Comitatus* 30 (1999): 96; Malcolm Andrews,

"Dickens, Comedy, and Disintegration," in *Dickens: The Craft of Fiction and the Challenges of Reading,* ed. Rossana Bonadei et al. (Milan, Italy: Unicopli, 2000), 125–39; B. M. Sagar, "Physical Appearance of Characters in Novels," *Literary Criterion* 26, no. 3 (1991): 53–55.

6. Henry Taylor, "The Halt Shall Be Gathered Together: Physical Deformity in the Fiction of Flannery O'Connor," *Western Humanities Review* 22 (1968): 325; for discussion of Hulga Hopewell's disability, see Anthony Di Renzo, *American Gargoyles: Flannery O'Connor and the Medieval Grotesque* (Carbondale: Southern Illinois University Press, 1993), 73ff.; for discussion of Asbury Fox, see Jeffrey J. Folks, "'The Enduring Chill': Physical Disability in Flannery O'Connor's *Everything That Rises Must Converge,*" *University of Dayton Review* 22 (1993–1994): 81–88.

7. See the treatment of Mrs. May's "iron hand" in Hsiu-chih Tsai, "Disrupted Narratives: O'Connor's Feminine Grotesque," *Concentric: Literary and Cultural Studies* 30, no. 2 (2004): 43; Mary Glenn Freeman, "Flannery O'Connor and the Quality of Sight: A Standard for Writing and Reading," *Flannery O'Connor Bulletin* 16 (1987): 26–33; Miles Orvell, *Invisible Parade: The Fiction of Flannery O'Connor* (Philadelphia: Temple University Press, 1972), 83–86, 140; Marshall Bruce Gentry, *Flannery O'Connor's Religion of the Grotesque* (Jackson: University Press of Mississippi, 1986), 120–21; James M. Mellard, "Framed in the Gaze: Haze, *Wise Blood,* and Lacanian Reading," in *New Essays on* Wise Blood, ed. Michael Kreyling (Cambridge: Cambridge University Press, 1995), 51–69; Larue Love Sloan, "The Rhetoric of the Seer: Eye Imagery in Flannery O'Connor's 'Revelation,'" *Studies in Short Fiction* 25, no. 2 (1988): 135–45.

8. Folks, "'The Enduring Chill,'" 83. Others who have analyzed the effects of lupus on O'Connor's fiction include Josephine Hendin, *The World of Flannery O'Connor* (Bloomington: Indiana University Press, 1970), 39–40; Susanna Gilbert, "'Blood Don't Lie': The Diseased Family in Flannery O'Connor's *Everything That Rises Must Converge,*" *Literature and Medicine* 18, no. 1 (1999): 114–31; William Frank Monroe, "Bringing the Script to Life: The Case of Flannery O'Connor," *Journal of Medical Humanities* 15, no. 2 (1994): 101–11; Monroe, "Flannery O'Connor and the Celebration of Embodiment," in *The Good Body: Asceticism in Contemporary Culture,* ed. Mary G. Winkler and Letha B. Cole (New Haven: Yale University Press, 1994), 171–88; Sue Walker, "Spelling Out Illness: Lupus as Metaphor in Flannery O'Connor's 'Greenleaf,'" *Chattahoochee Review* 12, no. 1 (1991): 54–63.

9. Hendin, *The World of Flannery O'Connor,* 28, 63; Laurence Enjolras, *Flannery O'Connor's Characters* (New York: University Press of America, 1998), 14; Martha Stephens, *The Question of Flannery O'Connor* (Baton Rouge: Louisiana State University Press, 1973), 9–10; Lake, *Incarnational Art,* 9, 190, 193.

10. Barbara Korte, *Body Language in Literature* (Toronto: University of Toronto Press, 1997), 29–30, 34.

11. Stephen R. Portch, *Literature's Silent Language: Nonverbal Communication* (New York: Peter Lang, 1985), 152.

12. Joanne Halleran McMullen, *Writing against God: Language as Message in the Literature of Flannery O'Connor* (Macon, Ga.: Mercer University Press, 1996), 12–13, 97–98; Leech and Short, *Style in Fiction,* 189–91; Chris Kennedy, "Systemic Gram-

mar and Its Use in Literary Analysis," in *Language and Literature: An Introductory Reader in Stylistics,* ed. Ronald Carter (London: Allen and Unwin, 1982), 83–99; Walter Nash, "On a Passage from Lawrence's 'Odour of Chrysanthemums,'" in *Language and Literature,* ed. Carter, 101–20.

13. M. A. K. Halliday, "Linguistic Function and Literary Style: An Inquiry into the Language of William Golding's *The Inheritors,*" in *Literary Style: A Symposium,* ed. Seymour Chatman (New York: Oxford University Press, 1971), 330–65; David Hoover, *Language and Style in* The Inheritors (Lanham, Md.: University Press of America, 1999), 69.
14. Di Renzo, *American Gargoyles,* 66; Mikhail Bakhtin, *Rabelais and His World,* trans. Helene Iswolsky (Bloomington: Indiana University Press, 1984), 125–26.
15. Frederick Asals, *Flannery O'Connor: The Imagination of Extremity* (Athens: University of Georgia Press, 1982), 65ff.; Robert H. Brinkmeyer, Jr., "'Jesus, Stab Me in the Heart!': *Wise Blood,* Wounding, and Sacramental Aesthetics," in *New Essays on* Wise Blood, ed. Michael Kreyling (Cambridge: Cambridge University Press, 1995), 71–89; Thomas M. Carlson, "Flannery O'Connor: The Manichaean Dilemma," *Sewanee Review* 77, no. 2 (1969): 254–76; Hendin, *The World of Flannery O'Connor,* 62–96.
16. John Hawkes, "Flannery O'Connor's Devil," *Sewanee Review* 70, no. 7 (1962): 399.
17. Edward Kessler, *Flannery O'Connor and the Language of Apocalypse* (Princeton: Princeton University Press, 1986), 79–80; Monroe, "Bringing the Script to Life," 106.
18. Paula M. Uruburu, *The Gruesome Doorway: An Analysis of the American Grotesque* (New York: Peter Lang, 1987), 8.
19. Sally Fitzgerald, "Note on the Text," in *Collected Works,* by Flannery O'Connor (New York: Library of America, 1988), 1260.
20. Ben Satterfield, "*Wise Blood,* Artistic Anemia, and the Hemorrhaging of O'Connor Criticism," *Studies in American Fiction* 17, no. 1 (1989): 45, 37, 33; Irving Malin, "Flannery O'Connor and the Grotesque," in *The Added Dimension: The Art and Mind of Flannery O'Connor,* ed. Melvin J. Friedman and Lewis A. Lawson (New York: Fordham University Press, 1966), 112; Hendin, *The World of Flannery O'Connor,* 63–64; McMullen, *Writing against God,* 62, 70.
21. Wilson Yates, "An Introduction to the Grotesque: Theoretical and Theological Considerations," in *The Grotesque in Art and Literature: Theological Reflections,* ed. James Luther Adams and Wilson Yates (Grand Rapids, Mich.: Eerdmans, 1997), 61; Roger Hazelton, "The Grotesque, Theologically Considered," in *The Grotesque in Art and Literature: Theological Reflections,* ed. James Luther Adams and Wilson Yates (Grand Rapids, Mich.: Eerdmans, 1997), 76.
22. William Van O'Connor, *The Grotesque: An American Genre and Other Essays* (Carbondale: Southern Illinois University Press, 1962), 3–19; Brinkmeyer, "'Jesus, Stab Me in the Heart!,'" 81; Ralph C. Wood, "The Catholic Faith of Flannery O'Connor's Protestant Characters: A Critique and Vindication," *Flannery O'Connor Bulletin* 13 (1984): 23.
23. Portch, *Literature's Silent Language,* 122; Folks, "The Enduring Chill," 84; Gary M. Ciuba, "From Face Value to the Value in Faces: *Wise Blood* and the Limits of Literalism," *Modern Language Studies* 19 (1989): 72; Di Renzo, *American Gargoyles,* 81, 73, 91; Stephens, *The Question of Flannery O'Connor,* 4; Lake, *Incarnational Art,* 210.

24. Carol Shloss, *Flannery O'Connor's Dark Comedies: The Limits of Inference* (Baton Rouge: Louisiana State University Press, 1980), 44–45.
25. Uruburu, *The Gruesome Doorway*, 127.
26. Jeanne Perreault, "The Body, the Critics, and 'The Artificial Nigger,'" *Mississippi Quarterly: The Journal of Southern Cultures* 3 (2003): 402. Perreault uses some of the quotations from O'Connor's letter in her argument (391–92).
27. Orvell, *Invisible Parade,* 46.
28. See Suzanne Kemmer, *The Middle Voice* (Amsterdam: John Benjamins, 1993), 53, on the term *body action,* which will be explained in depth in chapter 2.
29. Gérard Genette, *Narrative Discourse: An Essay in Method,* trans. Jane E. Lewin (Ithaca: Cornell University Press, 1972), 31, 186–87; see also Gerald Prince, *A Dictionary of Narratology* (Lincoln: University of Nebraska Press, 2003), 104.
30. Bakhtin, *The Dialogic Imagination: Four Essays,* trans. Caryl Emerson and Michael Holquist (Austin: University of Texas Press, 1981), 284–85.
31. Donald E. Hardy, "The Dialogic Repetition of Free Indirect Discourse in Oral and Literary Narrative," in *Repetition in Dialogue,* ed. Carla Bazzanella (Tübingen: Niemeyer, 1996), 90–103.
32. Gregory Ward, Betty Birner, and Rodney Huddleston, "Information Packaging," in *The Cambridge Grammar of the English Language,* ed. Huddleston and Geoffrey K. Pullum (Cambridge: Cambridge University Press, 2002), 1427. See also Leonard Bloomfield, *Language* (New York: Holt, 1933), 258, and John Lyons, *Introduction to Theoretical Linguistics* (Cambridge: Cambridge University Press, 1968), 372ff.
33. Huddleston, "The Clause: Complements," in *The Cambridge Grammar of the English Language,* ed. Huddleston and Pullum, 307.
34. James D. Benson, William S. Greaves, and Glenn Stillar, "Transitivity and Ergativity in 'The Lotos-Eaters,'" *Language and Literature* 4, no. 1 (1995): 31–35.
35. See Susan Hunston's *Corpora in Applied Linguistics* (Cambridge: Cambridge University Press, 2002), 128–30, for a short overview of the use of corpora in stylistics.
36. John Sinclair, *Corpus, Concordance, Collocation* (Oxford: Oxford University Press, 1991), 170; see Masahiro Hori, *Investigating Dickens' Style: A Collocational Analysis* (New York: Palgrave, 2004), 3–29, for a history of collocational analysis; see also the remainder of the book for an approach to the stylistic analysis of collocation that is different from my own in many interesting ways.
37. Ted Dunning, "Accurate Methods for the Statistics of Surprise and Coincidence," *Computational Linguistics* 19, no. 1 (1993): 71

Chapter 2: Grammatical Voice

1. See Michael Stubbs, *Text and Corpus Analysis: Computer-Assisted Studies of Language and Culture* (Cambridge, Mass.: Blackwell, 1996), 132–34, 154–56, for discussion of the "terminological confusion" surrounding linguistic analysis of the passive, the middle, the ergative, and other manifestations of linguistic voice.
2. See M. A. K. Halliday and Christian M. I. M. Matthiessen, *An Introduction to Functional Grammar* (London: Edward Arnold, 2004), 180–82, for discussion of the terms *actor* and *goal.* Terminology is also a problem with designations for semantic roles such as *actor* and *goal,* which are referred to sometimes in others' works as

agent and *patient,* respectively. Because I will need the term *agent* later for a different semantic role and because systemic linguistics recognizes all of the differences among the roles that I need in this study, I will be using the systemic terms.

3. T. Givón, *English Grammar: A Function-Based Introduction,* vol. 2 (Amsterdam: John Benjamins, 1993), 46–48. Givón uses the terms *agent* and *patient* (see note 2 above).
4. Kemmer, *The Middle Voice,* 1, 16.
5. E. J. W. Barber, "Voice—beyond the Passive," *Proceedings of the First Annual Meeting of the Berkeley Linguistics Society* 1 (1975): 16–24; William A. Foley and Robert D. Van Valin, Jr., *Functional Syntax and Universal Grammar* (Cambridge: Cambridge University Press, 1984), 322; M. H. Klaiman, "Affectedness and Control: A Typology of Voice Systems," in *Passive and Voice,* ed. Masayoshi Shibatani (Philadelphia: John Benjamins, 1988), 33.
6. Huddleston, "The Clause," 307; Randolph Quirk, et al., *A Comprehensive Grammar of the English Language* (London: Longman, 1985), 735–36.
7. Dominick LaCapra, *Writing History, Writing Trauma* (Baltimore: Johns Hopkins University Press, 2001), 19.
8. Data and some analysis from Donald E. Hardy, "Middle Voice in Creek," *International Journal of American Linguistics* 60 (1994): 39–68.
9. The subjects in (10) and (11) are actually a medium and an agent, respectively, rather than a goal and an actor. I do not introduce the terms *medium* and *agent* until later in this chapter, when the distinction is important. Because I have not yet introduced the crucial pattern of ergativity, the pairs *goal/medium* and *actor/agent* are effectively synonymous here. See Kemmer, *The Middle Voice,* on the terms *facilitative* and *body action,* 147, 53.
10. Kristin Davidse and Leisbet Heyvaert, "On the Middle Construction in English and Dutch," in *Corpus-Based Approaches to Contrastive Linguistics and Translation Studies,* ed. Sylviane Granger, Jacques Lerot, and Stephanie Petch-Tyson (Amsterdam: Rodopi, 2003), 61ff.; Givón, *English Grammar,* vol. 2, 75.
11. Davidse and Heyvaert, "On the Middle Construction," 12; Lindsay J. Whaley, *Introduction to Typology: The Unity and Diversity of Language* (Thousand Oaks, Calif.: Sage, 1997), 158–59;
12. R. M. W. Dixon, "Ergativity," *Language* 55 (1979): 61.
13. The terms *medium* here and *agent* below are both explained in greater depth in Halliday and Matthiessen, *An Introduction to Functional Grammar,* 282–90; Davidse, "Transitivity/Ergativity: The Janus-Headed Grammar of Actions and Events," in *Advances in Systemic Linguistics: Recent Theory and Practice,* ed. M. Davies and Louise Ravelli (London: Pinter, 1992), 108–9.
14. Halliday and Matthiessen, *An Introduction to Functional Grammar,* 286, 289; Davidse, "Transitivity/Ergativity," 109.
15. See Davidse, "Transitivity/Ergativity," 109, and Halliday and Matthiessen, *An Introduction to Functional Grammar,* 288, for similar demonstrations.
16. Davidse, "Transitivity/Ergativity," 118.
17. Davidse, "Transitivity/Ergativity," 118; Davidse and Heyvaert, "On the Middle Construction," 68.

18. Davidse and Heyvaert ("On the Middle Construction," 61) reference Samuel J. Keyser and Thomas Roeper for the "all by itself" test: Keyser and Roeper, "On the Middle and Ergative Constructions in English," *Linguistic Inquiry* 15 (1984): 381–416.
19. Davidse, "Transitivity/Ergativity," 109.
20. Davidse and Heyvaert, "On the Middle Construction," 68–69; Leonard Talmy, "Semantic Causative Types," in *Syntax and Semantics: The Grammar of Causative Constructions,* ed. Masayoshi Shibatani (New York: Academic, 1976), 76–78; Givón, *English Grammar,* vol. 2, 9–10; data from Eric Buyssens, "The Active Voice with Passive Meaning in Modern English," *English Studies* 60, no. 6 (1979): 748. See Leech and Short, *Style in Fiction,* 88, for the term *quasi simile,*
21. Buyssens, "The Active Voice with Passive Meaning," 748.
22. Givón, *English Grammar,* vol. 2, 75.
23. Kemmer, *The Middle Voice,* 73, 207–10.
24. The facilitative construction is also variously called the "medio-passive" or the "patient-subject" construction. For the resultative middle, see Hardy, "Middle Voice in Creek," 45–47. For the facilitative middle, as well as "passive-middle" types, which include what I refer to here as the resultative middle, see Kemmer, *The Middle Voice,* 147–49. For the medio-passive and patient-subject constructions see, respectively, Michael Grady, "The Medio-Passive Voice in Modern English," *Word* 21 (1965): 270–72, and Jeanne Van Oosten, "Subjects and Agenthood in English," *Proceedings of the Chicago Linguistic Society* 13 (1977): 459.
25. Kemmer, *The Middle Voice,* 53, 68, 209.
26. Kemmer, *The Middle Voice,* 72–73.
27. Halliday and Matthiessen, *An Introduction to Functional Grammar,* 285; Davidse, "Transitivity/Ergativity," 109; Kemmer, *The Middle Voice,* 73, 207–10.
28. Barbara Fox, "Body Part Syntax: Towards a Universal Characterization," *Studies in Language* 5, no. 3 (1981): 331.
29. Davidse, "Transitivity/Ergativity," 118; Davidse and Heyvaert, "On the Middle Construction," 61; Keyser and Roeper, "Middle and Ergative Constructions," 405; Leonard Faltz, *Reflexivization: A Study in Universal Syntax* (New York: Garland, 1985) 13, 128; Kemmer, *The Middle Voice,* 147; Davidse, "Transitivity/Ergativity," 114.
30. Davidse and Heyvaert, "On the Middle Construction," 68.
31. For general discussion of ergativity and the semanitcs of the medium, see Kristin Davidse and Sara Geyskens, "*Have You Walked the Dog Yet?* The Ergative Causativization of Intransitives," *Word* 49 (1998): 161.

Chapter 3: The Statistical Body

1. Mutual information scores and t-scores are sometimes used to analyze collocations, as in K. W. Church and P. Hanks "Word Association Norms, Mutual Information, and Lexicography," *Computational Linguistics* 16, no. 1 (1990): 22–29. We will not do so in this book because mutual information scores have the same problems demonstrated later in this chapter for χ^2, that is, overestimation of significance with low-frequency events (Christopher D. Manning, and Hinrich Schütze, *Foundations of Statistical Natural Language Processing* [Cambridge: MIT Press, 2001], 181). As

also detailed by Manning and Schütze, t-scores are specifically used to test the probability of collocations, as in Elisabeth Breidt, "Extraction of V-N-Collocations from Text Corpora: A Feasibility Study for German," Seminar für Sprachwissenshaft, Universität Tübingen, 1995 http://arxiv.org/PS_cache/cmp-lg/pdf/9603/9603006v1.pdf (8.9.07); because we will not be testing probability, for the reasons outlined in this chapter we will also not be using t-scores.

2. See Tony McEnery and Andrew Wilson, *Corpus Linguistics* (Edinburgh: Edinburgh University Press, 1996), 4–10, and Graeme Kennedy, *An Introduction to Corpus Linguistics* (London: Longman, 1998), 23–24, for discussions of Chomsky's turn of linguistics towards rationalism and the influence of that turn on corpus linguistics. The ANC is available through http://americannationalcorpus.org/ (8.11.06); the BNC through http://www.natcorp.ox.ac.uk/ (8.11.06); COBUILD through http://www.collins.co.uk/ (8.11.06); and Brown through the International Computer Archive of Modern and Medieval English at http://nora.hd.uib.no/icame.html (8.11.06).
3. The LOB is also available through the International Computer Archive of Modern and Medieval English at http://nora.hd.uib.no/icame.html (8.11.06). The *Brown Corpus Manual* is available at http://khnt.hof.uib.no/icame/manuals/brown/INDEX.HTM (6.30.06). A bibliography of texts sampled for the Brown texts appears in the appendix of this book.
4. For MonoConc, see http://www.athel.com/ (8.11.06); for WordSmith, see http://www.lexically.net/wordsmith/ (8.11.06). For discussions of the advantages of writing one's own program for text analysis, see Douglas Biber, Susan Conrad, and Randi Reppen, *Corpus Linguistics: Investigating Language Structure and Use* (Cambridge: Cambridge University Press, 1998), 255–56.
5. For stoplists see Manning and Schütze, *Foundations of Statistical Natural Language Processing*, 533–34. For keywords see Mike Scott "Comparing Corpora and Identifying Key Words, Collocations: Frequency Distributions through the WordSmith Tools Suite of Computer Programs," in *Small Corpus Studies and ELT: Theory and Practice*, ed. Mohen Ghadessy, Alex Henry, and Robert L. Roseberry (Amsterdam: Benjamins, 2001), 47–67, and Paul Baker "Querying Keywords: Questions of Difference, Frequency, and Senses in Keyword Analysis," *Journal of English Linguistics* 32, no. 4 (2004): 346–59.
6. Adam Kilgarriff, "Comparing Corpora," *International Journal of Corpus Linguistics* 6, no. 1 (2001): 97–98.
7. Michael P. Oakes, *Statistics for Corpus Linguistics* (Edinburgh: Edinburgh University Press, 1998), 9–10. See also Kilgarriff, "Which Words Are Particularly Characteristic of a Text? A Survey of Statistical Approaches," *Information Technology Research Institute Technical Report Series, ITRI-96–08* (Brighton: University of Brighton, 1996), 2, for discussion of hypothesis testing and randomness. See also Kay Wikberg, "The Style Marker *As If (Though)*: A Corpus Study," in *Out of Corpora: Studies in Honour of Stig Johansson*, ed. Hilde Hasselgard and Signe Oksefjell (Amsterdam: Rodopi, 1999), 303; Randolph Quirk, *Grammatical and Lexical Variance in English* (London: Longman, 1995), 113–19; Charles F. Meyer, *English Corpus Linguistics: An Introduction* (Cambridge: Cambridge University Press, 2002), 100–37;

Donald E. Hardy, *Narrating Knowledge in Flannery O'Connor's Fiction* (Columbia: University of South Carolina Press, 2003); for WordSmith, see http://www.lexically.net/wordsmith/ (8.11.06).

8. Anne De Roeck, Avik Sarkar, and Paul H. Garthwaite, "Defeating the Homogeneity Assumption," *7es Journées Internationales d'Analyse Statistique des Données Textuelles* (2004): 282–94 http://www.cavi.univ-paris3.fr/lexicometrica/jadt/jadt2004/pdf/JADT_026.pdf (1.7.07); John F. Burrows, "Numbering the Streaks of the Tulip? Reflections on a Challenge to the Use of Statistical Methods in Computational Stylistics," *Centre for Computing in the Humanities Working Papers* (1996). http://www.chass.utoronto.ca/epc/chwp/burrows/ (8.11.06).
9. Sinclair, *Corpus, Concordance, Collocation,* 109–10.
10. Kilgarriff, "Which Words."
11. Oakes, *Statistics for Corpus Linguistics,* 9–10; Burrows, "Numbering the Streaks of the Tulip?"
12. Dunning, "Accurate Methods," 64, 71; Paul Rayson and Roger Garside, "Comparing Corpora Using Frequency Profiling," *Proceedings of the Workshop on Comparing Corpora* (2000). http://www.comp.lancs.ac.uk/computing/users/paul/publications/rg_acl2000.pdf (11.23.04); Geoffrey Leech, Paul Rayson, and Andrew Wilson, *Word Frequencies in Written and Spoken English: Based on the British National Corpus* (Harlow, U.K.: Longman, 2001), 16–17; Kilgarriff and Tony Rose, "Measures for Corpus Similarity and Homogeneity," *Information Technology Research Institute Technical Report Series, ITRI-98–07* (Brighton: University of Brighton, 1998). http://www.itri.brighton.ac.uk/techindex.html (3.17.05).
13. Oakes, *Statistics for Corpus Linguistics,* 200–201.
14. Lake, *Incarnational Art,* 55–56, 59–60.
15. Hardy, *Narrating Knowledge in Flannery O'Connor's Fiction,* 114ff.
16. Sinclair, *Corpus, Concordance, Collocation,* 170.
17. Muller, *Nightmares and Visions,* 10–11; Di Renzo, *American Gargoyles,* 25.
18. Susan Hunston, "Review of *Word Frequencies in Written and Spoken English: Based on the British National Corpus,*" *Language Awareness* 11, no. 2 (2002): 155; Elena Semino and Mick Short, *Corpus Stylistics: Speech, Writing, and Thought Presentation in a Corpus of English Writing* (London: Routledge, 2004), 66; Hunston's own *Corpora in Applied Linguistics,* 70ff., takes care to explain the significance and calculation of t-score and mutual information, which are the measures of collocation that she uses.
19. McEnery and Wilson, *Corpus Linguistics,* 68.
20. Knut Hofland and Stig Johansson, *Word Frequencies in British and American English* (Bergen: Norwegian Computing Centre for the Humanities, 1982), 14; G. Udny Yule, *The Statistical Study of Literary Vocabulary* (Cambridge: Cambridge University Press, 1944); Rayson and Garside, "Comparing Corpora"; Rayson, "Matrix: A Statistical Method and Software Tool for Linguistic Analysis Through Corpus Comparison" (Ph.D. diss., Lancaster University, 2003), 43.
21. Yule, *Statistical Study,* 57; Rayson and Garside, "Comparing Corpora"; Rayson, "Matrix," 43; Hofland and Johansson, *Word Frequencies,* 14.

22. For the importance of the amount of information in statistical tests, see variously Rayson and Garside, "Comparing Corpora"; Kilgarriff, "Which Words," 2; and Kilgarriff, "Comparing Word Frequencies across Corpora: Why Chi-Square Doesn't Work, and an Improved LOB-Brown Comparison," *ALLC-ACH '96* (1996): 170. http://gandalf.aksis.uib.no/allc/kilgarny.pdf (8.11.06).
23. See Rayson, "Matrix," 196; Kilgarriff, "Comparing Corpora," 2; Christopher Butler, *Statistics in Linguistics* (Oxford: Blackwell, 1985), 118–23.
24. Oakes, *Statistics for Corpus Linguistics,* 25.
25. Butler, *Statistics in Linguistics,* 119.
26. Many references contain the details of the χ^2 calculation, including Oakes, *Statistics for Corpus Linguistics,* 24–27; Butler, *Statistics in Linguistics,* 118–23; the particular formula here is from Manning and Schütze, *Foundations of Statistical Natural Language Processing,* 169.
27. For what is called the "Yates's correction," see Oakes, *Statistics for Corpus Linguistics,* 25. Because of rounding in the calculation of χ^2 expected frequencies in the sample calculation, the equation will not equal 7.21 although 7.21 is the accurate value.
28. Kilgarriff, "Comparing Word Frequencies," 170; Rayson, "Matrix," 97.
29. Kilgarriff, "Comparing Corpora," 7; Oakes, *Statistics for Corpus Linguistics,* 172; Dunning "Accurate Methods"; Kilgarriff, "Which Words"; Rayson, Damon Berridge, and Brian Francis, "Extending the Cochran Rule for the Comparison of Word Frequencies between Corpora," *7es Journées Internationales d'Analyse Statistique des Données Textuelles* (2004): 929; Béatrice Daille, "Combined Approach for Terminology Extraction: Lexical Statistics and Linguistic Filtering," Technical Paper (Lancaster, U.K.: University Centre for Computer Corpus Research on Language, Lancaster University, 1995), 22. http://www.comp.lancs.ac.uk/ucrel/papers/techpaper/vol5.pdf (8.11.06).
30. Leech, Rayson, and Wilson, *Word Frequencies,* 17; Rayson and Garside, "Comparing Corpora"; Rayson, "Matrix," 97.
31. Dunning, "Accurate Methods," 71.
32. Kessler, *Language of Apocalypse,* 15; David R. Mayer, "'Like Ticks off a Dog': Flannery O'Connor's 'As If,'" *Christianity and Literature* 33, no. 4 (1984): 17; Melvin J. Friedman, "Flannery O'Connor's Sacred Objects," in *The Vision Obscured: Perceptions of Some Twentieth-Century Catholic Novelists,* ed. Friedman (New York: Fordham University Press, 1970), 71.
33. Dunning, "Accurate Methods," 71; Manning and Schütze, *Foundations of Statistical Natural Language Processing,* 181–82; Oakes, *Statistics for Corpus Linguistics,* 171–72.
34. See Dunning, "Accurate Methods," 70–71, not only for the contingency table but also for discussion of the logic behind comparing distributions of bigrams (two-word combinations) within a single corpus, a discussion that I summarize below table 7.
35. See Dunning, "Accurate Methods," 71–73, for similar proof and results with different data.
36. Tony Berber-Sardinha, "Comparing Corpora with WordSmith Tools: How Large Must the Reference Corpus Be?" *Annual Meeting of the ACL: Proceedings of the*

Workshop on Comparing Corpora 9 (2000): 7; Rayson, "Matrix," 128–29.

37. See Manning and Schütze, *Foundations of Statistical Natural Language Processing,* 533–34, on the use of stoplists.
38. Leech, Rayson, and Wilson, *Word Frequencies,* 17; Rayson, "Matrix," 36, 93.
39. Anthony A. Lyne, *The Vocabulary of French Business Correspondence: Word Frequencies, Collocations, and Problems of Lexicometric Method* (Paris: Slatkine, 1985), 102–3; Oakes, *Statistics for Corpus Linguistics,* 190; Leech, Rayson, and Wilson, *Word Frequencies,* 18; Rayson, "Matrix," 93–94; Lyne, "In Praise of Juilland's 'D': A Contribution to the Empirical Evaluation of Various Measures of Dispersion Applied to Word Frequencies," in *Méthodes Quantitatives et Informatiques dans l'Étude des Textes,* ed. Etienne Brunet (Geneva: Slatkine-Champion, 1986), 589.
40. Rayson, "Matrix," 93–94; Oakes, *Statistics for Corpus Linguistics,* 190.

Chapter 4: The Body

1. Srigley, *Sacramental Art,* 18; Avis Hewitt, "'Ignoring Unmistakable Likeness': Mark Fortune's Miss-Fortune in 'A View of the Woods,'" in *"On the Subject of the Feminist Business": Re-Reading Flannery O'Connor,* ed. Teresa Caruso (New York: Peter Lang, 2004), 144; Natalie Wilson, "Misfit Bodies and Errant Gender: The Corporeal Feminism of Flannery O'Connor," in *"On the Subject of the Feminist Business": Re-Reading Flannery O'Connor,* ed. Caruso, 107; Lake, *Incarnational Art,* 36.
2. See Hardy, *Narrating Knowledge in Flannery O'Connor's Fiction,* 46ff., for a full discussion of assumptions, such as this, as linguistic presuppositions.
3. Gentry, *Flannery O'Connor's Religion of the Grotesque,* 58.
4. See Gentry, *Flannery O'Connor's Religion of the Grotesque,* 59, both for the connection between religion and sex for Mrs. May as well as for Mrs. May's reaction to Mrs. Greenleaf.
5. Ciuba, "Face Value," 73.
6. Yaeger "The Woman without any Bones," 105; Brinkmeyer, "'Jesus, Stab Me in the Heart!,'" 80–81.
7. Kemmer, *The Middle Voice,* 25–28, 34–35, 63. Kemme notes, ". . . English maintains a similar meaning distinction between zero-marked and reflexive-marked verbs in these classes" (63).
8. Penelope Brown and Stephen Levinson, *Politeness: Some Universals in Language Usage* (Cambridge: Cambridge University Press, 1987), 13–15.
9. Some of the many critical discussions of "intellect" and "knowledge" in O'Connor's fiction include the following: Stephen C. Behrendt, "Knowledge and Innocence in Flannery O'Connor's 'The River,'" *Studies in American Fiction* 17, no. 2 (1989): 143–55; Desmond, *Risen Sons,* 34ff.; Bob Dowell, "The Moment of Grace in the Fiction of Flannery O'Connor," *College English* 27 (1965): 236; Hardy, *Narrating Knowledge in Flannery O'Connor's Fiction,* 1–8; Kessler, *Language of Apocalypse,* 75–112; John F. McCarthy, "Human Intelligence versus Divine Truth: The Intellectual in Flannery O'Connor's Works," *English Journal* 55 (1966): 1143; Michael L. Schroeder, "Ruby Turpin, Job, and Mystery: Flannery O'Connor on the Question of Knowing," *Flannery O'Connor Bulletin* 21 (1992): 79; Shloss, *Flannery O'Connor's Dark Comedies,* 48.

10. Horton, "Flannery O'Connor's Hermaphrodite," 33.
11. Yaeger, "The Woman without any Bones," 109.
12. Thomas H. Brown, "O'Connor's Use of Eye Imagery in *Wise Blood*," *South Central Bulletin* 37 (1977): 138–40; Freeman, "Flannery O'Connor and the Quality of Sight," 26; William E. Meyer, Jr., "Flannery O'Connor's 'Two Sets of Eyes,'" *Southern Studies* 25 (1986): 284; Mellard, "Framed in the Gaze," 55; Orvell, *Invisible Parade*, 168.
13. Patricia D. Maida, "Light and Enlightenment in Flannery O'Connor's Fiction," *Studies in Short Fiction* 13 (1979): 32; Sloan, "The Rhetoric of the Seer," 135–36; Hardy, *Narrating Knowledge in Flannery O'Connor's Fiction*, 114–57; Malin, "The Grotesque," 113; Gentry, *Flannery O'Connor's Religion of the Grotesque*, 113; Mellard, "Framed in the Gaze," 55.
14. John Sinclair, *Trust the Text: Language Corpus, and Discourse* (London: Routledge, 2004), 32–33, 142.
15. Van O'Connor, *The Grotesque*, 18.
16. Ward, Birner, and Huddleston, "Information Packaging," 1436–37; Givón, *English Grammar*, vol. 2, 76–77.

Chapter 5: The Bifurcated Self

1. See Hardy, *Narrating Knowledge in Flannery O'Connor's Fiction*, 166–67, for a discussion of this and other manipulations of point of view in "A Circle in the Fire."
2. John Haiman, *Talk Is Cheap: Sarcasm, Alienation, and the Evolution of Language* (Oxford: Oxford University Press, 1998), 74.
3. George Lakoff, "Sorry, I'm Not Myself Today: The Metaphor System for Conceptualizing the Self," in *Spaces, Worlds, and Grammar*, ed. Gilles Fauconnier and Eve Sweetser (Chicago: University of Chicago Press, 1996), 92–95, 101–2, 109–13; Horton ("Flannery O'Connor's Hermaphrodite") explores some of the same dichitomous "head" vs. "body" issues in "A Temple of the Holy Ghost" using the terms *subject* and *object*.
4. Faltz, *Reflexivization*, 239 (qtd. in Saha); Givón, *English Grammar*, vol. 2, 94–95; P. K. Saha, "Strategies of Reflexivization in American English," *American Speech* 62, no. 3 (1987): 216.
5. Kaoru Fukuda, "On Emphatic Reflexives," *English Linguistics* 6 (1989): 38.
6. Givón, *English Grammar*, vol. 2, 89.
7. Kemmer, *The Middle Voice*, 34–35, 63, 64–65.
8. Kemmer, *The Middle Voice*, 64–65.
9. Kemmer, *The Middle Voice*, 34–35, 64–65.
10. McMullen, *Writing against God*, 132–33.
11. Suzanne Morrow Paulson, "Apocalypse of Self, Resurrection of the Double: Flannery O'Connor's *The Violent Bear It Away*," in *Flannery O'Connor: New Perspectives*, ed. Sura P. Rath and Mary Neff Shaw (Athens: University of Georgia Press, 1996), 122; Mellard, "Flannery O'Connor's Others: Freud, Lacan, and the Unconscious," *American Literature* 61, no. 4 (1989): 632ff.; Hendin, *The World of Flannery O'Connor*, 63; Horton "Flannery O'Connor's Hermaphordite."
12. In a 1955 letter to Robie Macauley O'Connor used the phrase in a description of an upcoming television interview: "Everybody who has read *Wise Blood* thinks I'm a

hillbilly nihilist, whereas I would like to create the impression over the television that I am a hillbilly Thomist . . ." (*HB*, 81).

13. Srigley, *Sacramental Art*, 5; Monroe, "Flannery O'Connor's Sacramental Icon: 'The Artificial Nigger,'" *South Central Review* 1, no. 4 (1984): 71; Paul W. Nisly, "The Prison of the Self: Isolation in Flannery O'Connor's Fiction," *Studies in Short Fiction* 17, no. 1 (1980): 51–54; Lake, *Incarnational Art*, 36–37.
14. John R. Clark, *The Modern Satiric Grotesque and Its Traditions* (Lexington: University Press of Kentucky, 1991), 15.
15. Lake, *Incarnational Art*, 141–78.

Chapter 6: Conclusions

1. Daniel Kies, "The Uses of Passivity: Suppressing Agency in *Nineteen Eighty-Four*," in *Advances in Systemic Linguistics: Recent Theory and Practice*, ed. Martin Davies and Louise Ravelli (London: Pinter, 1992), 231–32; M. Angeles Martínez, "From 'Under the Rose' to *V*: A Linguistic Approach to Human Agency in Pynchon's Fiction," *Poetics Today* 23, no. 4 (2002): 644–49.
2. Zelda Boyd, "The Grammar of Representation in Psychoanalysis and Literature," in *The Psychoanalytic Study of Literature*, ed. Joseph Reppen and Maurice Charney (Hillsdale, N.J.: Analytic Press, 1985), 115–16, qtd. in McMullen, *Writing against God*, 23–24; Halliday and Matthiessen, *An Introduction to Functional Grammar*, 284–85.
3. McMullen, *Writing against God*, 22–24.
4. Jacqueline M. Henkel, "Linguistic Models and Recent Criticism: Transformational-Generative Grammar as Literary Metaphor," *PMLA* 105, no. 3 (1990): 448.
5. Henkel, "Linguistic Models and Recent Criticism," 449, 455; Jonathan Culler, *Structuralist Poetics: Structuralism, Linguistics, and the Study of Literature* (London: Routledge, 1975), 113; Ellen Schauber and Ellen Spolsky, *The Bounds of Interpretation: Linguistic Theory and Literary Text* (Stanford: Stanford University Press, 1986), 9; Gerald Prince, *Narratology: The Form and Functioning of Narrative* (Berlin: Mouton, 1982), 80–81; Roger Seamon, "Poetics against Itself: On the Self-Destruction of Modern Scientific Criticism," *PMLA* 104, no. 3 (1989): 298–99; Henkel, "Linguistic Models and Recent Criticism," 454.
6. Prince, *Narratology*, 83ff., 81; Culler, *Structuralist Poetics*, 113–30; Henkel, "Linguistic Models and Recent Criticism," 454–55; Seamon, "Poetics against Itself," 298.
7. Genette, *Narrative Discourse*, 31–32, 212; Lorna Hutchison, "The Book Reads Well: Atwood's *Alias Grace* and the Middle Voice," *Pacific Coast Philology* 38 (2003): 40.
8. Roland Barthes, "To Write: An Intransitive Verb?," in *The Structuralist Controversy: The Languages of Criticism and the Sciences of Man*, ed. Richard Macksey and Eugenio Donato (Baltimore: Johns Hopkins University Press, 1972), 142, 136; Emile Benveniste, *Problems in General Linguistics*, trans. Mary Elizabeth Meek (Coral Gables: University of Miami Press, 1971), 59–60, 145–51.
9. Hayden White, "Historical Emplotment and the Problem of Truth," in *Probing the Limits of Representation: Nazism and the "Final Solution,"* ed. Saul Friedlander (Cambridge: Harvard University Press, 1992), 47, 50–51; White, "Writing in the Middle Voice," *Stanford Literature Review* 9, no. 2 (1992): 179–87; Berel Lang, *Act*

and Idea in the Nazi Genocide (Chicago: University of Chicago Press, 1990), xii, referenced in White, "Historical Emplotment," 47.

10. LaCapra, *Writing History,* 29–30; Hans Kellner, "'Never Again' Is Now," *History and Theory* 33, no. 2 (1994): 133–35.
11. Jacques Derrida, *Speech and Phenomena: And Other Essays on Husserl's Theory of Signs,* trans. David B. Allison (Evanston: Northwestern University Press, 1973), 130, 137; for discussion of Derrida and the middle voice, see LaCapra, *Writing History,* 20ff., in addition to Pecora and Pepper (cited in note 12 below), both of whom are footnoted by LaCapra (*Writing History,* 20, 199) as sources he encountered after completing his own writing. Also for discussion of this passage, see White, "Historical Emplotment," 49.
12. Vincent P. Pecora, "Ethics, Politics, and the Middle Voice," *Yale French Studies* 79 (1991): 207 (Pecora quotes from a different translation); Thomas Pepper, *Singularities: Extremes of Theory in the Twentieth Century* (Cambridge: Cambridge University Press, 1997), 52, 72.
13. Herwig Friedl, "Thinking in Search of a Language: Pragmatism and the Muted Middle Voice," *Amerikastudien* 47, no. 4 (2002): 478, 480, 486; Bradford Vivian, *Being Made Strange: Rhetoric Beyond Representation* (New York: State University of New York Press, 2004), 60; Pepper, *Singularities,* 52 n. 4.
14. J. M. Coetzee, "A Note on Writing," in *Momentum: On Recent South African Writing,* ed. M. J. Daymond, J. U. Jacobs, and Margaret Lenta (Pietermaritzburg, South Africa: University of Natal Press, 1984), 11; Coetzee is quoted in Teresa Dovey, "J. M. Coetzee: Writing in the Middle Voice," in *Essays on African Writing: A Re-Evaluation,* ed. Abdulrazak Gurnah (Oxford: Heinemann, 1993), 57; Brian Macaskill, "Charting J. M. Coetzee's Middle Voice," *Contemporary Literature* 25, no. 3 (1994): 450, 466.
15. David C. Kress, "Middle Voice Moves in Nathaniel Mackey's *Djbot Baghostus's Run,*" *Callaloo: A Journal of African-American and African Arts and Letters* 23, no. 2 (2000): 778–79; Hutchison, "The Book Reads Well," 55; Minrose C. Gwin, "Racial Wounding and the Aesthetics of the Middle Voice in *Absalom, Absalom!* and *Go Down, Moses,*" *Faulkner Journal* 20 (Fall 2004 / Spring 2005): 23, 30.
16. Harbour Fraser Hodder, "In the Middle Voice: Philologies of Poesis in Dickinson, Whitman, and Hopkins" (Ph.D. diss., Harvard University, 1991); Yael Katz, "Configuring Crisis: Writing, Madness, and the Middle Voice" (Ph.D. diss., University of British Columbia, 2000), 66; Katz also briefly appeals to Kemmer's semantic view of the middle ("Configuring Crisis," 200–202.
17. Thomas M. Kavanaugh, "The Middle Voice of Film Narration," *Diacritics* 9, no. 3 (1979): 58; Michael Joyce, "New Stories for New Readers: Contour, Coherence, and Constructive Hypertext," in *Page to Screen: Taking Literacy into the Electronic Era,* ed. Ilana Snyder (London: Routledge, 1998), 176–77.
18. Judith Wilt, "The Cave of the Body: The Heart of the Matter," *Religion and the Arts* 1, no. 3 (1997): 73; Daniel Punday, *Narrative Bodies: Toward a Corporeal Narratology* (New York: Palgrave, 2003), 2–3.
19. Patricia Yaeger, "Flannery O'Connor and the Aesthetics of Torture," in *Flannery O'Connor: New Perspectives,* ed. Sura P. Rath and Mary Neff Shaw (Athens: University of Georgia Press, 1996), 192, 191, 195; Elaine Scarry, *The Body in Pain: The Making*

and Unmaking of the World (New York: Oxford University Press, 1985), 57; Barthes, *The Pleasure of the Text,* trans. Richard Miller (New York : Hill and Wang, 1975), 6–7.

20. Perreault, "The Body, the Critics, and 'The Artificial Nigger,'" 402, 404, 390.
21. Rachel Carroll, "Foreign Bodies: History and Trauma in Flannery O'Connor's 'The Displaced Person,'" *Textual Practice* 14, no. 1 (2000): 102; Gwin, "Racial Wounding," 23–24.
22. Punday, *Narrative Bodies,* 58–61, 63–66; Bakhtin, *Rabelais and His World,* 315; Di Renzo, *American Gargoyles,* 67.
23. Arthur F. Kinney, *Flannery O'Connor's Library: Resources of Being* (Athens: University of Georgia Press, 1985), 72; see Lake, *Incarnational Art,* 18, 203, for similar passages marked by O'Connor in Pegis and Aquinas.
24. Derrida, *Speech and Phenomena;* Leena Kore Schröder, "Virginia Woolf and the Body: Corporeality, Metaphor, and the In-Between," *Virginia Woolf Bulletin* 3 (2000): 17; John Crowe Ransom, *The New Criticism* (Norfolk, Conn.: New Directions, 1941), 281; see Donald E. Hardy, "Linguistics and Literary Theory: The Dancer and the Dance," *Southwest Journal of Linguistics* 10, no. 2 (1991), for details on the New Criticism and linguistics; Martin Gliserman, *Psychoanalysis, Language, and the Body of the Text* (Gainesville: University Press of Florida, 1996), 10.
25. See Stanley Fish, "What Is Stylistics and Why Are they Saying Such Terrible Things about It?," in *Approaches to Poetics,* ed. Seymour Chatman (New York: Columbia University Press, 1973), for one of the best-known of these caricatures.
26. Cleanth Brooks, *The Well Wrought Urn: Studies in the Structure of Poetry* (New York: Harcourt, 1947), 3; also see Hardy, "Linguistics and Literary Theory," for discussion of Brooks, paradox, and linguistics.

Bibliography

Andrews, Malcolm. "Dickens, Comedy, and Disintegration." In *Dickens: The Craft of Fiction and the Challenges of Reading,* edited by Rossana Bonadei et al., 125–39. Milan, Italy: Unicopli, 2000.

Asals, Frederick. *Flannery O'Connor: The Imagination of Extremity.* Athens: University of Georgia Press, 1982.

Baker, Paul. "Querying Keywords: Questions of Difference, Frequency, and Senses in Keyword Analysis." *Journal of English Linguistics* 32, no. 4 (2004): 346–59.

Bakhtin, Mikhail. *The Dialogic Imagination: Four Essays.* Translated by Caryl Emerson and Michael Holquist. Austin: University of Texas Press, 1981.

———. *Rabelais and His World.* Translated by Helene Iswolsky. Bloomington: Indiana University Press, 1984.

Barber, E. J. W. "Voice—beyond the Passive." *Proceedings of the First Annual Meeting of the Berkeley Linguistics Society* 1 (1975): 16–24.

Barthes, Roland. *The Pleasure of the Text.* Translated by Richard Miller. New York: Hill and Wang, 1975.

———. "To Write: An Intransitive Verb?" In *The Structuralist Controversy: The Languages of Criticism and the Sciences of Man,* edited by Richard Macksey and Eugenio Donato, 134–45. Baltimore: Johns Hopkins University Press, 1972.

Behrendt, Stephen C. "Knowledge and Innocence in Flannery O'Connor's 'The River.'" *Studies in American Fiction* 17, no. 2 (1989): 143–55.

Benson, James D., William S. Greaves, and Glenn Stillar. "Transitivity and Ergativity in 'The Lotos-Eaters.'" *Language and Literature* 4, no. 1 (1995): 31–48.

Benson, Sean. "'Even to the Gates of Rome': Grotesque Bodies and Fragmented Stories in *Coriolanus.*" *Comitatus* 30 (1999): 95–112.

Benveniste, Emile. *Problems in General Linguistics.* Translated by Mary Elizabeth Meek. Coral Gables: University of Miami Press, 1971.

Berber-Sardinha, Tony. "Comparing Corpora with WordSmith Tools: How Large Must the Reference Corpus Be?" *Annual Meeting of the ACL: Proceedings of the Workshop on Comparing Corpora* 9 (2000): 7–13.

Biber, Douglas, Susan Conrad, and Randi Reppen. *Corpus Linguistics: Investigating Language Structure and Use.* Cambridge: Cambridge University Press, 1998.

Bloomfield, Leonard. *Language.* New York: Holt, 1933.

Boyd, Zelda. "The Grammar of Representation in Psychoanalysis and Literature." In *The Psychoanalytic Study of Literature,* edited by Joseph Reppen and Maurice Charney, 107–24. Hillsdale, N.J.: Analytic Press, 1985.

Breidt, Elisabeth. "Extraction of V-N-Collocations from Text Corpora: A Feasibility Study for German." Seminar für Sprachwissenshaft. Universität Tübingen, 1995. http://arxiv.org/PS_cache/cmp-lg/pdf/9603/9603006v1.pdf (8.9.07).

Brinkmeyer, Robert H., Jr. "'Jesus, Stab Me in the Heart!': *Wise Blood,* Wounding, and Sacramental Aesthetics." In *New Essays on* Wise Blood, edited by Michael Kreyling, 71–89. Cambridge: Cambridge University Press, 1995.

Brooks, Cleanth. *The Well Wrought Urn: Studies in the Structure of Poetry.* New York: Harcourt, 1947.

Brown, Penelope, and Stephen Levinson. *Politeness: Some Universals in Language Usage.* Cambridge: Cambridge University Press, 1987.

Brown, Thomas H. "O'Connor's Use of Eye Imagery in *Wise Blood.*" *South Central Bulletin* 37 (1977): 138–40.

Burrows, John F. "Numbering the Streaks of the Tulip? Reflections on a Challenge to the Use of Statistical Methods in Computational Stylistics." *Centre for Computing in the Humanities Working Papers,* 1996. http://www.chass.utoronto.ca/epc/chwp/burrows/ (11.23.04).

Butler, Christopher. *Statistics in Linguistics.* Oxford: Blackwell, 1985.

Buyssens, Eric. "The Active Voice with Passive Meaning in Modern English." *English Studies* 60, no. 6 (1979): 745–61.

Cameron, Sharon. *The Corporeal Self: Allegories of the Body in Melville and Hawthorne.* Baltimore: Johns Hopkins University Press, 1981.

Carlson, Thomas M. "Flannery O'Connor: The Manichaean Dilemma." *Sewanee Review* 77, no. 2 (1969): 254–76.

Carroll, Rachel. "Foreign Bodies: History and Trauma in Flannery O'Connor's 'The Displaced Person.'" *Textual Practice* 14, no. 1 (2000): 97–114.

Church, K. W., and P. Hanks. "Word Association Norms, Mutual Information, and Lexicography." *Computational Linguistics* 16, no. 1 (1990): 22–29.

Ciuba, Gary M. "From Face Value to the Value in Faces: *Wise Blood* and the Limits of Literalism." *Modern Language Studies* 19 (1989): 72–80.

Clark, John R. *The Modern Satiric Grotesque and Its Traditions.* Lexington: University Press of Kentucky, 1991.

Coetzee, J. M. "A Note on Writing." In *Momentum: On Recent South African Writing,* edited by M. J. Daymond, J. U. Jacobs, and Margaret Lenta, 11–13. Pietermaritzburg, South Africa: University of Natal Press, 1984.

Culler, Jonathan. *Structuralist Poetics: Structuralism, Linguistics, and the Study of Literature.* London: Routledge, 1975.

Daille, Béatrice. "Combined Approach for Terminology Extraction: Lexical Statistics and Linguistic Filtering." Technical Paper. Lancaster, U.K.: University Centre for Computer Corpus Research on Language, Lancaster University, 1995. http://www.comp.lancs.ac.uk/ucrel/papers/techpaper/vol5.pdf (8.11.06).

Davidse, Kristin. "Transitivity/Ergativity: The Janus-Headed Grammar of Actions and Events." In *Advances in Systemic Linguistics: Recent Theory and Practice,* edited by M. Davies and Louise Ravelli, 105–35. London: Pinter, 1992.

Davidse, Kristin, and Leisbet Heyvaert. "On the Middle Construction in English and Dutch." In *Corpus-Based Approaches to Contrastive Linguistics and Translation Studies,* edited by Sylviane Granger, Jacques Lerot, and Stephanie Petch-Tyson, 57–73. Amsterdam: Rodopi, 2003.

Davidse, Kristin, and Sara Geyskens. "*Have You Walked the Dog Yet?* The Ergative Causativization of Intransitives." *Word* 49 (1998): 155–80.

De Roeck, Anne, Avik Sarkar, and Paul H. Garthwaite. "Defeating the Homogeneity Assumption." *7es Journées Internationales d'Analyse Statistique des Données Textuelles* (2004): 282–94. http://www.cavi.univ-paris3.fr/lexicometrica/jadt/jadt2004/pdf/JADT_026.pdf (1.7.07).

Derrida, Jacques. *Speech and Phenomena: And Other Essays on Husserl's Theory of Signs.* Translated by David B. Allison. Evanston: Northwestern University Press, 1973.

Desmond, John F. *Risen Sons: Flannery O'Connor's Vision of History.* Athens: University of Georgia Press, 1987.

Di Renzo, Anthony. *American Gargoyles: Flannery O'Connor and the Medieval Grotesque.* Carbondale: Southern Illinois University Press, 1993.

Dixon, R. M. W. "Ergativity." *Language* 55 (1979): 59–138.

Dovey, Teresa. "J. M. Coetzee: Writing in the Middle Voice." In *Essays on African Writing: A Re-Evaluation,* edited by Abdulrazak Gurnah, 56–69. Oxford: Heinemann, 1993.

Dowell, Bob. "The Moment of Grace in the Fiction of Flannery O'Connor." *College English* 27 (1965): 235–39.

Dunning, Ted. "Accurate Methods for the Statistics of Surprise and Coincidence." *Computational Linguistics* 19, no. 1 (1993): 61–74.

Enjolras, Laurence. *Flannery O'Connor's Characters.* New York: University Press of America, 1998.

Faltz, Leonard M. *Reflexivization: A Study in Universal Syntax.* New York: Garland, 1985.

Feeley, Kathleen. *Flannery O'Connor: Voice of the Peacock.* New Brunswick, N.J.: Rutgers University Press, 1972.

Fish, Stanley. "What Is Stylistics and Why Are they Saying Such Terrible Things about It?" In *Approaches to Poetics,* edited by Seymour Chatman, 109–52. New York: Columbia University Press, 1973.

Fitzgerald, Sally. "Note on the Text." In *Collected Works,* by Flannery O'Connor, 1257–64. New York: Library of America, 1988.

Foley, William A., and Robert D. Van Valin, Jr. *Functional Syntax and Universal Grammar.* Cambridge: Cambridge University Press, 1984.

Folks, Jeffrey J. "'The Enduring Chill': Physical Disability in Flannery O'Connor's *Everything That Rises Must Converge.*" *University of Dayton Review* 22 (1993–1994): 81–88.

Fox, Barbara. "Body Part Syntax: Towards a Universal Characterization." *Studies in Language* 5, no. 3 (1981): 323–42.

Francis, W. N., and H. Kucera. *Brown Corpius Manual.* Providence, R.I.: Department of Linguistics, Brown University, 1979. http://khnt.hit.uib.no/icame/manuals/brown/INDEX.HTM (8.9.07)

Freeman, Mary Glenn. "Flannery O'Connor and the Quality of Sight: A Standard for Writing and Reading." *Flannery O'Connor Bulletin* 16 (1987): 26–33.

Friedl, Herwig. "Thinking in Search of a Language: Pragmatism and the Muted Middle Voice." *Amerikastudien* 47, no. 4 (2002): 469–90.

Friedman, Melvin J. "Flannery O'Connor's Sacred Objects." In *The Vision Obscured: Perceptions of Some Twentieth-Century Catholic Novelists,* edited by Melvin J. Friedman, 67–77. New York: Fordham University Press, 1970.

Fukuda, Kaoru. "On Emphatic Reflexives." *English Linguistics* 6 (1989): 36–51.

Genette, Gérard. *Narrative Discourse: An Essay in Method.* Translated by Jane E. Lewin. Ithaca: Cornell University Press, 1972.

Gentry, Marshall Bruce. *Flannery O'Connor's Religion of the Grotesque.* Jackson: University Press of Mississippi, 1986.

Gilbert, Susanna. "'Blood Don't Lie': The Diseased Family in Flannery O'Connor's *Everything That Rises Must Converge.*" *Literature and Medicine* 18, no. 1 (1999): 114–31.

Givón, T. *English Grammar: A Function-Based Introduction.* 2 vols. Amsterdam: John Benjamins, 1993.

Gliserman, Martin. *Psychoanalysis, Language, and the Body of the Text.* Gainesville: University Press of Florida, 1996.

Grady, Michael. "The Medio-Passive Voice in Modern English." *Word* 21 (1965): 270–72.

Gwin, Minrose C. "Racial Wounding and the Aesthetics of the Middle Voice in *Absalom, Absalom!* and *Go Down, Moses.*" *Faulkner Journal* 20 (Fall 2004 / Spring 2005): 21–33.

Haiman, John. *Talk Is Cheap: Sarcasm, Alienation, and the Evolution of Language.* Oxford: Oxford University Press, 1998.

Hall, Jonathan. "The Evacuations of Falstaff (*The Merry Wives of Windsor*)." In *Shakespeare and Carnival: After Bakhtin,* edited by Ronald Knowles, 123–51. New York: Macmillan, 1998.

Halliday, M. A. K. "Linguistic Function and Literary Style: An Inquiry into the Language of William Golding's *The Inheritors.*" In *Literary Style: A Symposium,* edited by Seymour Chatman, 330–65. New York: Oxford University Press, 1971.

Halliday, M. A. K., and Christian M. I. M. Matthiessen. *An Introduction to Functional Grammar.* London: Edward Arnold, 2004.

Hardy, Donald E. "Collocational Analysis as a Stylistic Discovery Procedure: The Case of Flannery O'Connor's *Eyes.*" *Style* 38, no. 4 (2004): 410–27.

———. "The Dialogic Repetition of Free Indirect Discourse in Oral and Literary Narrative." In *Repetition in Dialogue,* edited by Carla Bazzanella, 90–103. Tübingen: Niemeyer, 1996.

———. "*Face* and the Middle Voice in Flannery O'Connor's Fiction." *Journal of Literary Semantics* 32 (2003): 133–50.

———. "Linguistics and Literary Theory: The Dancer and the Dance." *Southwest Journal of Linguistics* 10, no. 2 (1991): 1–29.

———. "Middle Voice in Creek." *International Journal of American Linguistics* 60 (1994): 39–68.

———. *Narrating Knowledge in Flannery O'Connor's Fiction.* Columbia: University of South Carolina Press, 2003.

———. "The Role of Linguistics in Interpretation: The Case of Grammatical Voice." *Belgian Journal of English Language and Literatures. Thematic Issue: The Linguistics/Literature Interface* 2 (2004): 31–48.

Hawkes, John. "Flannery O'Connor's Devil." *Sewanee Review* 70, no. 7 (1962): 395–407.

Hazelton, Roger. "The Grotesque, Theologically Considered." In *The Grotesque in Art and Literature: Theological Reflections,* edited by James Luther Adams and Wilson Yates, 75–81. Grand Rapids, Mich.: Eerdmans, 1997.

Hendin, Josephine. *The World of Flannery O'Connor.* Bloomington: Indiana University Press, 1970.

Henkel, Jacqueline M. "Linguistic Models and Recent Criticism: Transformational-Generative Grammar as Literary Metaphor." *PMLA* 105, no. 3 (1990): 448–63.

Hewitt, Avis. "'Ignoring Unmistakable Likeness': Mark Fortune's Miss-Fortune in 'A View of the Woods.'" In *"On the Subject of the Feminist Business": Re-Reading Flannery O'Connor,* edited by Teresa Caruso, 129–54. New York: Peter Lang, 2004.

Hodder, Harbour Fraser. "In the Middle Voice: Philologies of Poesis in Dickinson, Whitman, and Hopkins." Ph.D. diss., Harvard University, 1991.

Hofland, Knut, and Stig Johansson. *Word Frequencies in British and American English.* Bergen: Norwegian Computing Centre for the Humanities, 1982.

Hoover, David. *Language and Style in* The Inheritors. Lanham, Md.: University Press of America, 1999.

Hori, Masahiro. *Investigating Dickens' Style: A Collocational Analysis.* New York: Palgrave, 2004.

Horton, James W. "Flannery O'Connor's Hermaphrodite: Notes toward a Theology of Sex." *Flannery O'Connor Bulletin* 23 (1994–95): 30–42.

Huddleston, Rodney. "The Clause: Complements." In *The Cambridge Grammar of the English Language,* edited by Huddleston and Geoffrey K. Pullum, 213–321. Cambridge: Cambridge University Press, 2002.

Hunston, Susan. *Corpora in Applied Linguistics.* Cambridge: Cambridge University Press, 2002.

———. "Review of *Word Frequencies in Written and Spoken English: Based on the British National Corpus.*" *Language Awareness* 11, no. 2 (2002): 152–57.

Hutchison, Lorna. "The Book Reads Well: Atwood's *Alias Grace* and the Middle Voice." *Pacific Coast Philology* 38 (2003): 40–59.

Joyce, Michael. "New Stories for New Readers: Contour, Coherence, and Constructive Hypertext." In *Page to Screen: Taking Literacy into the Electronic Era,* edited by Ilana Snyder, 163–82. London: Routledge, 1998. .

Katz, Yael. "Configuring Crisis: Writing, Madness, and the Middle Voice." Ph.D. diss., University of British Columbia, 2000.

Kavanaugh, Thomas M. "The Middle Voice of Film Narration." *Diacritics* 9, no. 3 (1979): 54–61.

Kellner, Hans. "'Never Again' is Now." *History and Theory* 33, no. 2 (1994): 127–44.

Kemmer, Suzanne. *The Middle Voice.* Amsterdam: John Benjamins, 1993.

Kennedy, Chris. "Systemic Grammar and Its Use in Literary Analysis." In *Language and Literature: An Introductory Reader in Stylistics,* edited by Ronald Carter, 83–99. London: Allen and Unwin, 1982.

Kennedy, Graeme. *An Introduction to Corpus Linguistics.* London: Longman, 1998.

Kessler, Edward. *Flannery O'Connor and the Language of Apocalypse.* Princeton: Princeton University Press, 1986.

Keyser, Samuel J, and Thomas Roeper. "On the Middle and Ergative Constructions in English." *Linguistic Inquiry* 15 (1984): 381–416.

Kies, Daniel. "The Uses of Passivity: Suppressing Agency in *Nineteen Eighty-Four.*" In *Advances in Systemic Linguistics: Recent Theory and Practice,* edited by Martin Davies and Louise Ravelli, 229–50. London: Pinter, 1992.

Kilgarriff, Adam. "Comparing Corpora." *International Journal of Corpus Linguistics* 6, no. 1 (2001): 97–133.

———. "Comparing Word Frequencies across Corpora: Why Chi-Square Doesn't Work, and an Improved LOB-Brown Comparison." *ALLC-ACH '96* (1996): 169–72. http://gandalf.aksis.uib.no/allc/kilgarny.pdf (8.11.06)

———. "Which Words Are Particularly Characteristic of a Text? A Survey of Statistical Approaches." *Information Technology Research Institute Technical Report Series, ITRI-96–08.* Brighton: University of Brighton, 1996.

Kilgarriff, Adam, and Tony Rose. "Measures for Corpus Similarity and Homogeneity." *Information Technology Research Institute Technical Report Series, ITRI-98–07.* Brighton: University of Brighton, 1998. http://www.itri.brighton.ac.uk/techindex .html (3.17.05).

Kinney, Arthur F. *Flannery O'Connor's Library: Resources of Being.* Athens: University of Georgia Press, 1985.

Klaiman, M. H. "Affectedness and Control: A Typology of Voice Systems." In *Passive and Voice,* edited by Masayoshi Shibatani, 25–83. Philadelphia: John Benjamins, 1988.

Korte, Barbara. *Body Language in Literature.* Toronto: University of Toronto Press, 1997.

Kress, David C. "Middle Voice Moves in Nathaniel Mackey's *Djbot Baghostus's Run.*" *Callaloo: A Journal of African-American and African Arts and Letters* 23, no. 2 (2000): 765–83.

LaCapra, Dominick. *Writing History, Writing Trauma.* Baltimore: Johns Hopkins University Press, 2001.

Lake, Christine Bieber. *The Incarnational Art of Flannery O'Connor.* Macon, Ga.: Mercer University Press, 2005.

Lakoff, George. "Sorry, I'm Not Myself Today: The Metaphor System for Conceptualizing the Self." In *Spaces, Worlds, and Grammar,* edited by Gilles Fauconnier and Eve Sweetser, 91–123. Chicago: University of Chicago Press, 1996.

Lang, Berel. *Act and Idea in the Nazi Genocide.* Chicago: University of Chicago Press, 1990.

Leech, Geoffrey N., and Michael H. Short. *Style in Fiction: A Linguistic Introduction to English Fictional Prose.* London: Longman, 1981.

Leech, Geoffrey N., Paul Rayson, and Andrew Wilson. *Word Frequencies in Written and Spoken English: Based on the British National Corpus.* Harlow: Longman, 2001.

Lyne, Anthony A. "In Praise of Juilland's 'D': A Contribution to the Empirical Evaluation of Various Measures of Dispersion Applied to Word Frequencies." In *Méthodes Quantitatives et Informatiques dans l'Étude des Textes,* edited by Etienne Brunet, 589–97. Geneva: Slatkine-Champion, 1986.

———. *The Vocabulary of French Business Correspondence: Word Frequencies, Collocations, and Problems of Lexicometric Method.* Paris: Slatkine, 1985.

Lyons, John. *Introduction to Theoretical Linguistics.* Cambridge: Cambridge University Press, 1968.

Macaskill, Brian. "Charting J. M. Coetzee's Middle Voice." *Contemporary Literature* 25, no. 3 (1994): 441–75.

Magee, Rosemary M., ed. *Conversations with Flannery O'Connor.* Jackson: University Press of Mississippi, 1987.

Maida, Patricia D. "Light and Enlightenment in Flannery O'Connor's Fiction." *Studies in Short Fiction* 13 (1979): 31–36.

Malin, Irving. "Flannery O'Connor and the Grotesque." In *The Added Dimension: The Art and Mind of Flannery O'Connor,* edited by Melvin J. Friedman and Lewis A. Lawson, 108–22. New York: Fordham University Press, 1966.

Manning, Christopher D., and Hinrich Schütze. *Foundations of Statistical Natural Language Processing.* Cambridge: MIT Press, 2001.

Martínez, M. Angeles. "From 'Under the Rose' to *V:* A Linguistic Approach to Human Agency in Pynchon's Fiction." *Poetics Today* 23, no. 4 (2002): 633–56.

Mayer, David R.. "'Like Ticks off a Dog': Flannery O'Connor's 'As If.'" *Christianity and Literature* 33, no. 4 (1984): 17–34.

McCarthy, John F. "Human Intelligence versus Divine Truth: The Intellectual in Flannery O'Connor's Works." *English Journal* 55 (1966): 1143–48.

McEnery, Tony, and Andrew Wilson. *Corpus Linguistics.* Edinburgh: Edinburgh University Press, 1996.

McMullen, Joanne Halleran. *Writing against God: Language as Message in the Literature of Flannery O'Connor.* Macon, Ga.: Mercer University Press, 1996.

Mellard, James M. "Flannery O'Connor's Others: Freud, Lacan, and the Unconscious." *American Literature* 61, no. 4 (1989): 625–43.

———. "Framed in the Gaze: Haze, *Wise Blood,* and Lacanian Reading." In *New Essays on* Wise Blood, edited by Michael Kreyling, 51–69. Cambridge: Cambridge University Press, 1995.

Meyer, Charles F. *English Corpus Linguistics: An Introduction.* Cambridge: Cambridge University Press, 2002.

Meyer, William E., Jr. "Flannery O'Connor's 'Two Sets of Eyes.'" *Southern Studies* 25 (1986): 284–94.

Meyers, Jeffrey. "Introduction." *Winesburg, Ohio,* by Sherwood Anderson. New York: Bantam, 1995, ix–xx.

Monroe, William Frank. "Bringing the Script to Life: The Case of Flannery O'Connor." *Journal of Medical Humanities* 15, no. 2 (1994): 101–11.

———. "Flannery O'Connor and the Celebration of Embodiment." In *The Good Body: Asceticism in Contemporary Culture,* edited by Mary G. Winkler and Letha B. Cole, 171–88. New Haven: Yale University Press, 1994.

———. "Flannery O'Connor's Sacramental Icon: 'The Artificial Nigger.'" *South Central Review* 1, no. 4 (1984): 64–81.

Muller, Gilbert H. *Nightmares and Visions: Flannery O'Connor and the Catholic Grotesque.* Athens: University of Georgia Press, 1972.

Nash, Walter. "On a Passage from Lawrence's 'Odour of Chrysanthemums.'" In *Language and Literature: An Introductory Reader in Stylistics,* edited by Ronald Carter, 101–20. London: Allen and Unwin, 1982.

Nisly, Paul W. "The Prison of the Self: Isolation in Flannery O'Connor's Fiction." *Studies in Short Fiction* 17, no. 1 (1980): 49–54.

Oakes, Michael P. *Statistics for Corpus Linguistics.* Edinburgh: Edinburgh University Press, 1998.

O'Connor, Flannery. *Collected Works*. New York: Library of America, 1988.

———. *The Complete Stories.* New York: Farrar, Straus and Giroux, 1971.

———. *Everything That Rises Must Converge.* New York: Farrar, Straus and Giroux, 1965.

———. *A Good Man Is Hard to Find and Other Stories.* New York: Harcourt, Brace and World, 1955.

———. *The Habit of Being,* edited by Sally Fitzgerald. New York: Vintage, 1979.

———. *Mystery and Manners: Occasional Prose,* edited by Sally Fitzgerald and Robert Fitzgerald. New York: Farrar, Straus and Giroux, 1969.

———. *The Violent Bear It Away.* New York: Farrar, Straus and Cudahy, 1960.

———. *Wise Blood.* New York: Harcourt, Brace and World, 1952. Reprint, New York: Farrar, Straus and Cudahy, 1962.

Orvell, Miles. *Invisible Parade: The Fiction of Flannery O'Connor.* Philadelphia: Temple University Press, 1972.

Paulson, Suzanne Morrow. "Apocalypse of Self, Resurrection of the Double: Flannery O'Connor's *The Violent Bear It Away.*" In *Flannery O'Connor: New Perspectives,* edited by Sura P. Rath and Mary Neff Shaw, 121–38. Athens: University of Georgia Press, 1996.

Pecora, Vincent P. "Ethics, Politics, and the Middle Voice." *Yale French Studies* 79 (1991): 203–30.

Pepper, Thomas. *Singularities: Extremes of Theory in the Twentieth Century.* Cambridge: Cambridge University Press, 1997.

Perreault, Jeanne. "The Body, the Critics, and 'The Artificial Nigger.'" *Mississippi Quarterly: The Journal of Southern Cultures* 3 (2003): 389–410.

Portch, Stephen R. *Literature's Silent Language: Nonverbal Communication.* New York: Peter Lang, 1985.

Prince, Gerald. *A Dictionary of Narratology.* Lincoln: University of Nebraska Press, 2003.

———. *Narratology: The Form and Functioning of Narrative.* Berlin: Mouton, 1982.

Punday, Daniel. *Narrative Bodies: Toward a Corporeal Narratology.* New York: Palgrave, 2003.

Quirk, Randolph. *Grammatical and Lexical Variance in English.* London: Longman, 1995.

Quirk, Randolph, Sidney Greenbaum, Geoffrey Leech, and Jan Svartvik. *A Comprehensive Grammar of the English Language.* London: Longman, 1985.

Ransom, John Crowe. *The New Criticism.* Norfolk, Conn.: New Directions, 1941.

Rayson, Paul. "Matrix: A Statistical Method and Software Tool for Linguistic Analysis Through Corpus Comparison." Ph.D. diss., Lancaster University, 2003.

Rayson, Paul, Damon Berridge, and Brian Francis. "Extending the Cochran Rule for the Comparison of Word Frequencies between Corpora." *7es Journées Internationales d'Analyse Statistique des Données Textuelles* (2004): 926–36.

Rayson, Paul, and Roger Garside. "Comparing Corpora Using Frequency Profiling." *Proceedings of the Workshop on Comparing Corpora* (2000): 1–6. http://www.comp.lancs.ac.uk/computing/users/paul/publications/rg_acl2000.pdf (11.23.04).

Rickels, Milton. "The Grotesque Body of Southwestern Humor." In *Critical Essays on American Humor,* edited by William Bedford Clark and W. Craig Turner, 155–66. Boston: G. K. Hall, 1984.

Sagar, B. M. "Physical Appearance of Characters in Novels." *Literary Criterion* 26, no. 3 (1991): 53–55.

Saha, P. K. "Strategies of Reflexivization in American English." *American Speech* 62, no. 3 (1987): 211–34.

Satterfield, Ben. "*Wise Blood,* Artistic Anemia, and the Hemorrhaging of O'Connor Criticism." *Studies in American Fiction* 17, no. 1 (1989): 33–50.

Scarry, Elaine. *The Body in Pain: The Making and Unmaking of the World.* New York: Oxford University Press, 1985.

Schauber, Ellen, and Ellen Spolsky. *The Bounds of Interpretation: Linguistic Theory and Literary Text.* Stanford: Stanford University Press, 1986.

Schröder, Leena Kore. "Virginia Woolf and the Body: Corporeality, Metaphor, and the In-Between." *Virginia Woolf Bulletin* 3 (2000): 15–20.

Schroeder, Michael L. "Ruby Turpin, Job, and Mystery: Flannery O'Connor on the Question of Knowing." *Flannery O'Connor Bulletin* 21 (1992): 75–83.

Scott, Mike. "Comparing Corpora and Identifying Key Words, Collocations: Frequency Distributions through the WordSmith Tools Suite of Computer Programs." In *Small Corpus Studies and ELT: Theory and Practice,* edited by Mohen Ghadessy, Alex Henry, and Robert L. Roseberry, 47–67. Amsterdam: Benjamins, 2001.

Seamon, Roger. "Poetics against Itself: On the Self-Destruction of Modern Scientific Criticism." *PMLA* 104, no. 3 (1989): 294–305.

Semino, Elena, and Mick Short. *Corpus Stylistics: Speech, Writing, and Thought Presentation in a Corpus of English Writing.* London: Routledge, 2004.

Shloss, Carol. *Flannery O'Connor's Dark Comedies: The Limits of Inference.* Baton Rouge: Louisiana State University Press, 1980.

Sinclair, John. *Corpus, Concordance, Collocation.* Oxford: Oxford University Press, 1991.

———. *Trust the Text: Language Corpus, and Discourse.* London: Routledge, 2004.

Sloan, Larue Love. "The Rhetoric of the Seer: Eye Imagery in Flannery O'Connor's 'Revelation.'" *Studies in Short Fiction* 25, no. 2 (1988): 135–45.

Srigley, Susan. *Flannery O'Connor's Sacramental Art.* Notre Dame, Ind.: University of Notre Dame Press, 2004.

Stephens, Martha. *The Question of Flannery O'Connor.* Baton Rouge: Louisiana State University Press, 1973.

Stubbs, Michael. *Text and Corpus Analysis: Computer-Assisted Studies of Language and Culture.* Cambridge, Mass.: Blackwell, 1996.

Talmy, Leonard. "Semantic Causative Types." In *Syntax and Semantics: The Grammar of Causative Constructions,* edited by Masayoshi Shibatani, 43–116. New York: Academic, 1976.

Taylor, Henry. "The Halt Shall Be Gathered Together: Physical Deformity in the Fiction of Flannery O'Connor." *Western Humanities Review* 22 (1968): 325–38.

Toolan, Michael. "Syntactical Styles as a Means of Characterization in Narrative." *Style* 19, no. 1 (1985): 78–93.

Tsai, Hsiu-chih. "Disrupted Narratives: O'Connor's Feminine Grotesque." *Concentric: Literary and Cultural Studies* 30, no. 2 (2004): 35–54.

Uruburu, Paula M. *The Gruesome Doorway: An Analysis of the American Grotesque.* New York: Peter Lang, 1987.

Van O'Connor, William. *The Grotesque: An American Genre and Other Essays.* Carbondale: Southern Illinois University Press, 1962.

Van Oosten, Jeanne. "Subjects and Agenthood in English." *Proceedings of the Chicago Linguistic Society* 13 (1977): 459–71.

Vivian, Bradford. *Being Made Strange: Rhetoric Beyond Representation.* New York: State University of New York Press, 2004.

Walker, Sue. "Spelling Out Illness: Lupus as Metaphor in Flannery O'Connor's 'Greenleaf.'" *Chattahoochee Review* 12, no. 1 (1991): 54–63.

Ward, Gregory, Betty Birner, and Rodney Huddleston. "Information Packaging." In *The Cambridge Grammar of the English Language,* edited by Rodney Huddleston and Geoffrey K. Pullum, 1363–447. Cambridge: Cambridge University Press, 2002.

Whaley, Lindsay J. *Introduction to Typology: The Unity and Diversity of Language.* Thousand Oaks, Calif.: Sage, 1997.

White, Hayden. "Historical Emplotment and the Problem of Truth." In *Probing the Limits of Representation: Nazism and the "Final Solution,"* edited by Saul Friedlander, 37–53. Cambridge: Harvard University Press, 1992.

———. "Writing in the Middle Voice." *Stanford Literature Review* 9, no. 2 (1992): 179–87.

Wikberg, Kay. "The Style Marker *As If* (*Though*): A Corpus Study." In *Out of Corpora: Studies in Honour of Stig Johansson,* edited by Hilde Hasselgard and Signe Oksefjell, 93–105. Amsterdam: Rodopi, 1999.

Wilson, Natalie. "Misfit Bodies and Errant Gender: The Corporeal Feminism of Flannery O'Connor." In *"On the Subject of the Feminist Business": Re-Reading Flannery O'Connor,* edited by Teresa Caruso, 94–119. New York: Peter Lang, 2004.

Wilt, Judith. "The Cave of the Body: The Heart of the Matter." *Religion and the Arts* 1, no. 3 (1997): 73–95.

Wood, Ralph C. "The Catholic Faith of Flannery O'Connor's Protestant Characters: A Critique and Vindication." *Flannery O'Connor Bulletin* 13 (1984): 15–25.

Yaeger, Patricia. "Flannery O'Connor and the Aesthetics of Torture." In *Flannery O'Connor: New Perspectives,* edited by Sura P. Rath and Mary Neff Shaw, 181–206. Athens: University of Georgia Press, 1996.

———. "The Woman without any Bones: Anti-Angel Aggression in *Wise Blood.*" In *New Essays on* Wise Blood, edited by Michael Kreyling, 91–116. Cambridge: Cambridge University Press, 1995.

Yates, Wilson. "An Introduction to the Grotesque: Theoretical and Theological Considerations." In *The Grotesque in Art and Literature: Theological Reflections,* edited by James Luther Adams and Wilson Yates, 1–68. Grand Rapids, Mich.: Eerdmans, 1997.

Yule, G. Udny. *The Statistical Study of Literary Vocabulary.* Cambridge: Cambridge University Press, 1944.

Index

About the Author

Donald E. Hardy is a professor of English at the University of Nevada, Reno, and the author of *Narrating Knowledge in Flannery O'Connor's Fiction.*